One of the Neighbors' Children

One of the

Neighbors' Children

by Robert Mason

Introduction by Tom Wicker

Algonquin Books of Chapel Hill
1987

published by
Algonquin Books of Chapel Hill
Post Office Box 2225
Chapel Hill, North Carolina 27515-2225

in association with
Taylor Publishing Company
1550 West Mockingbird Lane
Dallas, Texas 75235

Library of Congress Cataloging-in-Publication Data

Mason, Robert, 1912–
  One of the neighbors' children.

    1. Mason, Robert, 1912–   2. Journalists—
United States—Biography.   I. Title.
PZ4874.M48355A3   1987   070'.92'4   [B]   86-26563
ISBN 0-912697-56-3

For Frances, Fran, and Mason

Contents

Introduction
Tom Wicker

This book settles a personal mystery that I've brooded about for nearly thirty years. Sometime in 1959, I was being considered for the post of editorial-page editor of the Norfolk, Virginia, *Ledger-Star*. I was then working for the Winston-Salem, North Carolina, *Journal*, and I really wanted that job in Norfolk. Nothing against the *Journal*, a newspaper I loved, but I thought I'd been in Winston-Salem long enough and was ready to move up.

Frank Batten, the publisher of the Norfolk papers, sent an aide down to look me over. I managed to work him for a free dinner and during the course of a pleasant evening registered some complaints against various editors of the *Journal* for being too cooperative with the Winston-Salem business community—a real powerhouse that included the R. J. Reynolds Tobacco Company, Western Electric, Wachovia Bank, and Goody's Headache Powder.

Breathes there a reporter with soul so dead that he has never gotten that kind of stuff off his chest once in a while? But I had no sooner set foot in the *Journal* newsroom the next day than I was summoned to the presence of the executive editor, the late Reed Sarratt. I listened in amazement as Sarratt rather irately recounted to me every word of criticism I had uttered, I thought in private, the night before. I knew Mr. Batten's emissary, who had already returned to Norfolk, wouldn't have violated my confidence, and Sarratt adamantly refused to tell me who had betrayed me, and how he or she knew what I had said.

Bob Mason, now retired, was then managing editor of the Norfolk *Virginian-Pilot*, the sister publication of the *Ledger-Star*. In this detailed but ever-fascinating account of his long career on North Carolina and Virginia newspapers, Mason solves my little mystery at last.

"A former *Richmond Times-Dispatch* reporter who had hired out to the cigarette lobby and moved to Winston-Salem," he writes, had been dining at the next table and overheard my complaint against the business community and the *Journal*. "He felt constrained," Mason adds dryly, "in the light of who paid his salary, to report in detail this blasphemy to Tom's editor."

Well, time heals all wounds—even the outrage I felt at the time, and the disappointment that soon arrived with news that someone else had been given that job in Norfolk. But I'm so grateful to know at last what happened that I don't even mind an error—for which he's not responsible—in Bob Mason's account of the story. Sarratt didn't fire me, as "the editor" told Mason he had; I resigned in August 1959 to move to the Nashville *Tennesseean*.

This book is full of such yarns, large and small, amiably retold by an old reporter and editor who appears to be afflicted with nearly total recall. It's not exactly an autobiography; Mason doesn't tell us much about his private life, although some passages suggest he knows and appreciates more about his family genealogy than most of us ever learn. You could call it a memoir, I suppose, but it's organized and reads more like a collection of tales of a long and richly enjoyed life spent largely in three pursuits—newspapers, the U.S. Navy, and fishing.

Well, I too served in the Navy, but not, I fear, with as much enjoyment as Bob Mason found in his World War II years in the Pacific, as well as his later Reserve years, all jovially recalled here. And I too am a devoted fisherman—though not so devoted, I confess, as to plunge into a Knotts Island marsh pond in pursuit of a largemouth bass and despite the immediate presence (it says here) of a cottonmouth moccasin "nearly as thick and buoyant as the truck inner tube" Mason was using for a float.

But as for journalism, I sense a kindred soul in these pages. I never had the privilege of working with or for Bob Mason—owing, perhaps, to that tobacco-lobby informer all those years ago—but anybody knocking around on North Carolina newspapers as I did in the 1940s and 1950s knew of him as the able editor of the *Sanford Herald*, and later of the *Virginian-Pilot*.

The latter is by no means a small-town paper, and by his own account Mason brought to it many of the useful innovations and attitudes that brought it into modern times (no small feat in Virginia). Yet *One of the Neighbors' Children* retains a real flavor of the kind of small-town journalism I cherish in my own background.

Mason's account of his two separate stretches in Sanford—as a reporter at ten dollars a week when the *Herald* was a weekly and as editor when it went daily—particularly appealed to me, and not just because I know the place well; these chapters reminded me of my own years in Aberdeen and Lumberton, nearby towns with not dissimilar newspapers. Mason obviously learned in such environs what I did too: humility about his line of work. That comes inevitably when you have to face the people you write about next day in the drugstore or the post office—which is why it's easier to write mean things about, say, President Reagan than about your local alderman.

Mason was clearly a good reporter (read his account of a lynching he covered when he worked for the Raleigh *Times*), an editor of high standards, and—what's rarer and more important—a sensitive and sensible man about the other human beings on the various staffs he led. Yet, after a full career in journalism, he seems to reflect less on weighty matters like the First Amendment or The People's Right to Know—both of which I have no doubt he respects—than upon the life itself and the people who follow it. For example:

The *Virginian-Pilot*, long before Mason's tenure, had been the only newspaper to learn on December 17, 1903, that Wilbur and Orville Wright, that morning at nearby Kill Devil Hills, had made the first powered flight. Unfortunately, the *Pilot*'s story, Mason writes, "was wildly off the mark," claiming a three-mile flight instead of the one thousand feet actually covered; and over time even the story of the paper's journalistic coup had been as wildly distorted by bad memory, exaggeration and impostors.

Forty-seven years after the event, Mason set out to put the archives aright. Harry Moore, the reporter who supposedly had had the original news tip, was still, incredibly enough, on the news staff and accepting credit. Unfortunately, Mason's research—aided by the

Wright brothers expert, Fred Kelly—exploded Moore's claim. Edward O. Dean, another young *Pilot* reporter in 1903, later to work for the *New York Times*, actually had had the "leak" from a telegraph operator.

A scandal? Not as Bob Mason sees it. Harry Moore had been onto the story only a little later than Dean, and anyway:

"Moore was a worthy citizen and a fine companion. He also was a relic of when exactitude was not a newspaper priority and a little journalistic swaggering was acceptable, especially when details didn't seem to matter so much. He was before his time in recognizing the entertainment possibilities of a newspaper."

This refreshing—and, among editors, unusual—lack of piety about his calling is extended even to Mason's own rather notable career. He confesses that he "made no great discoveries and did not change the world or any of its parts" and quotes with approval an old schoolmate at Chapel Hill, George Bryant, Jr., later of the *Wall Street Journal*, who had preceded Mason into retirement.

"Just remember," Bryant told him, "if you hadn't done any of it, it wouldn't make a goddam bit of difference."

Maybe you have to be getting out toward the end of the string to appreciate *that*. But a lot of newspaper men and women, young or old, will know exactly what Bob Mason means when he writes that, in retrospect:

"It was a good feeling to be driving down a street in an early morning, on my way to some fishing spot when I was older and on my way home from work when I was younger, and to see stacks of newspapers at corners and to observe carriers making their rounds, and to know that all over the city and throughout the countryside people would read headlines I had scribbled or news or editorials I had written before they did much of anything else, even sipped their coffee."

Amen to that, and to this rewarding book about a craft that—like the people in it—seldom fails to be interesting; and may Bob Mason in retirement hook into many a largemouth and never step on a cottonmouth.

One of the Neighbors' Children

1 Kinfolks

December 23, 1918, was a Monday. Daddy came home at noon for dinner as usual, walking the three-quarters of a mile from the Mebane Bedding Company plant. He ate at the head of the dining room table with Mother at the foot and my three brothers and I, from nearly eight to barely two years old, balanced along the sides. The baby sat in a high chair. I was six, the second oldest.

Mother had gone back to the kitchen and Daddy was rising from the table when he saw Mr. E. Y. Farrell coming down the street. He called Mother. Together they stood at the window, in dread.

Mr. E. Y. Farrell was the stationmaster. Our parents knew he bore a death message. If the telegram that surely was in his pocket said anything else it would have been carried either by Uncle Bubba Holt, who swept and built the fires and did other light work at the depot, having been crippled in a section-gang accident a long time ago, or else Po'boy DeGraffenreid, who pulled the baggage wagon and helped with the freight. The one or the other of them would have waited, were the message for our family and not sad, until after Daddy had finished dinner and was back in his littered office, or in the cotton shed weighing bales to be stacked there, or in the felt room yelling to Rob or Scrooch or Highpockets or another hand what to do about a stalled machine; and the one with the telegram would have taken it there, saving himself the long walk to our house, at a far edge of Mebane, North Carolina, population 693, on a clay road without a sidewalk, maybe a hundred yards from the woods. Mr. E. Y. Farrell, in bringing the telegram himself, was showing respect.

He had already passed the house on the corner, which was the Baptist parsonage, after coming up Oliver's Hill, and was about opposite Mr. Les Ray's, with its yardful of red-headed children. He kept straight on. That brought him to Mayor Ben Stanfield's, which was an unlikely place for the telegram, the Stanfields being from out in the country toward Leesburg, where no railroad tracks or telegraph wires ran; kinfolks or neighbors there would have to come to town with whatever news there was to tell.

He could have turned then, but didn't, to the left into the gravelly driveway down to the Johnsons' big yellow house, where Miss Mattie looked after the old folks and kept Mr. Will Murray as a boarder, at the upper end of what had been a farm and to a degree was yet, with a stable and horse and cow and also a springhouse and a run-down apple and pear orchard, except that the fields, what was left of them and hadn't gone to sedgegrass, were rented to Mr. A. P. Long, a mostly retired farmer on the other side of town who still liked to fool with a little wheat, which he and his near-giant-size son Jack cut with scythes. Jack got into trouble sometimes.

And he didn't stop at the last house before ours, as he hardly could have been expected to, where Old Man Carter, a childless widower who was called Lexington Carter because of the make of the big touring car he drove, and who would marry again, a schoolteacher this go-round, and have progeny, but for the time being lived alone and was not known to have either kin or intimates.

Mr. E. Y. Farrell came on past the vacant lot that Mr. H. E. Wilkinson, the fertilizer agent, planted in corn to be tended by his two boys, Hughes and Robert, to keep them busy summers while going to high school and then Davidson College; and on to our property, which began with a persimmon tree in the corner of a field we used for playing baseball and would convert, when we were older, into a tennis court. He removed his hat as he approached our door.

"Ah, law," Daddy said. "Ah, law."

Later he said he thought it was his mother who had died, for she was believed to have a bad heart. It turned out to be Mother's father, Melville Brown Peterson, who never had been sick a day in his life.

Mother packed a suitcase and got ready to take the afternoon train to Charlotte, 130 miles away, where she would change cars for Stanley, twenty miles farther west, a village in Gaston County where she and Daddy were from and where she would be that night with her seven sisters and two brothers and their newly widowed mother. My brothers and I cried, not because our grandfather had died but because Christmas was two days away and we wanted Mother to be home. I suppose she cried too. But she did not let us see her crying, then or ever.

Virginia Holt was sent for to look after us, and came none too happily, as she and that crowd at Uncle Luther Holt's were getting ready for Christmas too, and everybody knew how colored folk enjoyed Christmas, worse in some ways than whites. Mother wore her brown coatsuit with two little slits at the bottom of the long skirt, and Old Lady Stanfield no doubt had something to say about the slits when she saw her hurrying past. The Stanfields were Methodists: shouting Methodists.

Grandpa Peterson, dead at age sixty-seven years and three days, was a Lutheran. His name and denomination would make him seem now to have been Scandinavian, only there were no Scandinavians where he lived or came from, which was along the Catawba River, on both sides of the boundary separating the Carolinas. Lutherans there were generally Germans. My Peterson cousins who care about such matters say the family was English, although Grandpa's father had been no casual Lutheran but a Lutheran parson-schoolmaster. There's really no use, though, trying to identify blood by religion; Grandma Peterson, for instance, on her father's side was granddaughter of a Presbyterian minister, the Reverend William N. Peacock; and on her mother's was great-great-granddaughter of Michael Braun, the German Lutheran who built the Old Stone House near Salisbury that the Rowan County Historical Society restored, and granddaughter of Michael II, who spelled his name Brown and was a Presbyterian convert; and Grandma still wound up a Lutheran by marrying one.

She was born Lillian White Peacock. Her father was William Mitchell Peacock, a graduate of the University of North Carolina who went to upper Florida to practice law near his father's home. There he died of pneumonia in 1864 after falling ill in a Confederate army camp, where he was a reluctant private. She was five.

Her mother, Virginia Brown Peacock, and a slave couple lifted

Lillian and her seven-year-old brother Robert Harley into a wagon and with them drove from Madison, Florida, back to Salisbury, upwards of 400 miles, through hard country, some of it war-torn. Virginia was the second of Michael Brown II's daughters to be widowed by the Civil War.

Lillian was eighteen when she married—beneath herself, people remembered—Brown Peterson, approaching twenty-seven. With her husband's death forty years later my brothers and I had no grandfather.

Our father was seven when his father died—when Marcus Lafayette Mason, forty-four, hawk-nosed, and bearded, left his wagon train somewhere between Asheville and Charleston and came home to Gaston County, where he had been sheriff as his father had before him, to breathe his last in painful gasps: victim, I am persuaded, of a collapsed lung—of spontaneous pneumothorax—on the evidence that I had a few attacks of that myself, as did my daughter Fran, until surgery cured us.

Grandpa Mason was called Fate, shortened from his second name; his first clearly was a stab at his namesake's title, Marquis, hung on him by his father, Lawson Anderson Mason, son of John, whose 400 acres of land in Lincoln County deeded to him in 1795 was the family seat. The property became part of Gaston County when Gaston was sliced from Lincoln in 1846. Lawson was the first elected sheriff of Gaston, succeeding the sheriff named by the legislature when it created the county. He also was the first Gaston man to be elected from that district to the state senate, where one of his sons, Oscar Ferdinand Mason, and Oscar's son, George Bason Mason, also sat—and where I did too, but as a newspaper reporter rather than a member. He was colonel of the Gaston home guard and was at Bentonville with Johnston's army when Sherman whipped it and ended the Civil War, and so was his son Fate, my grandfather.

How the old man got home I do not know. My grandfather walked. He was nineteen years old, first sergeant of Company C, Seventy-first North Carolina Regiment, Confederate States Army. On his last night on the road he slept in Goshen Presbyterian Church, where he had been baptized. Next morning his mother wept as she embraced him. He told her if she was going to carry on like that he would just go back.

He was nearly twenty-eight when he married Alice Pegram, who was twenty. The bride had these wishes from Maria Forney, her 1870 classmate at Davenport Female College in Lenoir, North Carolina: "Peace be around thee wherever thou rovest, / May thy life be as one summer's day, / And all that thou wishest and all that thou lovest / Come smiling around thy sunny way."

Alice was born in the brick house that Thomas Rhyne, a native of Germany, built in 1799 on land along Stanley Creek granted his family by the Crown. Only Rhynes have lived there to this day. Her mother, Juletta McGee Rhyne Pegram, was Daniel Rhyne's daughter and Thomas Rhyne's granddaughter. Juletta and Edward Larkin Pegram were married in the Rhyne kitchen while the rest of the house was being repaired after a dreadful fire.

Edward Pegram, my great-grandfather, at the outbreak of the Civil War, when he was thirty-three, sold a farm his wife had inherited, put the money in Confederate bonds, helped organize and was elected a second lieutenant of Company B, Twenty-eighth North Carolina Regiment, C.S.A., and marched off to defend the South. He was struck in the face by a minié ball but recovered and returned to the army as a quartermaster captain. His wife Juletta and their three little girls, Alice, Laura, and Ida, were staying in the Rhyne home when Major General William T. Sherman's Union army, coming up from Columbia in early March 1865, made feints toward Charlotte before swinging eastward in the direction of Fayetteville. Brigadier General Judson Kilpatrick's cavalry meanwhile poked violently at small towns and rural communities in the Charlotte area. A unit halted near tiny Dallas, then the Gaston County seat.

When Juletta and her parents "heard that the Yankees were camped near Dallas they gathered up all their valuables such as silver, jewelry and what money they had, and concealed it in a small dugout under the house," wrote my cousin Barbara Stowe Rhyne in *Thomas Rhyne and His Descendants* (1965). "Little Alice Pegram, being a small child, was lowered through the trap door and placed the articles in their hiding place." So both my grandmothers had a taste of the war.

The Daniel Rhyne family nevertheless lost most of its food and some livestock. "It kept a few horses and mules by hiding them in the woods," continued my cousin. Daniel's younger brother Michael Rhyne "had a beautiful horse, and he had also hidden it. One of the slaves told the soldiers where it was hidden, and it, of course, was taken. Some of the soldiers slept in the house and others slept in the barns. Having the enemy in their home was probably the hardest of all to take."

James Reston, Jr., wrote in *You Cannot Refine It* (1985), a meditation on Sherman's march to the sea, that the South's cherished myths about it are embedded in family narratives. "If the horrors dominate, then stories of slaves' loyalty to their masters run a close second," he reported. "Such loyalty . . . is usually associated with the recovery of valuable property." The Rhyne slave who ratted on Michael's horse was a notable exception. I commend him to the school of thinkers that would raise Old Prophet Nat Turner to sainthood.

After Appomattox and Bentonville, Great-grandpa Edward Pegram took off his gray uniform, put on a white shirt and alpaca coat, and sat on the gallery of the Hoffman House hotel in Dallas. He attended big-court sessions, Democratic conventions, and meetings of the Mecklenburg Presbytery—except for the year he got an infected toe from stumping it on a watermelon under his bed while fixing to say his prayers. He hunted some, and when he came to town toward the last he was accompanied by two of the best hounds in Gaston County, named Grover and Adlai, for President Cleveland and Vice-President Stevenson.

His father-in-law, Daniel Rhyne, recovered some of his wealth before dying at eighty in 1875. He and Juletta kept an eye on their widowed daughter, my grandmother Mason. Grandpa had left a farm and $2,000 in life insurance from the Knights of Honor. She had three daughters and two sons to raise. The oldest girl soon married and the baby boy died. She sent the two other girls to the Normal and Industrial School, which became the University of

North Carolina at Greensboro, and the surviving boy—my father, Walter Lafayette Mason—to the Agricultural and Mechanical College at Raleigh, now North Carolina State University, where he completed the two-year "short course" in mechanical engineering.

My father went into textile manufacturing in Charlotte. In 1913, when I was eleven months old, he moved his family to Mebane, where he built and equipped a cotton-batting factory for Mebane Bedding Company, manufacturers of mattresses and springs. When he finished it, the company asked him to stay and operate it. He never left.

Thus it was to Mebane that Irene Peterson Mason's family in Stanley sent the telegram telling her of her father's death that Mr. E. Y. Farrell brought to our house at noon on December 23, 1918. Thus it was that Mebane, rather than a place where we had kin, was my and my brothers' hometown.

On the second day of Mother's absence Daddy asked us if we wanted Santa Claus to wait until the night after Christmas, when she would be home, to bring our presents. Much upset, I voted no. At age six, my faith extended perfectly to the person of Santa Claus but fell short of his willingness to make a second trip from the North Pole just to drop off a bag of apples, oranges, raisins, and niggertoes, plus a popgun or two, perhaps a teddybear and a set of building blocks, and surely some pasteboard horns, to four obscure little boys living in a town without pavement, electricity, running water, or telephones.

I remained troubled as I lay in bed Christmas Eve with my older brother Walter, Jr. I couldn't sleep, and I doubt that I could have slept even if the noise of firecrackers hadn't been coming from town and, a little nearer, from Bingham School. I knew that Mr. Toody White's drugstore stayed open until late and that all the young bucks went there, and I supposed they were setting off firecrackers ordered from catalogues and shipped as freight in wooden boxes packed with sawdust. I had heard about Christmas firecrackers at school, where I was in Miss Gattis's first grade. Maybe some Bingham boys were staying over the holidays and having fun the best way they could. The school had been a military academy from 1864 until

1891, when Major Robert Bingham moved its academics to Asheville and his brother-in-law, Preston Gray, an eccentric lawyer from Kentucky, took over the ghost campus, which he hadn't improved much either as to student body and instruction or as to barracks and classrooms, most of them empty and falling apart. I had gone through the woods with Daddy for town baseball games played on the school's athletic field.

I wondered if Professor Gray and Police Chief Jim Patillo would let the Bingham boys and downtown sports shoot firecrackers all night. I wondered if Ed Graves, who was my age and lived beyond Miss Mattie Johnson's orchard, could hear them, and what Santa Claus was bringing him. I thought about the Crawford brothers, in the house on the next hill, toward the Rice neighborhood, who were cousins of the red-headed Rays up the street, and what they would think if they came to see us next morning and Santa Claus hadn't been there. I imagined that Virginia Holt, who had gone home, running, right after fixing our supper, and that crowd at Uncle Luther's were still up. Then the firecrackers made me think about the war that had been over for six weeks and the promise that Daddy's cousins, Calvin and Percy Pegram, had made to bring us some German helmets for souvenirs . . .

When I woke up it was Christmas dawn, and Santa Claus had come after all, and there was Mother in the living room warming at the fire, still wearing her brown coatsuit with the little slits at the bottom of the skirt, which was pretty rumpled from so much travel; she had come home on the early-morning train: on what Po'boy DeGraffenreid called the hooty-owl. I ran to her before I even looked at my Santa Claus things.

2 The Depot

If you count my hometown's age from the time the North Carolina General Assembly gave it a name and charter, it was much younger than I am now when I grew up there between 1913 and 1929. But if you consider it a far edge of the Hawfields community bulging four miles from the Presbyterian church, still active, that in effect was the Scotch-Irish settlers' governing as well as worshipping seat, then it goes back to before the Revolution. The "Church in the Old Fields," near the Haw River, was organized in 1750. Cornwallis' Redcoats marched past it to their appointment at Yorktown. So did Confederate artillery, raising dust clouds for thirty-six hours hurrying from the western theater to Virginia in the fall of 1864. Colonel George W. "Cut-Throat" Kirk's regiment of former Union bush-whackers from eastern Tennessee came there in 1870 to seize twelve Hawfields Ku Klux Klansmen, three church elders among them, under orders from North Carolina's scalawag governor, W. W. Holden, to put down a race-tainted, two-county rebellion in what is remembered as the Kirk-Holden War, principally because it led to Holden's impeachment.

My hometown owes its existence to Giles Mebane, of the namesake family, in that he used his influence in the House of Commons to have the North Carolina Railroad, linking Goldsboro to Charlotte, routed through Hillsborough and Greensboro rather than Pittsboro and Asheboro. The Honorable's speaking style was persuasive but less than elegant. Sidney Andrews, a roving journalist, observed him on a later public occasion yacking away while gesticulating vigorously "with his right hand, between the thumb and first finger of which he held an immense quid of tobacco taken from his mouth before he rose to speak."

The railroad construction crew in 1855 reached a point ten miles west of Hillsborough. Dr. Benjamin Franklin Mebane, a physician and farmer, moved there that same year from Hawfields into a square two-story house he built near the tracks on a lot big enough to accommodate modest slave quarters and a general store. He had one neighbor and soon acquired a second. The railroad constructed a station nearby. That was the beginning of Mebane, originally called Mebanesville. Bingham Military School, with support from the Confederate Army, moved in 1864 from The Oaks, on the Hillsborough road, to a grove half a mile below the Mebane place. In 1868 the Hawfields church planted an offshoot between Bingham School and the village forming about the depot. Mebanesville was incorporated in 1881, about the time that the brothers Dave and Will White opened a spindle factory that over the next fifteen years progressed into furniture. The legislature shortened Mebanesville to Mebane in 1883. But when I was a boy the old people in Hawfields still called the town "the Depot."

Hawfields is to the south of Mebane. The oldest community to the north of it, on the road to Roxboro and Yanceyville, is Cross Roads. For more than a hundred years the Hawfields and Cross Roads Presbyterian churches were served by the same pastor, who during one period lived in Mebane, midway between them. Early in this century Orange Presbytery separated the two, grouping Greers and Stony Creek with Cross Roads and Bethlehem, Saxapahaw and Bethany with Hawfields. The new arrangement was natural, wrote Professor Herbert Snipes Turner in *Church in the Old Fields: Hawfields Church and Community in North Carolina*: "The members of the Cross Roads field were now primarily tobacco-raising farmers, while the Hawfields group raised more grain and cattle."

That was true in my boyhood and, despite a fair dose of urban sprawl, remains so. Hawfields' soil is red clay; a sandy loam begins at and spreads northward from Mebane. The residents of the two communities I knew were as different as the land. The Hawfielders, Scotch-Irish for the most part, were a flinty sort, tilling small farms. Robert W. Scott, whose son Kerr and namesake grandson would become governors of the state, was an exception. In the state Senate, where he chaired the agriculture committee, he was known as "Farmer Bob." His large family occupied a compound close to the Hawfields church. His own house, with thirteen rooms and seven chimneys, stood on a knoll above a round pond. The Mebane Presbyterian church held its picnics at the pond. As an enthusiastic participant in them I gained the impression that Heaven's mansions must be much like Farmer Bob's and that among salvation's joys would be to roll down their grassy slopes into such a pond—a concept I have felt no urge to improve on.

Out toward Cross Roads and beyond to the Virginia border, fields were broader than those at Hawfields and dwellings less uniform: here big houses had satellites of tenant shacks. The tobacco planters and even the field hands were more inclined to socialize than the Hawfields bluestockings—the former somewhat grandly, the latter sometimes violently. The landowners sent their sons to Oak Ridge Military Academy and the University of North Carolina rather than to Davidson College or N.C. State College, where Hawfields boys were likely to go; among them were foxhunters, football enthusiasts, and whiskey-drinkers. Not all were Presbyterians; around Mebane a Presbyterian was occasionally defined (usually by a country cousin) as a "Hardshell come to town." The Great Awakening of the 1830s hit the Cross Roads vicinity hard, although not hard enough to be much reflected, outside the white and colored Primitive Baptists associations, when I came along.

"Come to town" did a considerable number of those tobacco families' offspring. Nearly every business in Mebane, including tobacco warehouses, fertilizer sheds, insurance agencies, automobile and oil dealerships, and hardware, grocery, apparel and drug stores was operated by someone with roots between Cross Roads and Roxboro or Yanceyville—Carr, Corbett, Hightowers, Frogsboro, Fitch, Hurdles Mill, Hesters Store.

During my babyhood the Mebane Presbyterian Church moved from the town's outskirts to Fifth Street, overlapping the sandclay road to Hawfields, where the nicest homes were being built. One reason for the move was the decline of Bingham School, whose cadet corps had once filled the middle pews. Families living near the original church objected. Outvoted, they acquired the building and shipped into the Christian denomination, sometimes called Campbellites. It was my first lesson in the importance of dissent in religion's spread. The old churchyard became Oakwood, the town cemetery. My parents and two of my four brothers lie there.

Edwin M. Yoder, Jr., who conducted the editorial page of the *Washington Star* until the paper perished in 1980 and who now is a nationally syndicated Washington columnist, is a Fifth Street product. After revisiting Mebane at Christmastime 1977, he wrote:

"When I was growing up there, the founding family—a branch of it anyway—survived in a reduced estate, living in a ramshackle house with slave quarters still standing behind it. One cold November night, in a year impossible to specify now, the lone male scion had too much to drink (as, by rumor, he often had) and fell in the way of a delivery truck. The line came abruptly to an end.

"The town was, as they say in the South, sot in its ways. The furniture factory whistle, summoning its craftsmen to 'The South's Oldest Makers of Fine Furniture,' punctuated the day, at seven, noon, and five—except for a two-week July holiday, when its silence became penetrating.

". . . All the town's known Republicans were tagged, like exotic migratory birds, and it was unkindly whispered that they were all descended from carpetbaggers. On a fine Sunday morning you could set your watch, the furniture factory whistle being silent, by the ferocious roar of Miss Emma H.'s old auto, as with elaborate stuttering and popping she readied her noon departure from the Presbyterian Church. Traffic parted to make way, like the Red Sea before the Children of Israel.

". . . In May . . . the dogwoods lining the main residential street blossomed in clouds of white; and in the fall, following the rhythms of the year, companion maples flamed in incandescent hues of red, yellow, and orange.

"The town where I grew up has changed now—as, no doubt, has the town where you grew up. We walked around it recently, on a quiet and misty Christmas Day, taking the old road through the woods that once led to the baseball park. The park is now strangely overgrown with pine . . .

"What we most noticed, as we walked, was how the new houses, all brick suburban look-alikes, are untidily jammed into the open spaces. On the main street, the prosperous old houses, still lined with maple and dogwood, look a bit forlorn. One doesn't know, as one certainly did thirty years ago, who lives in them, or how they spend their time, or what their family secrets are . . .

"Here, looking old and down at the joints, is Miss Ella B.'s big house, once a kindergarten where naughty boys were sent to stand, humiliated, behind the upright piano. Miss B. must be dead now. She seemed to be living on borrowed time thirty years ago, when behind her frail but straight back her charges mimicked her strange flapping footsteps. And here, a block or so beyond, stands the pleasing old bell tower of the church, showing its age, the window-casings blistered and yellow. Beside it the new church, more conventional and less pleasing in design, observes the execution of time's sentence on the mother church. . . ."

I departed Giles Mebane's legacy to civic order long before Ed Yoder's father assumed supervision of its schools and took up residence on "the main street"— on Fifth Street. I had commenced working on my fourth newspaper, which is to say I was twenty-five or so years old, when Ed did penance behind the upright piano in Miss Ella B.'s parlor. But Miss B.'s influence is upon me, too.

I had not known about the kindergarten. Miss B. must have started it after retiring, at whatever the mandatory age was, as a town teacher. I was seven and she in her crisp prime when we met on the oil-soaked floor of the second grade in the square two-story brick building that contained the entire ten grades that the Mebane free-school district judged to be sufficient for a proper education. Miss Bell, she was.

I remove, for a reason I straightaway will clarify, the anonymity that Ed Yoder lent her. Toward spring, when chickens from Mrs. Wiley J.'s house next door were pecking into the big-recess overstock of biscuits and sweet-potato hulls on the shower-drenched schoolyard and the wisteria vine at the doorway was nursing again, wondrously, light purple globs, and we had pasted cutout bluebirds along the wainscotting where pumpkins and then the Wise Men and finally snowflakes had matched the season, I, having been allowed to free my feet from the confinement of shoes and now could barely stand entrapment of the rest of me in my small, scarred desk—in that air at once soft and stifling I became giddy enough to write and pass to Alfred G., the child whose birthday-was-in-November-and-mine-in-September who sat next to me, this note: "Old lady Bell fell in a well and went to Hell."

Alfred, my best friend, betrayed me. And Miss B.—let her be that again—was a long way from mellowing to the state that she would trust the space behind a piano to shore up a boy's character. Thin as she was, she was competent with ruler, switch, and strap. Yet she did not as much as glance at me after peering through her spectacles at the blasphemous lines from my tablet. She held the page away from her, as if it were something unpleasant and unfortunate, and dropped it quickly into the green metal wastebasket and then briskly wiped her hands on her skirt as if they were soiled. My shame has lasted sixty-five years.

The time Miss B. lived as a kindergarten teacher was entirely as borrowed as young Ed Yoder supposed. By all logic she would have died that long-before day when she honked the horn of her 1934 Chevrolet coupe at a Southern Railway locomotive approaching the bedding factory crossing and kept going, as of course the train did too, until they met. An unusual gait was a cheap price to pay for what Miss B. survived.

Four passenger trains and uncounted freights daily passed through Mebane over tracks maintained by Captain W.'s section crew to the rhythm of Uncle Bubba H.'s bass singing. When they approached the depot in a din of whistle, steam, and rumble, old Crazy Bill, a bearded and grizzled black man with yellow eyes who did odd jobs along Center and Clay Streets, would kick and whinney like a colt. Miss B. was not the only motorist who failed to profit from Bill's alarm. Mr. Toody W., the druggist, was another. Scott L. lost a foot trying to hop a boxcar. I suppose Miss Emma H. escaped disaster on those wild Sunday rides of hers only because church let out at noon, half an hour after the eastbound local had left the depot.

Before Miss Emma H. drove a car to church, she drove a horse-and-buggy. Her car was a Nash, her horse—mare, really—was a bay and named Nancy. Miss Emma bought the car upon moving to town. Prior to that she had lived in a shed, having diagnosed herself as being tubercular and requiring fresh air in undiluted doses, next to the exquisite house occupied by her father, who was a Confederate veteran, and her brother Shakespeare and his wife and their son— and, for weeks at a time under an interfamily lend-lease arrangement, by me. There was a second horse in the stable, a claybank named McKinley—after, let me emphasize, not the Republican President but a South Carolina poet who as a boy soldier had been in old Mr. H.'s company—and there were two saddles in the tack room, Mr. Shake's McClellan and Miss Emma's sidesaddle. Inasmuch as the H. boy claimed the McClellan, I rode in the sidesaddle, right knee hooked over the horn, left foot in the stirrup.

In 1984 I told Michael Plum, the seven-time Olympic rider, of my sidesaddle experiences. Four of us were at lunch. He looked at me with great interest. "An athlete, then," he said. Surprised, I told him I didn't claim much prowess. "You should if you kept your tail in that thing," he said. His companion, Karen Stives, soon to be an Olympic Gold Medalist, explained to me that Plum, masquerading in skirt and veil, had ridden sidesaddle in a stunt.

Exactly when Miss Emma H. determined herself cured, I do not recall. Her brother was a banker. On that credential she was treasurer of the Presbyterian Sunday school. She stacked the class collections on her desk, a few dimes, a handful of nickels, and columns of pennies that seemed by comparison to be as tall as the marble ones that Samson pulled down upon his locks.

As Miss Emma overcame hypochondria and Miss Ella B. lived on borrowed time, so did Tom, the last of the founding family's line to dwell in town, excuse himself from death's first summons. "By rumor," was it now, that he drank too much? Ed Yoder wrote in charity. Ed's and my town never paid much attention to Prohibition, which would endure for six years after I went away and affect my life as much as the Depression, the Big War, and the Race Revolution. White lightning could be bought at the ice plant, at Norman W.'s cafe, and at practically any filling station where gasoline was still pumped by hand. Business at the bedding factory, where my teetotaler father was felt superintendent, often was done over a fruit jar. No warehouseman, auctioneer, buyer, book man, clip man, or pinhooker was likely to refuse a drink after a tobacco sale on a fall afternoon.

Barbecues and fish frys and baseball games hardly would have been worth the fuss had corn whiskey been lacking.

Even so, Tom's drinking was a subject of torment among his kin and of prayer among his neighbors. He was an alcoholic before alcoholism was established, when the whispered word for it was drunkard. The only time his addiction seemed funny was on the Sunday night that a 1923 Ford hit a magnolia tree in the yard of the old White place, next door to the White furniture factory, and the first ones to come upon the wreck, on their way home from evening services at the Presbyterian church, found Tom lying on the car's back seat a hundred or more feet from the rest of the Model-T, which was in bad shape, and supposed that he was dead and had been temporarily laid out, only to discover with the arrival of Mr. Luther S. from the undertaking parlor that Tom was merely asleep and, judging from the depth of his slumber, had been asleep when the car hit the tree and had slept through being hurled into the air on the back seat, in fetal position, and was still asleep when he landed, no better and no worse off than when the car, driven by party or parties unknown, had been cadillacking down Highway 10. So folks laughed. But they would not have laughed had they known that Tom's number, while not on the old Ford touring car, was on a delivery truck and coming up.

Giles Mebane was a Whig until the old party expired, and then a Democrat. His kin, Tom's daddy among them, kept the faith and meanwhile tagged the Republicans and passed down the history of how each had come to be so. Besides one black man, the sole member of his race allowed to register, they were for the most part scalawag stock, not carpetbagger as Ed Yoder thought. The wealthiest family in Mebane during my boyhood was still identified by the patriarch who had taken a local office in the Reconstruction government and arrested Major Robert Bingham when he came home from the Civil War, for which he had been kicked out of the Masonic lodge for certain and, in legend at least, from the Presbyterian session. The Major, upon getting straightened out, rejoined his brother William in the operation of the Bingham Military School. He had commanded, as a captain, Company G of the Forty-fourth

North Carolina Infantry; major was a tombstone title, which the governor would improve to colonel once the Democratic party had redeemed the state in 1898-1900. His son, Robert Worth Bingham, to be born in the headmaster's house in 1871, would become ambassador to the Court of St. James's.

My hometown, I can tell you, was mean in its politics. I suppose it was mean in several other ways—bigoted, narrow-minded, and nosy, the way all small towns are supposed to be. But it was forgiving, too, and understanding, else its Republicans would not have stayed on to prosper and be influential, and its strayed sons—I have not lived there since entering the University of North Carolina in 1929—would not regard it so warmly.

3 The Intruder

That summer I turned sixteen I was the youngest and next to the lightest member of the town baseball team. It did not bother me that I was barely five-foot-nine and a shade under 130 pounds. Muddy Ruel, who was catching then for the Washington Senators and was my ideal, was no taller, and I figured I would put on the twenty pounds I needed to match his weight before finishing Mebane High School the next spring, in 1929.

I claimed to be the second-string catcher. But the only times I got in a game were when we were laughably ahead or hopelessly behind. In such a case Hurley Riggs or Talmadge Jobe or Joe Sam Fox, who were the starting pitchers, would come out and Louis Dixon would move from second base to the mound. Chicken Cheek, the boy who was smaller than I despite being a year older, would take over second, prancing about like a colt and chattering away as if he were auctioneering tobacco at the High Dollar warehouse across town.

And I would put on the mitt for Louis Dixon's little mess of junk, which Fatty Wilkinson, the regular catcher, found to pose an un-acceptable risk to his meat hand and also his mobility. For me a torn fingernail or lunge in the dirt was a bargain price to pay for playing. To tell the truth, I didn't have too much trouble with those flutterballs, roundhouses, and dipsy-do's. For I had caught, and still did, a better pitcher than Louis Dixon—or, for that matter, better than any of the three members of the town baseball team's starting rotation.

I'm talking about Lacy Tate.

The Tates were a colored family that worked for Mr. Walter Crawford, our neighbor. There were two elderly sisters, Ata and Emma. Ata had a husband, Bethel, but no children. Emma had no husband but two sons, both grown though unmarried, Lacy and Tom. All were known as Tates, but Bethel's name, and hence Ata's, may have been something else.

Mr. Crawford had a cedar mill in town, with a population then of about 1,200, and a tobacco farm at the edge of it, where his and our families lived. The three Crawford boys overlapped me in age, and I spent about as much time with them as I did with my three brothers; the seven of us, indeed, sort of ebbed and flowed, in whole or in part, from one house to another.

The Tates occupied two log cabins near the Crawford house, the remnants of quarters going back to when all Mebane was farm and timber country extending from the Hawfields community four miles away, where a Presbyterian church was organized in 1750. Several other little clusters of former slave shacks were partially intact in and about town. One had been taken over by an old soldier—a Confederate veteran—and the flea-bitten horse that was his partner in the dray business.

Lacy and Tom Tate worked during the winter at the cedar mill. Come planting time they would shift to the farm. Sometimes one or two of my brothers and I would help them and the Crawford boys in the fields, especially during tobacco cutting and curing time.

Back then and there tobacco was harvested by slicing the stalk rather than pulling, or priming, the separate leaves as they ripened. Lacy and Tom took turns at cutting, which required some skill.

They would split the stalk from near the top to within about three inches of the ground, then, withdrawing and turning the hook-bladed knife, sever the entire plant. A boy or woman would receive the plant on a tobacco stick: hand-riven pine, three-fourths by an inch-and-a-half, and four-and-a-half feet long. When a stick was filled with six to eight plants, the person holding it would pass it to Bethel for careful placement on his mule-drawn sled. Later, at the curing barn, the tobacco-laden sticks would be hung on rafters. Bethel would tend the curing fires. That took real faculty.

Tobacco grew well where we lived. Much of it became wrappers—the smooth outer layer for chewing-tobacco plugs or twists and for cigars, as opposed to the lower-quality leaf for lump and filler. Operators of the four auction warehouses in Mebane bragged that they handled more wrappers than any other market in the Old Belt, including Danvillevirginia—it was always spoken that way—forty miles away, where three sets of buyers followed the auctioneers. Bethel was a wrapper man. He stoked the fires to his flues for a straw-tinted leaf. Of such color was Bethel himself, but with a peevish of brownish red, like burley. He was at least a quarter Indian. His sparse whiskers and fringe of hair were more like cotton than wool. His nose was thick but arched, his lips thin and pursed. Bethel spoke little and smiled less. His dark eyes, rheumy from hickory smoke and the years, were solemn as a baby's.

Ata and Emma Tate helped with the harvest and, after the curing, with the ordering and grading. At all other times they seemed to be at the Crawford place, cooking or washing-and-ironing or helping Mrs. Crawford and her nearly grown daughter or else caring for the baby, also a girl. They were big, bosomy, high-rumped women, elegantly black. Also, they were chatty and pleasant. The Crawford siblings and my brothers and I understood very well that we were to mind Aunt Ata and Aunt Emma.

When my brothers and I helped the Crawfords, we ate dinner at their house, along with the paid hands. Usually we filled our plates in the kitchen and took them to the grove between the house and barn. After eating a mound of beans, tomatoes, corn, okra, and chicken or ham, most of the workers would take off their brogans and stretch out on the grass in their gummy Blue Bell overalls and chambray shirts to nap.

But not Lacy Tate and me.

We would go down to the barn lot for a half-hour or so of battery practice, with a side of the barn serving as a backstop. Whenever one of Lacy's hummers got through me and banged against the planking, I would remember painfully the time Mr. Bill D. LeGrand, the town baseball team's manager, on observing my swing with a bat, said, shaking his head, that if I didn't level my arc I'd never hit the side of a barn.

Lacy was tall, big-boned and muscular. He had a square, handsome face. To guard his throwing arm against rheumatism, he wore on his right wrist a double strand of heavy copper wire twisted evenly at the ends. The bracelet might have been a chameleon, the way it blended with Lacy's skin. He threw the ball hard and with precision. It came like a bullet—like lightning. Thirty years later, working on a morning newspaper in another state, I would think immediately of Lacy's pitches when the managing editor one Christmas Eve at midnight saluted the composing room, in the spirit of the season and the nature of his calling, by dispatching to it, through the pneumatic tube linking it to his desk, a skyrocket, spewing flame and trailing smoke.

Yet I learned to receive the ball steadily and, I now like to think, gracefully, into my mitt. It was my mitt only in the sense that I wore it. Otherwise it belonged to Lacy's younger brother Tom, lying under the pin oak trees with the other field hands, if not sleeping then jabbering, as he did in all his waking hours. Both mitt and ball, hard used and showing it, benefited periodically from waxed twine applied with a stout needle by Crip Lester, the paraplegic sports authority who helped at Rembert's Shoe and Harness Shop on lower Clay Street, next to the livery stable.

As the mitt was Tom's, so was the catching job on the colored baseball team that Lacy pitched for. There was a second pitcher on that team, a curiously happy youth called Po'boy who worked at the railroad depot, across from the furniture factory—a second and third pitcher in one faded uniform, when you came right down to it, because Po'boy was ambidextrous: not just able with both hands, as every good baseball player is, but totally proficient with either: a switch pitcher as truly as Frankie Frisch, the infielder acquired by the St. Louis Cardinals from the New York Giants two years before, was a switch hitter. Usually, though, Lacy did the pitching to Tom.

The Mebane baseball park was at the other end of town from where we lived, in a little neighborhood of mill workers. It had a grandstand with about as many seats as the nearby Baptist church, two hundred or so, and narrow bleachers along the third base line. The infield was bare, the outfield weedy. A wooden fence enclosed the park.

Usually the Mebane town team traveled in a couple of automobiles, overflowing to the running boards, to one of the neighboring village or country fields for a midweek game. But it played at home most Saturdays, always in the afternoon. The colored team had the park Saturday mornings, grandstand included. Whites at the colored games sat in the little bleachers, to which colored people were relegated in the afternoons. After their game the white players would cold-shower and dress in a space under the water tank at the mattress factory. A few were college boys paid for playing at the scale of summer jobs provided them by the business community as a civic obligation. The colored team played but once a week, always at home, normally against country fellows who arrived in uniform, carrying their spikes on their shoulders and their gloves on their belts, and hung around town most of the night, still dressed and equipped that way.

Mr. Bill D. LeGrand, the white-team manager, never missed a colored game—or any other baseball game he could get to. Years before, he had reached the upper rungs of minor-league play as a hard-hitting catcher with a special knack at handling pitchers. The fingers of his right hand were crooked and knobby from foul-tip assaults. He was stockily built, not very tall, with sloping shoulders and round belly and bow legs, whose every movement was even and flowing, like a bear's. He was as much Indian as old Bethel, sitting over there with the colored people. Some springs he would take leave from his mattress-stitching job to coach the University of

North Carolina freshman baseball team, commuting the twenty-five miles between Mebane and Chapel Hill, through Hillsborough, in a Model-T Ford. He was a nice man with a nice family.

One Saturday morning of that summer when I turned sixteen and claimed to be backup catcher of the town baseball team, along about the middle of tobacco-cutting time in the Crawford fields with the Crawford boys and my brothers and the Tates, I sat in the bleachers with Mr. Bill D. LeGrand and a scattering of other all-day regulars. Lacy Tate was pitching to his brother Tom.

Tom could hardly have been more different from Lacy. He was the spitting image of his mother—round face, huge body, skinny legs, and narrow haunches halfway to his shoulders. His skin was dark. He was maybe fifty pounds heavier than Lacy. And he had none of Lacy's personal reserve or athletic discipline.

Lacy on that morning was mowing down the batters of a team from out near Prospect Hill, in Caswell County. Up in the grandstand, his mother was urging him to greater heroics still. "You better than he are!" she would shout. "All that plowboy seeing is after it gets there! Hold the ball up, Tommy, so he can see what your brother throwing!"

Preparing to pitch again, Lacy would crouch, hands on knees. "Put the hawk wings on it, Lacy," Emma would yell. "Let the hawk swoop to the biddy! Turn that hawk loose!"

A batter managed to reach first. With Lacy's next pitch, he headed for second. Trying to cut down the runner, Tom threw into center field.

"Good God, child, aim down lower!" screamed Emma. "Aim about where Lacy's at! You too strong like Samson!"

As play progressed, so did Tom's throwing errors. Any visiting player profiting from a hit or bobbled ball was sure to challenge Tom's arm. At length Emma stood and hollered loud enough to be heard even by the kids watching the game from the limbs of a big pine behind the center field wall:

"Good God-a'mighty, Tommy, you and me get home I grease down your arm like I ought to did last night! Get it loose! Get that soupbone limber! You aim that ball at Lacy's feet now! You got too much power for throwing high-up!"

Everybody in the grandstand laughed at Emma's antics. That egged her on. She shouted more advice to Tom. I slipped out of the bleachers and went to the edge of the grandstand to witness the fun.

Emma had moved down to the chicken-wire screen. Several rows back her sister Ata was clapping and stomping. A lot of people were. Even old Bethel, sitting with Ata, seemed tickled.

"Hey, Aunt Emma," I called.

Standing, she glanced toward me and said nothing. I waved. She looked straight at me—stared: glowered. Her silence spread over the grandstand. Heads turned to me. I knew a lot of the people—Rob Tinnen and his two boys, Pegleg Shelley, Little Tom McCullogh and his sister Mice, four or five of the light-skinned Holts from up the railroad tracks near the brickyard, Do-funny, Pockets, Buddy Evans, Bad Manx, John Packingham, Roxie Magee, Deacon Shaw, Crazy Bill, Bib DeGraffenreid, Bob Morrow and most of his family. None as much as nodded.

"Hey, there, Aunt Emma," I called again. "How you doing?"

This time she spoke. "White boy," she said, "I ain't yo mamma's sista. How come you call me 'Aunt'?"

I had sense enough to leave. I went back to the bleachers, trying to be natural, not walking too fast or too slow. My ears rang and my throat felt swollen.

As I sat down, Mr. Bill D. LeGrand asked me, "What was all that jubilee in the grandstand, Bobby?"

"Sir?" I replied. I heard him well enough. But I was afraid to speak right then for fear my voice would sound funny.

"Who was that shining their behind up there?" Mr. Bill D. LeGrand pressed me.

"Oh, you might know," I said. "Those goddam Tate niggers."

That was the first time in my life I ever said a cussword before a grown white man. Mr. Bill D. LeGrand looked sharply at me but said no more.

My words had come out without one bit of trouble. My voice was clear as a bell. I felt good.

4 A Damfool Thing

At Mebane High School we had no library and no laboratory. We didn't even have a gymnasium or athletic field. Our basketball team, which in my senior year won the state "B" class championship in the annual tournament at N.C. State College, played its home games in a low-rafter tobacco warehouse across town. The town baseball park, half a mile from school, served the school baseball and football teams. The school had a shower room but no hot water.

I was ill prepared for the University of North Carolina, which I entered in the fall of 1929. But after two years I managed to catch up with the boys who had attended city high schools or Virginia prep schools.

At the close of my sophomore year I collected enough nerve to approach Professor O. J. Coffin, who singlehandedly conducted the journalism department in one classroom and adjoining office on the second floor of the Alumni Building. I found him parking his red Chevrolet coupe under a live oak tree near Alumni's granite steps. He wore a bow tie and knickers, which were in some fashion on campuses. His nose was hawkish and his legs equally avian. I told him my name and who my father was and, I'm pretty sure, where my family went to church. Being used to country manners, he heard me politely. At length I blurted: "Sir, I'm doing pretty well in English and government and fair in history, and I thought maybe I'd like to study journalism."

Mr. Coffin put an arm about my shoulders and regarded me kindly. "Son," he said, "what do you want to do a damfool thing like that for?"

He nevertheless accepted me into his basic newswriting class the next fall. During that and the following year I sat at his feet almost daily.

He had grown up in Asheboro, a small town in Piedmont North Carolina. He worked in a wagon factory there for a year just prior to enrolling at Chapel Hill shortly before World War I. After graduating he became a reporter and desk editor in Winston-Salem, Charlotte, and Raleigh. He was editor of the Raleigh *Times*, an afternoon paper owned by John A. Park, when the university chose him to develop a journalism department. The subject for several years had been taught by part-time instructors with newspaper experience. At the *Times* he wrote all the editorials and some news as well.

His teaching was informal and occasionally ribald. Some mornings two or three students would join him in singing a hymn while the dozen or so others drifted into the classroom, which was distinguished by a spittoon up front ringed with tobacco stains and cigarette burns.

To start us off, Mr. Coffin would paraphrase a story from one of the morning papers and have us rewrite it. We pecked away on the old Underwood typewriters set on little stands facing the back wall. Later on he would assign us to cover a lecture or do an interview. Once I was foolish enough to fabricate an interview. Tossing my copy toward his oversize wastebasket, Mr. Coffin said, "Son, just because I'm a goddam college professor doesn't mean I don't know what that white stuff on chicken shit is."

The journalism department was no better equipped with teaching aids than Mebane High School. Its nearest thing to a library was a stack of North Carolina newspapers that waxed and waned, according to the janitor's humor, in the office where Mr. Coffin kept meager files. The only magazine I ever saw there was *War Cry*, which Mr. Coffin bought for twenty-five cents each Friday from a Salvation Army lassie. And the only reading I recall he recommended was the Book of Job.

Although he qualified as a printer, and indeed had printed, and even been offered the composing-room foremanship at the *Charlotte Observer* (which he scorned although it paid more than he was making as state editor), he had little interest in copyreading, headline-editing, or makeup.

During the North Carolina legislative session of 1933, which stretched through the winter and spring of my senior year, Mr. Coffin did more yarn-spinning than lecturing. Much of what he said remains in my head. His formula for covering the legislature was to play poker with the leadership and drink whiskey with as many of the honorables as possible. Original sin bound government at all levels, he taught us; the less we expected of succeeding officeholders and politicians generally, the less we would be disappointed.

He had one lecture on libel, the sum of a disjointed account he took up from time to time of a $25,000 suit brought against him and the Raleigh *Times* in 1926 by the Rev. James R. Pentuff, a much-traveled Baptist preacher tending just then a flock in Concord. Mr. Pentuff played a leading role in a fundamentalist effort to persuade the 1925 legislature to forbid any teaching of evolution in North Carolina public schools. Upon the campaign's narrow defeat in the House of Representatives he took it to the revival circuit. He claimed to hold a doctorate and to be an authority on creationism.

On the *Times* editorial page Mr. Coffin poked fun at the monkey bill and its sponsors. At one point he called the Rev. Mr. Pentuff "an immigrant ignoramus." The parson filed suit in the courthouse in Concord.

Mr. Coffin's counsel had the trial moved to Lexington, in an adjoining county. There it managed to stack the jury with Methodists, whose faith Mr. Coffin was known to share.

To those twelve good men and true the defense was able to show that the plaintiff was born in South Carolina and hence in North Carolina was an immigrant. Also, it placed in the record a clipping from a weekly newspaper indicating that Mr. Pentuff had bragged about a hen that laid two eggs a day—good evidence of his ignorance in biological matters. It traced his wanderings into eight states and his arrest in most of them: for bad checks, for adulterous behavior with church organists and choir members, and for swindling con-gregations in various ways, some ingenious. The trial judge dismissed the case. But his decision went to the North Carolina Supreme Court three times before it stuck.

Mr. Coffin told us he paid for his defense rather than be beholden to the *Times'* owner and publisher. He did not like publishers as individuals or as a class. In time a few minor ones tried to get him fired, but nothing came of that.

His disdain extended to civic clubs, patriotic orders, county fairs, and newspaper farm pages. Most civic club functions should be left to three-chair barbershops, he insisted. He believed fairs were basically money-stealing rackets especially profitable to publishers printing the catalogues. And he was persuaded that farmers, like everybody else, preferred murder and sex stories to the N.C. State Agricultural School's handouts that a lot of papers printed toward the back of their Monday morning editions.

Among his instructions to us was that we could write about anybody except whores and the insane. "They've withdrawn from society," he would say. "Leave them alone."

He prepared me to realize that a newsman should not look for appreciation or even fairness from anyone—not from his employers or his readers, certainly; and that he should work essentially for himself, setting his standards high and striving always to earn his own good opinion, or at least his self-respect.

In my senior year I was editor of *The Buccaneer*, the campus humor—make that "humor"—magazine, and drew cartoons as well as wrote a column for it. Mr. Coffin never mentioned them, although he commented at length on the *Daily Tar Heel's* news and editorials. He studiously ignored a controversy I kicked up as president of an honor society. How he judged me I was never sure.

He paid me a small compliment for noting, in a story about a campus political convention, that a football player's knees knocked when he made a nominating speech. And he found merit in my quotation of a little boy at a barbecue back home who wailed: "Mama, that dam dog stole my something-to-eat!" My mention that the Methodist church bell tolled at midnight, April 6, 1933, when three-point-two beer flowed in Chapel Hill with the first easing of

Prohibition, earned me an "A" on my final course—although Mr. Coffin took the precaution, inasmuch as nobody else seemed to have heard the solemn tones, of checking with the Methodist minister to be sure I wasn't fudging again. Usually he gave me a "B," partially in penalty for my tendency to spell originally.

Yet I was the first in my class he recommended for a job in a Depression year when work was so scarce that he lost, temporarily, his sole paying connection with the press—turning out three times a week "Shucks 'n' Nubbins," a column of doggerel, reflections, and one-liners that the *Greensboro Daily News* long had featured on its editorial page. I later learned that the prospective employer had inquired about my character.

"The boy ain't but twenty years old," Mr. Coffin replied. "I hope his character hasn't formed."

All right, what about drinking, the employer pressed him; did I drink liquor?

To which Mr. Coffin replied: "What the hell has drinking liquor got to do with character?"

5 One of the Neighbors' Children

The University of North Carolina awarded me a Bachelor of Arts degree and a compact edition of the King James Version of the Holy Bible on June 4, 1933. A week later O. J. Coffin, my old journalism professor at Chapel Hill, wrote me in Mebane to get in touch with W. E. Horner at the *Sanford Herald* if I was "desirous of coupling up with a semiweekly job—about ten dollars a week." Sanford, he noted, "is much like Mebane, but a bit more worthwhile as a community in that it has more advantages." Mebane then had a population of 1,568; Sanford was nearly three times as large and, unlike Mebane, was a county seat—or practically one: the Lee County courthouse sat in a field halfway between Sanford and Jonesboro, which long since have physically and legally merged.

"You may become a cosmopolitan in time—I hope you do if you want to," Mr. Coffin continued. "But just now you are a small-town lad, one of the neighbors' children, and that is what I believe Horner to need." He concluded: "I'd prefer, if you don't mind, that you said nothing to anyone save Horner of my interest in the matter—there aren't many jobs just now, and while I don't want you or anybody else to think I'm playing favorites, I do try to fit the job to the man."

In anticipation of graduating I had written, as far back as March, to five North Carolina newspapers announcing my availability. One was managed by a close relative married to the owner's daughter. None replied. So in gratification I took the cars to Sanford, near the center of North Carolina, about forty miles from Raleigh.

I arrived at the railroad station on a Sunday afternoon at dusk. Mr. Horner had arranged for me, at five dollars a week, a room and meals at a boarding house catering to railroad men and, during the fall and early winter, to middle-level personnel at the tobacco market—clip and book carriers, for example, but not the lordly buyers and auctioneers. A porter told me how to find it.

At the corner of the street facing the honeysuckle-covered railroad embankment was a furniture store-funeral home. Most of the buildings below it seemed to be empty. Lugging my single suitcase, I passed that corner on my way up the short block to Sanford's principal street, encountering a hotel that seemed to be relatively new, two movie theaters blinking across the pavement at each other, a luncheonette, a cobbler's shop, and a drugstore.

Along the principal street I walked past two more drugstores, two department stores, another furniture store, a real-estate and insurance office, a haberdashery and a shoe store, a lot vacant except for a taxi stand and several worn automobiles, a jeweler's, a dime store, a florist's, and at the far corner an imposing hotel. The street's upper-floor windows bore the names of lawyers, medical doctors, and a chiropractor. Down two intersecting streets I took note of several tobacco warehouses, one of them burned and ruined, a hardware and two grocery stores, a dry cleaner's, the post office, a veterinarian's, a blacksmith's, and a livery stable.

I saw no bank. Sanford had boasted two, but both had failed. The whole town, including a cotton mill and a sash-and-blind plant, and two large brickyards beyond its limits, had to depend on a country bank eight miles away.

Then I came to the red-brick Methodist church that the porter had described to me. My boarding house was next door—a large frame building with a broad porch lined with chairs and a swing. I rang the bell. The landlady appeared. She was a squat, elderly woman with streaks in her gray hair that matched in color the snuff stains at the corners of her wide mouth.

The first-floor room she showed me was furnished with two cots, two straight-back chairs, a bureau, a quite handsome wardrobe, and a little table sporting a blue-bound copy of *The Sinking of the Titanic*.

"I hear-tell you're a college boy," the landlady said.

I told her I had just finished at Chapel Hill.

"Well," she replied, "I hope that don't mean you drink liquor."

Oh, my goodness, no, I said, and showed her my graduation Bible. She didn't seem to be much assured. "I want you to know this is a respectable house," she said. "Some of the finest people in town take their meals with me." After a pause she added, "My husband is a merchant, but he's here every evening and Sunday." He owned a little hardware store in the mill section.

I had a roommate, she then informed me. I had wondered about that. At school I had slept in the Alpha Tau Omega attic with three other students, but the prospect of living with a stranger was a mite worrisome. "He's a very nice young man who's a brakeman with my son-in-law on the Atlantic and Yadkin," said my landlady, as if reading my mind. She had no idea when he would be in. And oh, yes, I should use the upstairs bathroom.

The first thing I did after the landlady left was to check the mattress on my cot. On its faded label I made out the brand name "Piedmont." That was the poorest among four grades of mattress that my father manufactured in Mebane. Then I looked for my grandmother's first cousin's picture in the *Titanic* book.

My grandmother's cousin was shown with her husband. He was Isidore Straus, a Jewish merchant and Congressman who had been a Confederate agent abroad. His family had left Georgia for New York City in 1864 and there acquired Macy's department store. She was Sadie Brown Straus, a great-granddaughter of Michael Braun, the German-born Lutheran master of the historic Old Stone House near Salisbury. How Isidore and Sadie met I do not know; perhaps Isidore's father had sent him peddling from Georgia into the Carolinas before the Civil War. Sadie must have loved her husband dearly. In my mother's family it was told that she chose to drown with him rather than enter a *Titanic* lifeboat without him.

Putting away the book, I undressed, slipped on one of my two pairs of pajamas, and tried the Piedmont. I had slept on worse at the fraternity house. I wished to be rested and fresh for my first day of serious work.

It was daylight when I awoke. My roommate was sitting on his rumpled cot. He wore only a black velveteen shirt, in which he evidently had slept. He was examining his genitals.

"Excuse me," he said upon realizing that I saw him. "I'm getting over a dose of clap." Carefully he fashioned a cloth sack over his penis.

I had paid the landlady a week in advance. It took me a week beyond that to accumulate enough money to move. Mr. Horner meanwhile had raised my pay to twelve dollars a week—half of it in scrip that the county had issued, and was legal tender only in the county, to help it through that Depression year. I was performing better, he explained, than he had expected.

With my prospects thus brightened, I took a room at the Carolina, the newer of the town's two hotels, with Aaron Ashley Flowers Seawell, Jr., who had just begun to practice law with his father's former partner, Judge Thomas J. McPherson. The senior Seawell lately had left Sanford for Raleigh, where, despite advancing age, he rose rapidly from assistant attorney general to attorney general to associate justice of the North Carolina Supreme Court. I had known the son—"Red," we called him—at Chapel Hill.

Red laid out a course of study in his law books for me, and when

I had nothing better to do at night I applied myself to it. Judge McPherson examined me in contracts by having me draw up papers for the sale of a farm. I neglected to include stable manure among the assets. The judge said I was a city slicker.

I was beginning to feel like one. After six months on the job I was making seventeen dollars a week plus an average of two or three dollars I picked up as a stringer for United Press. Never had I lived so well, and never have I since.

I paid the hotel thirty dollars a month for my share of the room, complete with bath and telephone, and three meals a day in the coffee shop, which was the best place in town to eat. Each Saturday morning Casey Trebuchon, who was descended from Frenchmen imported to work nearby gold and coal mines back before they either failed or flooded or blew up, brought me a quart of corn whiskey, for which I paid him fifty cents; about the best thing you could say for it was that it was as neatly wrapped in newspaper as anyone could manage. For another fifty cents a woman did my laundry, which her little boy collected and delivered. I also paid fifty cents a week to the butler-waiter-blouse presser at a big old house on a shaded street, where schoolteachers were received as paying guests, for coming Sunday mornings to brush my suit, polish my shoes, and help me out of bed, and for taking a note to my sweetheart when he left.

She didn't stay my sweetheart. The clearest thing in my mind about all these events of more than half a century ago is how she looked from the back one evening as she walked away, forever. She had a small waist and shapely hips.

6 Every Monday and Thursday

The *Sanford Herald*, a semiweekly, was housed in the basement of the Masonic Building under Crabtree's Drugstore, in a busy part of town. W. E. Horner had acquired it for $5,000 in 1930 from an itinerant printer-publisher who, unable to compete successfully with the venerable Sanford *Express*, a weekly occupying a sagging building across the railroad tracks, had suspended operations. Its equipment was limited to a passably serviceable Linotype machine, a protesting flatbed press, and several cases of type.

"I am going to expect you to take work and responsibility off me, instead of putting more on me," Mr. Horner had written to me in confirming my hiring. "That has been the trouble with the two girls I have been working. I had to lay out about all the work they did, and also worry about seeing that they did it. I am figuring that I will have to do neither with you. For instance, from the start you will be responsible for the news end of the paper."

One of the girls remained as a part-time society editor when I came aboard. Mr. Horner handled the advertising. A circulation agent working on commission scoured the countryside for subscriptions; he would return most evenings with the trunk of an old Chevrolet roadster loaded with corn, turnips, sweet potatoes, or chickens or eggs, to be converted to cash at W. R. Hartness's wholesale place or Munger's Grocery. The *Herald* owned the Chevy. Occasionally I would bribe the circulation agent into lending it to me for a night, solemnly vowing to have it at his house before dawn lest the boss learn of its extracurricular employment.

Mr. Horner was about ten years older than I, thirty or so. He had attended Trinity College before it became Duke University, graduated from the University of North Carolina, and studied journalism for a year at Columbia University. Then he had joined the *Durham Morning Herald*, in his home city, and risen to managing editor. He was a thin, intense man given to whines, rages, and penny-pinching. He longed for wealth and prominence, and pursued them systematically, vigorously, and intelligently. His friends called him Bill. I never did.

As long as I kept the Linotype operator busy when he wasn't plunking advertisement type, Mr. Horner pretty much left me alone. After making my rounds at the town hall and courthouse, lingering at the police station and sheriff's office, I would call a scattering of lawyers, doctors, and business people who kept up with politics and whatever else was going on around town. A favorite stopping place was the law office of Judge Thomas J. McPherson, who presided over the county court and practiced with my roommate, A. A. F. Seawell, Jr.

"Anything new, Your Honor?" I would inquire.

"Wal, y-a-a-s," Judge McPherson might reply. "You may announce in your columns that I now am in telephonic communication with the world." He would point to an upright transmitter with the receiver hanging on a hook. His judgeship was part-time, and I suppose he hadn't been able to afford a phone—lately, anyway.

"This is a wonderful instrument," the judge might go on. "It was invented, as every schoolboy knows, by Alexander Graham Bell and patented in 1875 or thereabouts, when the great State of North Carolina, need I remind you, was still struggling to throw off the yoke of Republican Reconstruction and my greatest pleasure, being just a tad in a starving land, was to jump off a rail fence and see my shirttail flap. The telephone also works on vibrations, but of a different sort, transmitted by wire and cable. By merely lifting that receiver I will attract the prompt and polite attention of a young woman in the telephone office, possibly an acquaintance of yours, who, at my bidding, will link my voice with your ear, assuming it's you I wish to speak with and you're where you should be and not in here, for instance, planning some mischief with my esteemed associate, Mr. Ashley Seawell. Or she may place me in vocal contact with Raleigh, Washington, or Chicago, or with such foreign capitals as London, Budapest, and Tokyo, Jay-pan. You may inform your readership that I now am available to calls from friends and advisers, but please not creditors, and from clients, if any, and that if they fail to find me in these precincts, well, why, my learned associate, the aforementioned Mr. Seawell, will receive their greetings and messages, and if he ain't here either, being professionally and profitably, I hope, engaged elsewhere, they should inquire of my wherebaouts from the telephone operator, sometimes referred to as central, whom I intend to keep advised of my goings and comings, which I don't calculate is too much to expect of the telephone company to honor and relay, considering that they made me pay a deposit on this here thing and what they charge me for using it."

On returning to my desk—or, rather, to the board attached to the wall that held my typewriter—I would write a little story about Judge McPherson's marvelous contraption to accompany my accounts of the town aldermen's deliberations, the state of the tobacco crop and repairs to a recently burned auction warehouse, the coroner's findings as to a hobo's severed body discovered on the railroad tracks near the Deep River bridge, a report by the grand jury on the sorry condition of the poorhouse roof, a listing by the clerk of the court of those lately convicted of assault and battery, or breaking and entering, or issuing and uttering worthless checks, or loitering and trespassing, or fornication and adultery, and about sundry other happenings, probabilities, and cancellations, good and bad, sufficient to fill, along with the advertisements that Mr. Horner could scrounge, the eight pages that the *Sanford Herald* produced each Monday and Thursday, come hell or high water, for the edification, amusement, and outrage of two thousand subscribers paying five cents a week, twenty cents a month, or one dollar a year, cash or its equivalent, with farm families receiving a five-pound bag of sugar as a bonus upon plunking down.

I also wrote the editorials, usually three for each edition, for which I allowed myself the morning after the paper came out. I soon learned that a brief piece about food, pie especially, or about a child, an animal, or a cemetery—that's right: graveyard, the countrier the better—very likely would be picked up by one of the state dailies and, over the next few weeks, further reprinted by several other newspapers. Content was less important than topic and length. I wrote enough brief reflections on peach and dogwood blossoms, mules and ponies, yaupon and sassafras tea, mistletoe and running cedar, migrating birds, hooting owls, flying squirrels, rabbits and foxes, dogs and cats, barbecue and chit'lins, cemetery beautifications, and cheerleaders, Girl Scouts, and little boys whose voices were changing to cut a pretty good swath through a stand of pulpwood. A protest I wrote against a metal device I saw a counterman place on a pie to guide his knife along a perfect geometric pattern of six triangles, suspending every customer's eternal hope of getting the biggest slice, plugged up spaces in so many editorial pages that I carelessly clipped it for reprinting, *Herald* credit line and all, in the column where it originally had appeared.

7 Where's the Editor?

Sanford and Jonesboro subscribers usually received the *Sanford Herald* by midafternoon on publishing days, Monday and Thursday. But occasionally the Linotype machine or the old flatbed press would fail and the paper would be late. Some carrier boys might become bored with waiting for their bundles and stray off to play. Rounding them up, once the press began to rumble, would be a major managerial problem. Now and then W. E. Horner, the *Herald*'s owner and publisher, would find it necessary to deliver a route in his family automobile, a black two-door Ford sedan with yellow wire spokes. Some of us hirelings in the basement printing plant might have performed the chore but Mr. Horner didn't like to entrust his car to us.

On one such occasion the *Herald* was delayed until nightfall. To my astonishment, Mr. Dan C. Lawrence stormed into the office and demanded to know what was the matter. He was ready for his paper, he fussed, and had been ready for it ever since coming home to supper two hours earlier.

Now Mr. Dan C. Lawrence was a wealthy and important man, a mite on the eccentric side, perhaps, but who wasn't. He invariably wore moleskin trousers and an Oxford gray coat, lived in a splendid house, and owned farms and businesses. His wife was an aristocrat. It had never occurred to me that the *Herald* meant much to the likes of Mr. Dan C. Lawrence. At that moment I began to take my work seriously.

Filling the eight-page newspaper twice a week required some

doing. The society editor took care of a page or two with ornate writeups of weddings, all of them pretty much alike except for differences there might be in what the ladies wore, and of bridge parties and tea-pourings and book club meetings, as well as a column of personals. Correspondents in rural communities sent in, at a nickel per published inch, handwritten accounts of home-demonstration club gatherings, church affairs, births and birthdays, first cotton bolls and tobacco curings, fox raids on hen houses, frost damage, thank-you notes, quilting bees, homecomings and dinners-on-the-grounds, house warmings and poundings (for preachers mostly: everybody bring a pound of something), visits, arrivals and departures, whose gardens were ready and who was canning what, which flowers were in bloom, and, in late July or August, organized prayers for rain.

I wrote the hard news. But there was only so much hard news in a town of 4,253 souls at the bottom of the Depression. I had to be resourceful. Some of the stuff I wrote got me or the *Herald* in trouble.

Judge Thomas J. McPherson summoned me to his bench at the close of a weekly session of county court. "Bob, you've embarrassed me," he said gloomily.

"How do you mean, sir?" I asked, much concerned. "I didn't mean to, and I apologize for whatever it was."

I was sorry indeed. Judge McPherson was one of my favorite news sources. He was a small man, no more than 120 pounds. Everything about him was dark—hair, eyebrows, eyes, sunken cheeks, clothing. A brown fedora made him seem topheavy when I met him in the street.

"Well, that piece you had in the paper about dogfighting upset me," the judge replied. Elbow on bench, he rested his head in a hand. "Dogfighting is against the law, and it's my sworn duty to punish and otherwise discourage lawlessness in this county. You described a crime and your participation in it. It occurs to me that you're in contempt of my court."

I had written a story about the dogfights that were held every Saturday morning in a meadow between Buffalo and Tramway. The town cobbler had taken me to one. The cobbler made a habit of stopping me as I passed his shop to take me to task for a *Herald* misspelling or a sentence structure that he found faulty. At the orphanage where he had learned his trade he also had learned English grammar.

During these encounters I discovered that the cobbler bred pit bulldogs. He told me a good bit about the care and training of puppies, including his rule never to apply a blade to one; he trimmed tails with his teeth. In my article I quoted the cobbler at some length, and Judge McPherson could have learned far more from him than from me about dogfighting in his judicial domain. Also, he might have found clues as to what went on by checking most Monday mornings on the condition of a brindle pit that was kept on a chain at a filling station in the middle of town. Only another pit could have inflicted the cuts, bruises, abrasions, and contusions that dog might show along its neck and on its legs.

Again I assured the judge that I was sorry to have troubled him. But I didn't feel I had written anything that wasn't in the public domain, I added.

"Well, I'm still thinking about holding you in contempt," he said.

That was the last I heard of it.

Toward the end of 1933 the $20,000 in scrip that the county, lacking funds to meet its obligations, had issued in April became scarce. Somebody, it was clear, was holding scrip with the intention of collecting the authorized 6 percent interest on it at the year-end redemption time. Whom it might be was of great interest in Sanford, among business people especially.

By February 1934 the county had enough money on hand to redeem the scrip. It announced it would call in the issue on March 1, a month early, and thereby save the taxpayers 0.5 percent interest— a whopping one hundred dollars. Soon $16,378.50 in scrip showed up.

The newly organized National Bank of Sanford had cornered $9,991.25 for a profit, at 5.5 percent interest, of $549.52. The next largest holder was a Sanford physician, Dr. John F. Foster, who turned in $2,132 and collected $117.30 in interest.

I got the list, a public record, from the county auditor, and of course published it.

A month later Dr. Foster paid me an office call. He was furious about my scrip story. I had intruded upon his privacy by exposing his personal affairs, he complained, and moreover had failed to give him the credit he deserved for, out of civic interest and at great sacrifice to himself, freeing the county of unpopular and stigmatizing funny money and of economic strain. Then he got down to brass tacks.

"Since you wrote that business about my scrip," he growled, "nobody will pay me his bills."

My heart didn't bleed for the doctor. He either had an extensive practice or was an expert at creating the illusion that he did—as every rival doctor in town, some of whom were struggling, believed to be the case. No meeting of any consequence was convened without his presence, whether civic, political, social, or religious. And none progressed far before he was urgently paged. It got to be a town joke.

Still, I was sorry to make him mad. He was the county coroner and often took me with him on his official rounds. Several times I was among his jurors.

So I took more of his guff than I cared for.

The county jack cost me a scolding, too.

The board of county commissioners observed that farmers' mule stock, like the price of tobacco and cotton, was in decline. This was not due, heaven knows, to a failure of the supply side. Among the advertisements that Mr. Horner hustled at the approach of tobacco marketing time, when cash would be least scarce, were announcements by sales stables of the arrival, fresh from Missouri, of a shipment of mules, their high quality and durability guaranteed. The trouble was that a farmer wasn't sure to have the price of a mule left in his pockets after he had paid his landlord and supplier and made his children decent for school.

So the commissioners bought a jack with county funds and made him available, without fee, to any farmer owning a brood mare. The mule colts thus produced, the commissioners figured, would brighten agriculture's future. I duly reported the commissioners' thoughts and actions. Editorially I noted that they were well within the spirit of the New Deal's Agricultural Adjustment Act and perhaps would inspire a new plank in Norman Thomas's Socialist platform the next time he ran for president.

Soon the jack arrived—and what a jack he was! He stood maybe fifteen hands, yet seemed to be all head. His ears were nearly as large as tobacco leaves. I didn't know that donkeys reached such proportions.

The jack was installed at the livery stable behind the Wilrik Hotel, near the center of the business district. His bray, he began to demonstrate, was as great as his brawn. Not even the siren atop the fire station was as ear-splitting—or as unpredictable. The jack would bray at any time and for any duration.

Guests at the stately Wilrik responded with a howl of their own. Was this an inn or a stable? they asked the management; should they expect to find pigs in the lobby and chickens in the hallways? Even the old-maid county home-demonstration agent, who was among the hotel's permanent residents, joined the protest, although the jack was in the department of her close colleague, the county farm agent.

In emergency session, the commissioners voted to transfer the jack to the county home, a few miles from town, where a farm was conducted to help feed the poor and infirm sheltered there. When word spread in and beyond town that a work order had been issued for the jack, traffic out that way would pick up. Men would leave their offices, shops, and fields to witness the carryings-on. Even the benches and checkerboard in the taxi lot would be abandoned.

But the jack, alas, was prone to disappoint all, man and beast. As George Washington wrote the Marquis de Lafayette about the ass he received from the King of Spain in 1788, "In appearance he is fine; but his Royal master, tho' past his grand climateric, cannot be less moved by female allurements than he is; or when prompted, can proceed with more deliberation and majestic solemnity to the work of procreation." Washington, though, remained optimistic. To a relative he confided in a letter, "I have my hopes that when the

Royal Gift becomes a little better acquainted with republican enjoyments, he will mend his manners and fall into our custom of doing business."

Our county jack continued to loaf on the job. I wrote on the *Herald* editorial page that he seemed to think he had hired out to the WPA, the most abused of the Roosevelt administration's boondoggles. I suggested also that he disgraced the symbol of the vigorous and creative Democratic party.

The chairman of the board of county commissioners, Mr. K. E. Seymour, ignored my earlier jabs concerning the county jack. But he took exception to what he perceived to be my doubts about his competence in animal husbandry. Coming upon me at the courthouse one day he bluntly inquired if I held any real estate in the county. I replied that I did not.

"That's one of the troubles with you, Mason," he said. "You never will amount to a damn until you own property."

I believe he was saying that, in his opinion, I wasn't qualified to cast a ballot, much less to comment on the affairs of government.

My critics were not confined to county officials and professional people. And I had no monopoly on their expression of outrage.

An overhead bulb usually lit the *Herald*'s basement office. I remember a time it did not.

I strolled in to do whatever it was I had in mind. In the dimness I saw Mr. Horner sprawled in his chair with his feet on his desk. His hat was tilted over his face, which was turned toward the ceiling. He was putting drops in his nose.

I started to switch on the light, but hesitated. I sensed that I was entering a grave and dangerous scene.

In one terrible movement Mr. Horner slammed his feet onto the cement and bolted upright. His face startled me. I had not seen him before without glasses. One eye was black. Both cheeks were swollen. His face was further distorted by anger.

"What in the goddam hell," Mr. Horner screamed, "did you write about that crazy blacksmith?"

It took me half an hour to sort out just what had happened. Part of it I winnowed from Mr. Horner's curses and threats. The rest I sifted, amid snickers and guffaws, from a rambling account provided by Mel Edwards from over behind the press, out of Mr. Horner's hearing. Mel was a printer. I wasn't sure which tickled him more: Mr. Horner's humiliation or my anxiety.

Mel had been the first to reach the shop that morning. He hardly had unlocked the door when a husky man slouched in and casually asked to see the editor.

The editor hadn't arrived, Mel said.

Well, when would he come?

It depended on several things, Mel replied, including just whom the caller had in mind: Mr. Horner owned the paper and called himself the publisher and editor, but a younger fellow named Mason did most of the writing.

"You tell the editor, then, whichever one it is, that I want to see him at my blacksmith shop next to the livery stable behind the Wilrik Hotel," the caller said. He went his way.

Mr. Horner arrived before I did. Mel Edwards told him about the caller. "Probably wants an ad," Mr. Horner said. "I'll take care of it—got to be down that way anyhow."

At about midmorning he stopped at the blacksmith shop and said he was from the *Herald*. The blacksmith promptly knocked him down. Mr. Horner got up and tried to scramble away. But the blacksmith grabbed him, struck him several more times, and threw him against the wall. Mr. Horner bounced off running.

The street in front of the blacksmith shop was unpaved. As Mr. Horner fled up it, the blacksmith followed, hurling cinders and clods at him.

I did not know the blacksmith. But I knew what I had written about him. He had been a defendant in criminal court that week, and I had embellished my report of his trial with some unsavory matter told me by the arresting deputy sheriff.

Also, I knew what I had to do at once, lest I never hear the end of the business.

"I'm going to see the blacksmith," I told Mr. Horner. "I'll tell him he jumped the wrong man."

The walk I took then was about as long as any I remember. Maybe the fellow would beat me up too, I thought, but there could be some doubt. I had been in a few fights and survived them, and I expected to survive whatever was in store. Also, I had more than half an idea that the blacksmith had got the meanness out of his system for the time being.

That turned out to be the case. When I entered his shop and announced that I was the one who had displeased him, he said, "You want me to whup you too?"

It was up to him, I said; I had come in realization that he might wish to do just that. But it seemed to me, I added, that he and I ought to be able to settle our differences without brawling.

He nodded and said he guessed so. We talked a while about nothing in particular. I was tempted to ask him what sort of target Mr. Horner had offered, scooting up the street like that, but thought better of it. The blacksmith didn't ask me for a retraction of anything, and I had no suggestion. So I left.

I learned two things from that experience. One was to make myself immediately available to anyone I had aggrieved. The other was to double check whatever a cop told me.

8 The Old Enemy

Whether North Carolina might join the parade of states ratifying the Twenty-first Amendment to the U.S. Constitution, repealing Prohibition, was the big issue in the November 1933 election. The *Sanford Herald*'s position was soaking wet.

Toward the end of October I wrote an editorial chiding preachers and deacons for teaming up with bootleggers to campaign for, in the name of the "Noble Experiment," crime and disorder. Mr. Paul Barringer, a Sanford leader of the United Dry Forces, replied with a letter upbraiding the *Herald* for bedding down with an unprincipled industry that would encourage wife-beating, furniture breaking, debt-defaulting, and great suffering among little children. He went at us pretty hard.

W. E. Horner, the *Herald*'s publisher, was stung. "You've got to come back with something a damsight smarter than you wrote the first time," he told me. I had been writing the editorials since midsummer. "There was the time," he raged on, "when the *Greensboro Daily News*, I think it was, said a candidate for something or other, governor maybe, wasn't fit to be a dogcatcher. The candidate threatened to sue for libel. So the *News* said that, on second thought, it believed the candidate would make a splendid dog-catcher and ought to run for that instead of governor. Now you write something sharp like that."

Whatever I produced extended no journalistic lore. It did not even persuade me that I, having turned twenty-one in September, should go to the courthouse and register to vote. For I did not wish to remember the rest of my life that the first ballot I ever cast was a disappointment to my Presbyterian-elder father.

If I ignored my editorial advice, my readers gave it shorter shrift still. On election day a choir of ladies from the Baptist church, dressed in white and carrying candles to light the spiritual way, marched along the streets singing "Yield Not to Temptation" and "Where He Leads I Will Follow." Sanford and Lee County voted overwhelmingly against the proposition of calling "a convention to consider the proposed amendment to the Constitution repealing the Eighteenth Amendment." So did the State of North Carolina—by more than two to one.

But the results were academic. Prohibition as a national policy collapsed early the following month when Utah became, by one convention vote, the thirty-sixth state to go wet, providing the necessary three-fourths majority to alter the Constitution.

Neighboring Virginia the next year created a system of state liquor stores. Their wares soon seeped into North Carolina as an illicit alternative to white lightning. In 1935 North Carolina introduced, on a limited local-option basis, stores like Virginia's. Sanford waited thirty more years to opt for legal liquor sales.

Clearly, then, the *Herald*'s wet stand in 1933 was bold. That was not lost on me. Liquor had been illegal in North Carolina since 1909, a full decade before the nation outlawed it. I was born in 1912 and was a senior at Chapel Hill when Congress modified the Volstead Act to permit the manufacture and sale of 3.2 beer. Thus my generation was unique, and remains so, for having grown up in a period when all intoxicating beverages were jail bait.

Prohibition and defiance of it were visible in Sanford almost constantly in the thirties. No issue of the *Herald* appeared without mention of a still-busting raid or an arrest for moonshining, blockading (also known as rum-running), or bootlegging. The taxis operating from a midtown stand delivered more "bootlegger pints"— 12 ounces—of stumphole than they did passengers. One day Rob Seymour, a tinsmith self-taught in copper, came to the office and asked me to address his paper for the next month in care of a general store a dozen or so miles down the road. "I'm going to be in the woods down there sugar-heading," he explained.

I was getting a haircut not long afterwards when a deputy sheriff entered the barbershop and addressed the customer in the chair next to mine. The dialogue went something like this:

"That your Studebaker out there?"

"What's left of it. A fender fall off or something?"

"Naw, not that. But it's squattin' kinda low on the springs, ain't it?"

"Got a load of stovewood in there for mama. She's been burnin' bark and fussin' for a month."

"I know what you got in there. I done pulled out the back seat and looked."

The customer was silent for a long moment, then he sighed: "Oh, goddam, goddam. Peas and onions for supper."

The county jail was a poor feeder.

And there was the ice-and-coal dealer who, running for the town board of aldermen, encountered a whispering campaign that he had been convicted of making liquor in the adjoining county where he had spent his early years. He acquired from the clerk of the court there an affidavit attesting to the purity of his record. It became the main plank of his platform.

I figured that federal revenue agents rather than the sheriff must have bagged that old boy. So I wrote a friend at the *Greensboro News* and asked him to check with the clerk of the U.S. District Court for the Middle District of North Carolina. There was our candidate's file—guilty as charged, fined $100, and placed on probation for three years.

The case was twelve years old. I did not print it.

But I did print a story about a farmer out toward Shallow Well who worked his old mule to death. When the poor thing wasn't pulling a plow it was hitched to a Hoover cart—to the sawed-off back part of an automobile with shafts bolted to it. Hoover carts were a depression phenomenon. The farmer buried his mule behind his barn.

Spring came. The farmer didn't put in a crop. Soon weeds overran his fields.

Toward summer, though, he acquired an automobile—second-hand, to be sure, but in fair shape. And a little later he patched his roof and porch. That fall, when his neighbors were moaning about twelve-cent tobacco, he put in a telephone.

The sheriff's office took note of the farmer's improvements and their contrast with his neglected acreage. It also became aware of the unusual comings and goings in the farmer's yard and between his house and barn.

So the chief deputy took a look. Behind the barn he observed that the mound over the mule's grave remained raw and unsunken. It appeared to have been shaped just that day.

As a matter of fact it had, as the chief deputy reckoned upon employing a shovel to the grave's soft dirt. A few feet down, and on to where bones and some mule-hide were struck, the chief deputy unearthed twenty-two half-gallon jars of moonshine.

"Some of the jars right there in the carcass, what of it hadn't rotted," the chief deputy said that night at the filling station where men gathered after work. "It's a mighty common son-of-a-bitch that will stash whiskey to sell inside a dead mule."

"That's so," agreed a man drinking a Nehi orange. "But you got to admire anybody who can get more results out of a dead mule than you usually can expect from a right nice team of horses."

The chief deputy was more likely than the high sheriff to root out stills and sweet mash. Church people complained that the sheriff courted moonshiners' votes. But he couldn't restrain the chief deputy without giving him good cause to run against him in the next election. Some of the sheriff's friends, admitting he showed little stomach for still-busting, said he simply wasn't hypocrite enough to suck up to the dry establishment.

For it was well known that the sheriff had wrestled hard, from time to time, with the Old Enemy. He claimed to have won, and that earned him some support, especially among good women who admired repentant men. The sheriff was a widower, a lean and handsome man with graying hair, a penchant for dressing well, and courtly manners.

Yet the church gossip that he was soft on moonshiners bothered him some. He had been elected narrowly and knew that his next race would be harder than the last. He had to campaign all the time.

Occasionally the sheriff made trouble for himself. One winter night, for example, while he was foxhunting with cronies and two packs of hounds near Lemon Springs—while the lot of them were banging over back roads in pickup trucks and automobiles, that is, stopping now and then to build a fire and take a drink or two and listen to the baying—one of the two huntsmen, a colored man riding a mule, came upon an abandoned still; and the sheriff, when he learned this, went in behind the huntsman with two or three others and brought out a submarine boiler and a Ford radiator used for the condenser and a mash barrel and a filthy straining bonnet, and lifted this junk onto a pickup, from which the sheriff heaved it all, toward morning, into the front yard of a Methodist steward who had been especially vocal in criticizing his inattention to swamp and stumphole duty.

There were four deputies, counting the chief deputy. One of them suggested to me that I join a still-raiding party the chief deputy would lead. I readily accepted. But when I chanced to mention the prospect to Judge Thomas J. McPherson, who presided over county court, he warned me that the operation might be in essence a snipe hunt—that I should expect to be led quickly to an idle still with no one about, which the raiders would then attack with axes, only to flush from nearby bushes a din of shouts and shotgun firing and leaf rattling. Lawmen delighted in scaring hell out of greenhorns, the judge warned me.

So I had my guard up. Nevertheless, I was surprised when the high sheriff himself asked me to go into the woods with him. I told him, fine!

He and I rode in his car down to the Fayetteville highway and onto a dusty road. Near a plank bridge he pulled into the edge of some piney woods. We got out and followed the branch that the bridge spanned. Soon we came upon a small pot still partly covered with brush. The cap and worm were missing.

"There's a house pretty near here," said the sheriff. "We'll just go back to the car and ride there."

The house was small but sturdy and pleasant. In its neat yard were magnolia and dogwood trees and shrubs and flowers. The outbuildings were in good repair.

The sheriff parked in the driveway near the house. He got out and called. A woman came onto the porch. She was almost pretty, forty-five or so, about the sheriff's age.

We went on up. "Hidy, Miss Martha," said the sheriff. "He here?"

"Sheriff," responded the woman. Then, giving herself time to take in the scene before her—the familiar form of the county's top law-enforcement officer and a perfect stranger—she asked, "He?"

"Yes'm," said the sheriff. "He. Him."

"Well, him then," replied the woman. "Him and his brother, they're at their daddy's, helping out today. Left early in the morning. Their daddy's poorly."

"I'm sorry to hear that," said the sheriff. He removed his hat in a gesture of sympathy. Then he jammed it back on his head and spoke in a businesslike way:

"Well tell him then, soon as he gets home, tell him he should come see me. It's Friday today. Tell him the sooner the better.

Monday will do. Tell him, too, I found that mess of his by the branch."

The woman's face remained expressionless. "I don't know about any mess," she said.

"No, I wouldn't expect you to," the sheriff answered, kindly. "But tell him just the same I found it, and tell him I want him to come see me and get right when he does. Just that.

"Now, you understand, there ain't one thing I can do about that mess, long as nobody was there. But this man with me here, that makes it another story. He's a federal agent, and under the United States Fresh Path Act, he can make an arrest where the path leads to, and that's to right here. He says he's got to get back to Greensboro this evening. Him and I will talk. We'll have us a talk.

"So you tell him, soon as he comes from his daddy's, I want him to come see me. Monday's fine."

We returned to the car and left. I said, "Sheriff, I want you to know I don't appreciate being used like that. She was a nice-looking lady, and the idea of her hating my guts for nothing I've done doesn't suit me. I know you've got to do your politicking, and I wish you well. But I don't like being used."

The sheriff drove on. "If I was you," he said at length. "I don't believe I'd say what you don't like or anything else. I believe I'd just keep my mouth shut about the whole thing. I'll remind you that it's against the law to impersonate a federal officer."

I couldn't believe my ears. Before I could think of anything to say, the sheriff added, in a drawling sort of way:

"And remember, I've got me a witness back there."

9 Statecraft

Life was lovely in Sanford. Yet when the *News and Observer* in Raleigh offered me a job in November 1935, I couldn't wait to go.

Having just had myself fitted for a forty-dollar suit of clothes, I was broke. In Raleigh I hocked the watch my father had given upon my graduation from the University of North Carolina to tide me over until I drew my first week's pay—twenty dollars.

The 1935 General Assembly was to convene in January. I wanted desperately to cover it. One of my father's cousins, George B. Mason, a Gastonia lawyer, was a member of the Senate. George's father, Oscar F. Mason, also a Gastonia lawyer, had been a Senator in the "Redemption" legislature of 1899, when Democrats regained control from the Republican-Populist "fusion" that grew out of Reconstruction. Uncle Oscar had become my father's guardian upon the death at an early age of his father. And Uncle Oscar's father, Lawson A. Mason, who was my great-grandfather, had been in the Senate before the Civil War.

But the *N&O*'s city editor intended to keep me on the police and courts beat. I heard that the Raleigh *Times*, down Martin Street from the *N&O*, was looking for a legislative reporter, and I went there and signed on for what I was making.

Two of my friends from college worked for the *Times*, one covering city hall and the other running the telegraph desk. I moved from the Y.M.C.A., where I had found temporary lodgings, into a boarding house with the telegraph editor—a considerable comedown from my Sanford life-style.

To my delight, the *Times* assigned me to the Senate. The city editor, who doubled as Capitol reporter, chose the House of Representatives for himself. I feared that my friend covering city hall, who had been on the paper a year, would resent what I perceived to be my jump over him. Later he told me he was glad to stay where he was, figuring that any reporter hired for the legislature would be fired at adjournment—a judgment not, alas, without foundation.

The legislature met in the lovely old Capitol chambers. Only four reporters had permanent seats at the little press table in the Senate, directly in front of the president's dais. I was among them. When any of the four wished to talk with a Senator, he simply went to his desk. From time to time one of us would substitute for the reading clerk. It wasn't unknown for a reporter to contribute to a voice vote.

Lieutenant Governor Alexander H. "Sandy" Graham, who presided over the Senate, was from Hillsborough, ten miles from Mebane, my hometown. He was grandson of a governor, and at the close of the session announced his candidacy, which did not pan out, for the office. If looks and bearing had counted for much, he would have won. He had been a captain in the First World War and was ramrod straight. Also, he was handsome and courtly.

My second cousin, the Senator from Gaston County, took little part in the proceedings. He sat silently during the squabbling over repeal or modification of the sales tax, which was new and controversial; on abolishing the absentee ballot, a perennial topic; on dampening the bone-dry Turlington Act, which would occur during the rush to adjournment; on licensing cosmetologists, who sent a bevy of lobbyists to the Sir Walter Hotel, where most legislators stayed; and on substituting a gas chamber for the electric chair, which was scandalously busy that year. Then someone introduced a bill to facilitate divorce from a mentally impaired spouse.

When that proposal came up for debate, so did my kinsman, his voice aquiver. The idea of abandoning a mate under any circumstances was bad enough, he cried, but to cast off a helpless one was unforgivably mean and hateful. When a man and woman plight their troth for good times and bad, in sickness and in health, their contract covers mental as well as physical ailment, he preached, and it ought to have legal as well as moral standing. "What therefore God has joined together, let no man put asunder," he recited. On and on he went. He raised hell. I do not know what got into my cousin—why that bill, to the exclusion of all others, fired him up.

The best speech I heard during that 1935 session was delivered by Senator U. L. Spence of Moore County. Mr. Spence was a trial lawyer from Carthage, the little county seat—a tall, spare man with a great bald head and staring eyes that steel-rimmed spectacles distorted. He was chairman of the Senate Roads Committee, a position of much importance in a state that set unusual store by its highway system—and spread about as much politics as asphalt onto it. The "U" of his initials stood for Union. Speculation at our press table was that the "L" stood for League, as the Spence family Bible probably would attest. On the Senate roll, however, Mr. Spence was listed as Union Lee. The difference could hardly have been greater. For Mr. Spence, like many another successful Southern politician born in the Reconstruction period, was something of a professional Confederate.

Immediately after the Senate's opening prayer on February 21, he stood. "Your Honor!" he thundered.

Sandy Graham's well-barbered head was still bowed and his eyes, a mite red, were still closed. His reactions were not sharp that day. After momentary befuddlement, he responded, "I beg your pardon, sir."

"I beg *your* pardon," Mr. Spence responded. "Mr. President!"

"The-Senator-from-Moore," answered the presiding officer.

"I rise on a point of personal privilege," boomed Mr. Spence.

"The-Senator-will-state-his-point-of-personal-privilege," rattled Mr. Graham.

"Mr. President," Mr. Spence said, lowering his voice somewhat, "on the twenty-eighth day of June in the Year of Our Lord 1857, in the town of Brockville, Penn-syl-vania, there was born a boy-child."

That was his term: boy-child. He continued something like this:

"And what a bright and perceptive boy he was! Although by the time he was eight years old he had lived in the North through the War Between the States, he instinctively was developing an affinity for the South.

"Yes, Your Honor—I beg your pardon, sir: Mr. President—this boy, when he engaged in his boyish pursuits, when he played about his good home, and when he explored the fields and meadows about his town, he was intrigued by the wind that blew from the South; for it seemed to him that the southern wind had a special softness, a certain sweetness, and he wondered of its source."

Lieutenant Governor Graham's eyes took on a glaze. He leaned upon his dais, supporting himself with outstretched arms and hands.

"And in time, Mr. President, that boy indeed sought out the source of the sweet and gentle wind from the South. But first he went in other directions. And sir, he went far; how very far he traveled!

"As a young man he affiliated himself with a Pennsylvania newspaper, the *Pittsburgh Times*, it was, and he was sent by it to Russia to inquire into and to learn its oil-producing methods, about which he proceeded to write to the edification of scientists and industrialists as well as the reading public. And that started his wanderlust, which took him to all parts of the North American continent, to New Mexico and Nevada and on to California, always craving for knowledge on all manner of subjects uppermost in his mind. Thus he built up a store of learning which few men have possessed.

"And then in the late eighteen-nineties, Your Honor—Mr. President—when the boy was no longer a boy but a man, and a married man, he realized that not the East, not the West, and not the North, but the South held what he wanted most, what in his mind he had always desired, which was home. Ah, sir, home!

"So southward he began his last and final trek. With his wife at his side he sought the source of those sweet and gentle winds that had stirred his boyish imagination and impulses. Down through Virginia he came.   .

"Ah, Virginia! That noble country where so many North Carolina boys shed their blood—boys from the state which was ninth in population among the Confederate eleven but which provided a sixth of their troops and lost upwards of 50,000 of them. The soil where Harvey Hill distinguished himself and his division before moving on to Chickamauga and at last to Bentonville; where Dorsey Pender fought so nobly at Seven Pines and Chancellorsville and died at Staunton; in the land where the beautiful Ramseur, wrapped in his long gray coat and saying the prayers he had learned at Davidson College, entered eternal sleep, both his lungs cruelly pierced; the land where Ransom led that marvelous cavalry of the Ninth North Carolina Volunteers; and where the bold Grimes unleashed one more time his fury in the last Confederate assault at Appomattox. Those gray giants! Those gray ghosts! And Hoke! And Bragg! And Barringer! Ah, sir. Ah, sir."

Those were Confederate generals from North Carolina. It must have pained Mr. Spence that his Pennsylvania boy-child's father fought the South as a lieutenant colonel in the Yankee army, a detail he did not mention.

"As I was remarking," Mr. Spence continued, "down through Virginia came this journalist, following the sweetness of the gentle breeze until it brought him into North Carolina and, near its center, into Moore County. And in Moore County, in the Sandhills and amid the longleaf pine, he stopped. He stopped! He had found his Valhalla—for such he named the home he at last had found. And in Moore County he lent his brains and his hands to the development of a winter resort appealing to gentlefolk from the harsher climes. I speak of Pinehurst and Southern Pines, sir.

"As a foremost journalist of this entire nation, he informed and enlightened the people through newspapers he established or joined, and in other papers he served as a correspondent. And when the sainted Woodrow Wilson summoned Josephus Daniels from Raleigh to be his Secretary of the Navy, this man who had come among us, this writing man, with the magnitude of his mind and the fluency of his pen, he became assistant editor and carried on, in editor Daniels's patriotic absence, the traditions of the *News and Observer*: of the 'Old Reliable'."

Lieutenant Governor Graham left his dais. He paced the little space behind it, wiped his brow, and adjusted his collar. Then he remounted the dais, drank from the pitcher of water there, and leaned again upon his hands, steadying his fingers.

"And sir, this splendid man, this good and wise journalist who had left his home to find a home, found also comfort and satisfaction where the soft wind had brought him; and now he has found peace as well. And it is fitting sir, that here he now shall sleep until his Maker calls, in the Sandhills, below the bough of a longleaf pine.

"And I think, sir, a little bird, a little songbird, perhaps a Carolina wren, will perch on that bough, and that the bird will warble, and that the bird's song will have an unusual sweetness—and sir, an unusual sadness.

"For Your Honor, I have received within this hour, by Western

Union telegram, the distressing news that Bion H. Butler has passed into eternity."

Senator Spence of Moore sat.

On the dais Lieutenant Governor Graham continued to stare downward. Then, suddenly aware of the silence, he looked up and about him.

"I beg your pardon, Senator," he said, "what bill was that you were talking about?"

10 Extra, Extra, Extra!

At about the time the legislature adjourned, the *Times* telegraph editor took a job in another city. I moved to his desk—much relieved, for I feared I was a short-timer. Whether I was or not, I wished to learn desk work. Good copyreaders, I had observed, were rare enough to have built-in job insurance.

On the *Times*, as on most newspapers of its category then, the telegraph editor moved all the wire copy without help. He designed the front page and wrote its headlines. Also, he placed secondary news inside the paper, seeing each page to completion except those devoted to editorials, local news, sports, and society.

Intricate rules guided headline-writing and makeup. Each line of a head, for example, had to contain the same number of letters, or of counts: 1½ for m and w, ½ for i and l. No line could end with a preposition or adjective; no phrase or term could be split. Below each head were one to four subheads, depending on the head's size and location as well as the paper's style; banks also had to be precise in grammatical and physical ways. I acquired style books from the *New York Times*, the *Washington Star*, and the *Chicago Tribune*, and set about to master them. Some of the old rules endure here and there; most have been relaxed and simplified, with the result that today's front pages are less mathematical and cluttered than yesterday's and all pages are more attractive and readable. The door guarding the copyreader's closed shop has been kicked down.

A single Associated Press teletype machine delivered to the *Times* all its wire news—state, national, world, and sports. The paper seldom printed more than sixteen pages. I found time to edit local as well as telegraph copy, working closely with both the managing and city editors. Occasionally they divided my usual work between them and sent me out of town to handle a special story, such as the opening in Wilson of the state's first post-Prohibition liquor store, swoops into mill towns of textile union "flying squadrons," tobacco-marketing crises, coastal storms, and major crimes.

Thus it came about that on July 30, 1935, an exceedingly hot day, I rushed off to adjoining Franklin County to cover a lynching.

A twenty-five-year-old Negro man known as Sweat Ward, whose first name was reported to be Govan and then Roosevelt, was the victim. Early in the day he struck his sister with a rock at their home. A man who happened by intervened, and Ward fought him off with a bottle.

Charles Stokes, white and elderly, was working in a field nearby. He too intervened. Ward felled him with a rock and cut off his head with an axe. Other men in the field, all Negroes, subdued Ward and held him, none too gently. Somebody called the sheriff's office in Louisburg, the county seat, eleven miles away.

Sheriff J. T. Moore and two deputies came for Ward. They took him to a physician's office in Louisburg for treatment of his roughing up. There Ward shoved aside the doctor's nurse, bruising and frightening her, and tried to flee. The lawmen dragged him to the county jail.

Word reached the sheriff that Charles Stokes's neighbors in the remote Epsom community were gathering. He and two deputies hustled Ward back into the sheriff's car and started with him to Rocky Mount, the nearest city, where jail security would be greater. Five miles out of town they were challenged by armed men in one of four cars that were traveling together.

Sheriff Moore yielded Ward to five men in the lead car. In the caravan were about fifteen other men. None wore a mask or other disguise. All carried guns. Away they sped with Ward.

The sheriff and two deputies returned to Louisburg to spread an alarm.

When they next saw Ward he was dead, hanging by his neck from a cotton plowline to a scrub oak tree near where he had decapitated Charles Stokes. One bullet wound was in his chest. His head and body were battered. He was handcuffed. One big toe was missing—and presumably in somebody's pocket.

On learning of the lynching at about noon, Governor J. C. B. Ehringhaus in Raleigh ordered the National Guard company at Henderson, near Louisburg, and all available highway patrolmen into Franklin County. The Raleigh patrol detail responded in twenty-six brand-new cruisers. I was a passenger in one. The *Times* had no staff car. I don't believe anyone on the news staff owned an automobile, either.

But Joynes MacFarland, head of the Raleigh Associated Press Bureau, did. Russell Rogers, the *Times* sports editor and sometime photographer, and Irving Cheek, a *Times* reporter, hitched a ride with him to the lynching scene. (Full-time news photographers were rare in North Carolina. The relatively big *Charlotte Observer* had just one, who dashed about in a car that resembled a fire chief's.)

The MacFarland team beat most of the patrol cars to the scene. Several hundred men and boys were milling about Ward's body, most of them farmers wearing overalls and straw hats. The body was left hanging for several more hours while Coroner R. A. Bobbitt collected a jury and conducted an inquest. Once empaneled, the jury returned a verdict in five minutes: death at the hands of a party or parties unknown.

I interviewed guardsmen and patrol commanders, picked up quotes from several early arrivals, and gave my notes to Cheek and Rogers, who returned to Raleigh with MacFarland. Three stories of the lynching and Rogers's full-length picture of the body hanging from the tree, feet about twelve inches from the ground, and a closeup of the head, partly obscured by manacled wrists across neck and shoulder, appeared under huge red headlines in the third extra edition that the *Times* printed that afternoon.

The *Times* was among few newspapers anywhere that could print in two colors. I'm not sure it had ever sported red streamers before. I know it went wild with the lynching accounts.

The managing editor ignored all mail schedules and concentrated on extras, replating as additional information was telephoned and eventually brought in. He kept the presses running. What the street sales were I have no idea.

They did not meet the managing editor's expectations. Next day the pressroom, the circulation manager's office, and the loading dock were jammed with stacks of all three extras. The publisher, returning from an out-of-town trip, was appalled at the waste. He straightaway fired the managing editor.

I meanwhile was still in Louisburg, having stayed overnight in a little hotel that was a favorite Sunday-night dining place for Raleigh residents. I gathered additional information about the lynching and events leading to it.

Franklin County's elected sheriff, T. N. Spivey, recently had died. Under the state constitution, his duties had fallen to the coroner, R. A. Bobbitt. The Franklin board of county commissioners on the Friday before the Tuesday lynching had appointed J. T. Moore as sheriff. But he had not got around to qualifying, and technically was a deputy under Coroner Bobbitt.

Prior to being named sheriff, Moore was in his second term as Louisburg constable. He was well acquainted among residents in and around the county seat, he told me, but he knew hardly anyone up in the northern corner where Charles Stokes had been decapitated and Sweat Ward had been lynched. That explained, he said, why he had not recognized any of the men who took his prisoner.

He thought the car into which Ward had been transferred was either a Buick or a Plymouth; he wasn't at all sure which, although any schoolboy in those days could identify any make of automobile. He hadn't taken down the license number. "I'm new on this job, and a lot was going on, and I couldn't think of everything," he said. With that he clammed up.

It was generally agreed among the Louisburg people that the men who lynched Sweat Ward were Charles Stokes's lodge brothers. Nobody I talked to was much disturbed about the lynching.

Being without a portable typewriter, I went to the office of the weekly *Franklin Times* to write my story. Just one typewriter was available there, an antique with an obsolete keyboard. So I wrote in longhand. Then I took my copy to the railway station and watched the station agent tap it out by Morse code. Later I boarded a train to Raleigh. The city editor, who was also acting managing editor, asked me not to put in an expense account until the publisher calmed down. "Just your room and train fare," he cautioned me. "You had to eat anyhow."

Governor Ehringhaus sternly called for an investigation of the lynching and a report to him. Attorney General A. A. F. Seawell responded vigorously. He organized a hearing in Louisburg in cooperation with Solicitor William Y. Bickett, whose prosecutory district included Franklin County, and Charles Green, attorney for Franklin County.

The courthouse in Louisburg was packed for the hearing. Sheriff Moore strutted about like a hero. Just three reporters were there— for the AP, the *News and Observer*, and I for the *Times* and, in violation of the *Times*'s AP charter but with the AP man's knowledge, the United Press. Sheriff Moore promptly threw us out.

Attorney General Seawell brought us back. He made Sheriff Moore fetch a table and chairs for us. He opened proceedings with a lecture to the sheriff on the First Amendment and the importance to a democratic government of a free press. It was the first speech on that topic I ever heard. None of the dozens I have heard since stirred me as much as it. Every so often during the hearing that ensued, Mr. Seawell would turn to the reporters and ask if we were comfortable or if the sheriff could do anything further for us. His sense of drama was as fine as his commitment to justice, a quality that all four of his sons inherited: A. A. F., Jr., my Sanford roommate; Malcolm, my college friend who also became attorney general as well as a candidate for governor; Donald, my college classmate and journalistic colleague, who became a New York and London attorney, a stage producer, and publisher of the *Denver Post*; and Billy, a naval casualty of World War II, who was a midshipman sharing a seat with me on a troop-packed train the last time I saw him.

Although Sheriff Moore was grilled and nearly thirty witnesses were questioned by Mr. Seawell and his associates, those findings so quickly arrived at by the coroner's jury at the lynching scene were not extended. The sheriff swore he had never seen before and never since the twenty unmasked men who seized Sweat Ward. His only concession was that he wished he had noted the kidnap car's number.

The lynching was the ninety-eighth recorded by North Carolina since it began keeping such records in 1882. The state has listed no subsequent lynching.

But it has run to 364 the number of persons it has executed since 1910, when it installed the electric chair at Central Prison in Raleigh and relieved the counties of the burden of hanging capital offenders. (The chair was replaced by a gas chamber in 1936; now condemned persons may choose a lethal injection.) In the year that Sweat Ward was hanged by a mob, North Carolina executed eleven persons; in the year before, twenty; and in the year following, a record twenty-three, to be tied in 1947 when nineteen blacks and four whites were gassed.

I was a witness to more of the 1935-36 executions than I would choose to be again. It was my judgment at the time that most of the convicts fared, as to the spirit of the law and goal of justice, only a little better than Sweat Ward.

One grizzled, yellow-eyed old Negro convicted of raping a white girl thought until the moment he was buckled into the electric chair that he was to be hanged. A wizened, parchment-skinned mill hand stood on tiptoes to kiss the burly executioner, a good-natured deputy warden, on the bulge made by a wad of chewing tobacco, and giggled at the commotion he caused. A swamp-countryman as crazy as a loon promised to hex himself into freedom with a black-cat's bones drawn through his teeth and left a triumphant note decorated with a pinned-on cutout of Felix the Cat, the cartoon character, but managed to extend his life only by the few seconds needed to replace, with the electricity cut off, the leg electrode after it slipped down his blistered calf. One execution was carried out six hours after the traditional Friday-at-ten A.M. schedule: the prisoner tried to escape the chair while being led to it by jumping from the death-row ledge to the concrete floor several tiers down; he was carried to the prison infirmary, extensively patched up, eventually pronounced conscious, and put to death.

Every person I saw die was, no matter what else, poor, unlettered, and despised. Of the 364 notched on the state's devices over the decades, 285 were black, 5 were Indians, and 74 were white.

Fairly typical of the lot was Little Bus Holt.

I knew Little Bus in school. I was among the 400 or so pupils in the Mebane public school system, that is, and he was the delivery boy at Mr. Pappy Clark's tiny grocery store across the street from the white schoolhouse. He could have been no more than twelve years old, and fourteen was the legal dropout age, but he was black—ginger-colored, really; there were three or so sets of Holts in Colored Town and all were light-skinned except for Uncle Max Holt and his crowd, who were ebony—and black children didn't have to go to school, to their ramshackle, plank, seven-grade building up the Southern Railway tracks beyond the brickyard, unless they wanted to or their parents made them. Little Bus Holt was proof of that. Our superintendant was in charge of the Negro as well as the white school, which was the basis of his being a superintendent rather than a principal, and could look from his office in our brick building straight at Little Bus Holt, in ragged clothes too big for him, resting on Mr. Pappy Clark's store porch without it ever crossing his mind that *Why, that child is a truant.*

Seven or eight years later Little Bus Holt murdered in cold blood the night fireman in the furniture factory boiler room, a feeble, Bible-quoting old colored man as pensioned off as the factory owner ever pensioned off anyone, and robbed of what he had in his pockets, which was one thin dime. I went to see Little Bus Holt on death row the night before he was to die. He hadn't grown much and, in his floppy brown prison suit, didn't seem any older than when I had joshed with him while buying penny candy or a nickel Chericola at Mr. Pappy Clark's store. He said he would feel better about tomorrow if I would come back and wave to him good-bye, and I went, although I didn't want to. The thing I remember most about his electrocution is the way the electrode cap swallowed his shaven head. I don't suppose that Little Bus Holt ever wore anything that fit him.

The last electrocution I wrote about was Bruno Richard Hauptmann's. My story was a plain fake.

Under the Associated Press's rules when it was an exclusive club, with membership determined by territory and vote, morning papers had exclusive use of copy transmitted between 6 P.M. and 2 A.M., with the afternoon papers controlling the other cycle. But big news labeled in the New York headquarters as EOS—extraordinary service—was available to all AP-member papers and could be printed by any that chose to in an extra edition—the gone and all-but-forgotten EXTRA-EXTRA-EXTRA-READ-ALL-ABOUT-IT! such as the *Times* had published after the Sweat Ward lynching.

All Hauptmann news on the night of April 3, 1936, was EOS. A skeleton staff gathered in the *Times* office to get out an extra as quickly as it could once Hauptmann was executed for the kidnap-murder of infant Charles Lindbergh, Jr. We assumed that the *News and Observer*, a block up Martin Street, also was preparing one.

The *N&O* had badly beaten the *Times* to the street with an extra the night of September 8, 1935, when Senator Huey P. Long was assassinated in Baton Rouge. This time we took precautions. I wrote a description of Hauptmann's death based on electrocutions I had seen at Central Prison, which was put into type, plated, and fixed on the press ready to be churned out on newsprint the moment we received the death flash from Trenton.

My story filled a double-column. It included a review of the legal and political maneuvers that took place in Trenton on that day, including this: "Not until moments before he gasped his last breath was it certain that Hauptmann would die tonight. It was for Col. Mark O. Kimberling, the prison warden, to make the final decision, State Supreme Court Justice Thomas Trenchard earlier in the day having refused to grant a stay . . ." But when I wrote, ". . . two thousand volts of electricity stiffened Hauptmann's body, and in a few moments he had paid the price . . ." I was assuming.

As the actual death story came over the wire, I sent it, take by take, to the composing room. I wrote new headlines for the complete account, and read proof on the new page.

I'm the only person who ever read that page. The managing editor replacing the one fired for packing the building with lynching extras didn't take a chance on a press overrun. He decided against replating. My disgust lingers.

The new managing editor was a cautious man. He almost never relieved me from the telegraph desk so I could report state stories. I hung on as telegraph for another year. Then I got a call from the *Durham Morning Herald*. Its managing editor wanted a good, fast, journeyman copyreader who knew all the rules and could take over any desk, including sports and, oh, lordy, society.

11 Good Morning, Your Honor

A. W. Stamey, who was the managing editor of both the *Durham Morning Herald* and the afternoon *Durham Sun* during the thirties, was a charming rascal. Everyone called him Coonie. His cheeks were broad, his nose and chin sharp, his eyes bright and crinkly behind rimless glasses; further, he was built on the order of a coon: short, broad, and easy moving.

Good manners and good taste were Coonie's guides as to what a newspaper should be. "Rape" was forbidden in headlines. Reports of any violence had to be restrained. Pictures showing corpses or carcasses, especially deer draped over automobile fenders, were not to be published. Coonie expected good taste to be applied to makeup—but it had to be somebody else's; he avoided desk work of any sort and was privately contemptuous of the headline-writing rules that fastidious copyreaders followed in protection of their turf.

He had joined the Durham papers upon graduating from Trinity College shortly before it became Duke University, and had been a local columnist as well as a reporter. He wrote as clearly and precisely as anyone I ever knew, absolutely free of journalese, including all-inclusive lead-sentences. I am haunted to this day by his account of the deaths by lightning of three pretty sisters, two of them home from college, as they huddled under a wagon to escape a shower while helping their father harvest tobacco. There was no sentiment, no bathos; just a stark report of what happened.

Why Coonie assigned himself to that tragedy I do not know. Usually he confined his writing to some matter involving the Durham establishment—for example, the planned construction of the University Apartments near the Duke campus, Durham's first multi-unit complex, and the defiance by Erwin Cotton Mills of Operation Dixie, mounted in 1937 by the Textile Workers Organizing Committee-CIO. As he typed, he loosely held a pencil in his right hand, a habit I picked up and have not overcome.

Durham was then a busy city of 52,037 (18,000 less than the Chamber of Commerce claimed), yet the *Herald* had only three reporters. One of them was Bernard Dekle, a Georgian who had gone to Oglethorpe College and worked briefly for a bank in Osaka, Japan. "Deke" covered courts. Somehow it fell to him to write a little piece about the death of a prize bull at Quail Roost Farm, a dairy and horse farm operated as a profitable hobby by George Watts Hill, a Durham industrialist and banker. Deke wrote that the animal was destroyed.

"What the hell do you mean—'destroyed'?" Coonie asked him the next day.

"That's the correct terminology in animal husbandry," Deke replied. "Shot. Killed. Put down. *Destroyed*."

"Shot is good enough," Coonie said. "You don't need jargon. Next time Watts Hill kills a bull just say it was shot. Everybody will understand that. Don't say a bull is destroyed unless Watts Hill shoves a stick of dynamite up its ass and lights the fuse."

Deke would join the Office of War Information during World War II and eventually return to Japan. When I last heard of him he was married to the Japanese star of a traveling company of *Teahouse of the August Moon* and was her manager. In Durham he had been wed to a pretty nurse who cooked fish that he and I caught in Lake Michie, the city's water source, out near Bahama community off the Roxboro Road.

I kept a twelve-foot juniper boat and 3½-HP Water Witch engine— the first of fourteen outboards I have owned—at the lake. Deke was my constant fishing partner. We brought to his apartment a lot of bream and crappie and occasionally a bass. They made us a fine midday meal.

Coonie surprised me one summer day by asking me to take him fishing. He was not your outdoor type. "Fine," I said. "I was going tomorrow, but Deke said he couldn't, so I'll come for you at 5 A.M., if that suits you." Coonie said he would be ready.

I usually left the office at 2:30 A.M., right after the last edition of the paper went to press. I'd eat then, and if I were going fishing I'd hang around the restaurant, talking with the all-night manager and the other customers, policemen mostly, until the approach of dawn, when I'd head for the lake. So when I called for Coonie I was on time. No one answered the doorbell. I tried again, hesitatingly; I didn't wish to disturb Stamey's wife, whose name was Eunice, or any of their three small children.

I was about to leave when Eunice appeared at the door, wearing a nightgown and robe but barefoot. "What in the name of heaven are you doing here?" she asked, incredulously.

"Coonie and I were going fishing," I said. "I told him I'd come by for him."

"Did he tell you to come here in the middle of the night?" she wished to know. She was pretty frosty.

"It's getting light," I replied. "He said he'd be ready at five o'clock."

"Well, just you wait a minute," said Eunice. "If he said he was going fishing, by God he's going!" Back into the house she flew.

Pretty soon Coonie appeared, looking foolish. He wore his regular street clothes, shoes and all, except for a sleeveless sweater instead of a jacket. The morning was chilly. The odor of stale whiskey was about him.

We got into my automobile, a 1934 Chevrolet coupe I'd bought secondhand before leaving Raleigh. I asked Coonie if he'd had breakfast. He said he didn't need any. He stretched out as best he could and closed his eyes.

About a mile from the lake I stopped long enough to pluck two dozen catalpa worms from a tree in a farmer's yard and to leave fifty cents at his door. Deke and I had an arrangement with the farmer. I put the soft worms in a paper bag.

At the landing I stowed my fishing gear in my boat and asked Coonie to sit forward. As usual, I had some trouble starting the motor. But it wasn't long before we were off.

Lake Michie covers several miles. We were fifteen minutes downstream when the little motor conked out. I checked the fuel setting, adjusted the carburetor, and jiggled the choke needle. All this time my back was to Coonie. I didn't see him stand.

Then I started pulling the cord. The engine caught. It only had a forward gear, so the boat lunged. Coonie fell overboard. We were in about forty feet of water.

The boat kept going. But I turned it about, shut off the engine, and glided quickly to Coonie.

His head bobbed up. He made no effort to swim or even tread, but adjusted his glasses on his nose. Then he sank again. On resurfacing, he readjusted his glasses.

I got Coonie to the stern and, with his help, hauled him into the boat. I burned an arm on the engine, but my boat was narrow and I was afraid to land Coonie any other way.

"You want me to take you home?" I asked.

"Oh, hell, no," Coonie said. "I've already heard enough about this fishing trip there. Just get me to where I can dry out. I'm freezing." The water was fairly warm. Still, Coonie was shaking.

I took him to a point down the lake where a rock as large as a houseboat protruded. We scrambled ashore. Coonie stripped to his one-piece BVDs, placing each item of clothing in a separate place, on a limb or a rock. He took great care and was very neat. He spread the bills from his wallet just so, and patted flat his handkerchief on a tree stump.

I left him with two cane poles and half the catalpa worms. Working my boat with the paddle, I cast toward the banks with a split-bamboo flyrod that had cost me a week's pay. To keep the worm from tearing off, I turned it wrong-side out by pressing a matchstick against its head and applied its fairly tough lining to the hook. If that sounds grim, the fish weren't in for a very good deal either.

At about noon I went back to Coonie. He had taken off his BVDs and was stretched out, buck-naked, on the big rock, sound asleep. He was pink all over. The sun had become bright.

It had dried his clothes, and he dressed gingerly. In the boat and then the car, he was grumpy. I didn't say much. Driving home, though, I got to sniggering.

"What's so goddam funny?" Coonie asked.

"I was thinking about the way you kept adjusting your glasses in the water," I said. "That's all you did, just kept pushing up your glasses."

"Well, I can't swim a lick," Coonie replied. "I figured if I was going to drown I might as well see what was going on."

I didn't see much of him the next few days. The truth is, I stayed away from him. I was sure his discomfort from the sunburn made him irritable. And anyway, my working contacts with the managing editor were limited under ordinary circumstances.

He kept day hours for the most part. I had come to the *Herald* two years earlier as swing editor, filling in on their nights off for the telegraph editor, the city editor, the sports editor, the state editor and the society editor, and on Saturday night lending a hand wherever it was needed. I still did that, and meanwhile had become the nightside straw boss. The Fair Labor Standards Act of 1938 provided for a forty-four-hour work week to be cut in two years to forty, and most North Carolina daily papers had adopted a five-day week. But at the *Herald* we hacked away six days for at least forty-eight hours, with the overtime pay due us rigged into our weekly salaries—which didn't take much doing, considering that the minimum hourly wage was just forty cents. The *Herald* wasn't a good place to work. But jobs were still scarce in the late thirties.

I think I was making $42.50 a week at the start of 1939 when I asked Coonie for a few days off in mid-February. "I'm going to get married," I explained.

Coonie gave me a hard look. "You ought to see a doctor," he said. "He might save you a lot of trouble. It could be that it's just your liver acting up."

No, I told him, I was serious. "The Bishop told me he'd swap a day off on the telegraph desk, and I'll leave a Sunday feature story, and the rest can take care of itself for a couple of days." The Bishop is what we called the former Morse man who was the regular telegraph editor.

"Ah, hell, take a week," said Coonie. "A honeymoon ought to last a week."

I was overwhelmed. Also, I was a mite cautious. Holidays were rare at the *Herald*. Vacations there were ten days rather than the two weeks that most papers gave. Carl C. Council, the *Herald*'s publisher, was a modest, polite, and attractive man, but he dearly believed in a long day's work and a short day's pay.

"You reckon Mr. Council will mind?" I asked, impulsively.

That irritated Coonie. He didn't like having his authority questioned—although I knew sometimes it was questionable.

"What the hell has Mr. Council got to do with it?" he asked gruffly. "It ain't his funeral."

A little later Coonie told me he'd like to give me a bachelor's party on Wednesday, my night off, just before the Saturday I was to be married. "I'll talk the hotel into lending us the bridal suite as a matter of public relations," he said. "We'll have us a few drinks of liquor, and smoke us a few cigars, and eat us some cheese sandwiches, and romance around." That's how he described every party, from a Sunday school picnic to the Chamber of Commerce annual dinner, which in Durham was pretty big stuff.

He meant the Washington Duke Hotel, which was just across

narrow Market Street from the *Herald*. The printers kept a pair of binoculars for looking into hotel rooms.

The party got off to a wretched start and ended just as awkwardly. Coonie bought a batch of whiskey the day before and took it home for safekeeping. There he and Oakey Mitchell, the *Herald* sports editor, got into it, and Mrs. Stamey threw them out. Coonie was in temporary residence at the bridal suite when the guests arrived there. Three of them were from the Raleigh papers, the others from the *Herald* and the Carolina and Duke news bureaus, maybe a dozen in all. Things got pretty loud. At about 3 A.M., shortly after the appearance of the last of the *Herald*'s night staff, the hotel's manager asked us to leave.

On the street, Coonie said he missed his home cooking and was hungry. The restaurant down the street where I usually ate wouldn't do him, and nothing else was open except a hot dog stand. So he, Oakey Mitchell, and I drove to Raleigh in my car to have breakfast at the Sir Walter Hotel.

I parked on Martin Street, near the *Times* building, and we walked to the hotel a block away. When we came back an hour later the car was on the other side of the street with a lamp post bent across its top. Waiting at it was a police cruiser. My brakes had slipped.

The police cruiser was unmarked but I recognized it—a limousine, practically, used for night prowling in the Negro neighborhoods by Sergeant Joe Lowe and his vice squad. Pickings must have been lean that night, or Joe wouldn't have fooled with a traffic case. I knew him and one of the two cops with him, a thin man so elderly that even Joe called him Mr. Peebles. They took us to jail.

The bullpen where we were locked up had no bunks or chairs. Eight or nine bums lay on the concrete floor. Coonie and Oakey were indignant, loudly so. I made myself as comfortable as I could and pondered how I should approach Judge Wiley G. Barnes when Police Court opened at 10 A.M. He was a good friend of mine.

I had dozed off when a great commotion awakened me. I opened my eyes just in time to see the turnkey slam Oakey Mitchell into the bullpen, where he had been with Coonie and me when I fell asleep. Oakey landed on his face. He was a frail, graying man of middle age, with a purse mouth, pop eyes, and a nose bent like a corkscrew. He could be explosive. Also, he could be funny.

"What happened, Oakey?" I inquired as things settled down.

"I escaped and was recaptured," he said, a bit smugly.

"How the hell did you get out?" I asked, really astonished.

"It was easy," replied Oakey. "While you were snoozing the cops brought in those new fellows over there. I walked out the cell door backwards and the cops thought I was another drunk coming in." He seemed to be quite pleased with himself.

Judge Barnes was on the bench when the bullpen was emptied into his court. Instead of sitting with the other members of the night's haul, I went up to him, guiding Coonie and Oakey along.

"Good morning, Your Honor," I said, trying to make humor of the classic phrase.

"Why, Bob," said the Judge, "what brings you here?"

"Well, sir," I replied, "it's a fairly long story, but the essence of it is that my car rolled down the street and hit a lamp post in front of the *Times* building while my friends here and I were having an early breakfast—late supper, in my case—at the Sir Walter. I'd like you to meet them. This is Mr. A. W. Stamey, the distinguished managing editor of the *Durham Morning Herald* and the *Durham Sun*, and this is Mr. Oakey Mitchell, the *Herald* sports editor; I imagine you've read Mr. Mitchell . . ."

Just then the prosecutor joined us. He was Sam Ruark, with whom the distinguished Mr. Stamey had gone to Trinity College.

"Hello, Coonie," the prosecutor said, obviously surprised.

Coonie was surprised too. "Good God-a'mighty, Sam," he gasped, "what have they got you for?"

The upshot was that Judge Barnes let us go. "Do you think you ought to let Anthony McKevlin drive you out of town?" he asked me. Tony McKevlin, the *News and Observer* sports editor, was widely known to have sworn off the hard stuff half a dozen years before, at approximately the hour that he stood before Judge Barnes to answer for urinating into a barrel of flour after failing to locate the men's room in the cafe across from the *N&O* where he had been a regular customer for a decade. I told the judge I was sure I'd be fine.

I had to pay three dollars to the garage for towing in my car. Sergeant Joe Lowe was furious that Judge Barnes didn't make me pay for the broken lamp post, but he kept his mouth shut about that until he was back on the street.

The garage charged me another four dollars for straightening my bumper so the car would steer. We had to wait an hour for the work to be done. To kill time and meanwhile get the kinks out of our backs and legs, Coonie, Oakey, and I walked down Fayetteville Street. Anyone who saw us could have guessed where we'd bedded down. Oakey had turned up his overcoat collar in a jailbird's reflexive affectation.

Up near the Capitol, directly across the street from where we strolled, Governor Clyde R. Hoey and his administrative assistant, Robert L. Thompson, emerged from a drugstore where the Governor came each morning for a Coca-Cola. "Let's duck," I said to Coonie, much alarmed. "It won't do for Bob Thompson to see us." Bob had left the *News and Observer* political beat in 1936 to handle Mr. Hoey's campaign publicity, and, upon his election, joined his staff. He could find out everything there was to know of our presence in Raleigh so early, unshaven, forty miles from where we ought to be.

Oakey, unfortunately, had other thoughts. Away he dashed, right hand extended, calling out, "Governor Hoey! My dear Governor Hoey! How nice it is to see you! I'm E. V. Mitchell." That's exactly who he was. Oakey was a family name that somehow had become glued to him.

There was nothing for Coonie and me to do but follow Oakey. Governor Hoey spoke politely with us. He wore, as always, high-laced shoes, striped pants, claw-hammer coat with a red carnation in the lapel, bat-wing collar and red four-in-hand, and a fuzzy fedora atop his shoulder-length gray hair: how corny can you get? Bob Thompson, who had been in a scrape or two himself, didn't ask too many questions; for that at least I was thankful. I was nearly as uncomfortable as I'd been in Judge Barnes's court.

At work that night, gloomy and remorseful, I decided that pretty soon I would climb upon the wagon with Tony McKevlin. Not just now, I told myself, in the spirit of St. Augustine's youthful prayer, but pretty soon, pretty damned soon.

12 Gentlemen of the Press

Frances Fulton and I were married in the little Episcopal church in Walnut Cove, North Carolina, in February 1939, my twenty-seventh year. I had been courting Frances, off and on, since we were teenagers. Her people were merchants, bankers, and landowners. After college she worked in the bank at Walnut Cove and for an architectural firm in Roanoke, Virginia, where one of her three brothers operated an automobile dealership handy to his cattle farm in West Virginia. She had seven sisters.

Nothing had prepared her for a Durham night newspaperman's lot. I promised her I would look for day work on a better newspaper, and was committed to the pledge's latter part. We moved into the brand-new University Apartments. The first thing she did was hire a little colored girl to help her keep house. Amid a marvelous variety of Duke University graduate students and their wives, we were happy and carefree.

My single night off was Wednesday. But inasmuch as on Saturday I got off early and on Sunday went to work late, we could enjoy some of the weekend—about as much as, indeed, our late-lamp-burning neighbors, the medical students in particular.

When I arrived at the office on Sunday shortly before 6 P.M., to edit the copy coming over the Associated Press teletypes, Mr. Henry B. would be winding up his day's self-appointed chore. Well, I would reflect, that takes care of two columns in tomorrow's newspaper.

Always on Monday, God's in the morning papers; / On Page 27, just opposite the Fashion Trends, / One reads at a glance how He scolded the Baptists a little . . . Phyllis McGinley wrote those lines back then, in reference to reviews of Sunday sermons appearing in the far back pages of the week's slimmest edition of the American press—metropolitan journals as well as Bible Belt bugles. If she had substituted Presbyterians for Baptists, she might have been kidding Mr. Henry B.

Mr. B. was a New Englander who had graduated from Yale in 1896 and had been "connected with editorial depts. Chicago *Tribune*, New York *Evening Post* and *Commercial West*, Minneapolis, to 1904." The quoted clause is from the 1928-29 *Who's Who in America*. I never have quite understood Mr. B.'s journalistic background.

After a hitch "in spl. lit. work, 1904-07," Mr. B. entered the consular service. He was posted to Hobart, Nassau, Bombay, Petrograd, and Trinidad, with side excursions to New Zealand and other far places. He married an Australian.

Travel was not kind to Mr. B. Although he was no older than sixty-five when I knew him, he was bent, tottering, and rheumy at eyes and mouth. By then a widower, he lived with his only daughter, a pretty woman wed to a university professor.

Each Sunday his daughter would accompany him to the First Presbyterian Church of Durham and, after services there and lunch nearby, deposit him at the newspaper building. There he would remain all afternoon, creating, no doubt, a cherished hiatus in the routine at home by his absence. Slumped before a vintage L. C. Smith, glasses slipped to the tip of his round nose, a cigar dangling from his lips and spilling ashes onto his vest, erratically tapping with one or two gnarled fingers, he presented a cherubic figure.

What he was doing was something else again. Invariably he began his exercise by citing the First Presbyterian minister's text and quoting a few of his remarks, imprecisely remembered, and hastily got down to what cheered him most: to quarreling with the Calvinistic theology he believed to have been propounded. In the process he might become personal, turning experiences, observations, and, I suspect, illusions into parables that discredited the New Deal, European intervention, and the morning's host. On and on he would go.

At last the thus-abused divine got enough of it and protested to the *Herald*'s managing editor, the gifted and rascally Coonie Stamey. He demanded that he be accorded responsible attention or else left alone—that, in short, he be relieved of Mr. Henry B.'s biases and ineptitude.

"But Mr. B. loves to write those little pieces," Coonie objected. "He's a nice old gentleman, as everybody agrees, with nothing else to do. Covering your sermons is the highlight of his week. And I don't think anybody much reads him, tell you the truth."

The clergyman was firm. "Tell him to stop," he said.

Genuinely shocked, Coonie threw up his hands. "Good God-a'mighty, Doctor," he cried. "I can't tell Mr. B. to stop. YOU tell him!"

Few people indeed could have read God's scolding of the Presbyterians as interpreted by Mr. Henry B. In a city of nearly 60,000 souls, the *Herald* had a circulation of less than 15,000. Josephus Daniels wrote in *Tar Heel Editor*, a volume of his memoirs, that progressive elements in Durham urged him to give up the Raleigh *News and Observer* and establish a newspaper among them. He declined. "And the result proved the wisdom of my decision," he continued. "I probably would have made more money in Durham . . . but the paper would of necessity have been localized." Besides being parochial, the *Herald* cared little for editorial quality or influence. Some brilliant young men from neighboring Chapel Hill and next-door Duke drifted through the dreary city room that the *Herald* shared with the *Sun*, but few stayed.

The night staff was pretty gamy. The telegraph editor was a former AP Morse man, the city editor was a failed baseball player demoted—I mean it—from the sports desk, and the sports editor who succeeded him had worked his way up and down, from paper to paper, after starting out as a copyboy on the *Richmond Times-Dispatch*. The police reporter carried a pistol; late one night, for the hell of it, he put a slug through the inverted demijohn of spring water that served as the office drinking fountain: the *Herald*'s single refinement. The first night I worked there I wrote a letter applying for a job in another city. Relief was five years away.

We would get out the last of three editions a little after 2 A.M., when the wire closed. Then two or three newsmen and as many printers, plus a bucket-shop telegrapher who had worked for the AP until the teletype displaced him, would cut the cards.

They were playing poker and I was writing a Sunday piece one Wednesday morning when the city editor blew in. Tuesday had been his night off. He was drunk—soused, cockeyed.

"This is a hell of a note," he said. "The old editor died yesterday and is lying in a box six blocks from here without a soul sitting up with him, and here you all are gambling and not giving a good goddam."

The old editor had been retired a long time. Some of us had never met him. But the city editor had known him well. They had worked together. The city editor had been on the paper since shortly after World War I, when he came up from the Atlanta sandlots to try out for the Durham Bulls, of the old Piedmont baseball league, and didn't make it. He was tall and big-bellied. The only sparse thing about him was his vocabulary.

"It's in the paper," said a printer. "We saw it."

He wasn't kidding. Newspaper beat reporters and copy editors are among the most provincial people to be found. They hardly know anyone except colleagues, politicians, and bureaucrats. Let a policeman, or fireman, or dog warden, or overseer of the poor die and the desk will treat it as a topic of public grief. It used to be that if a two-thirder in the composing room came to an untimely end the newspaper would reward him with a two-column headline. Even the office cat would rate nine or ten inches of lament. The *Herald* had spread the old editor across the top of page one and had turned the rules—had made black borders for the account.

The city editor said, "You saw the story but you ain't seen the remains. And the one that wrote the story ain't wrote anything in the memory book at the funeral home. So I've written everybody's name for you, to show some respect."

Somebody said he must be out of his mind.

"Like hell I am," said the city editor. "There wasn't a goddam name in the book when I got to the sitting-up room, so I put in some—the mayor's, the city manager's, the sheriff's, the fire chief's, everybody's I could think of. And Doris Duke's too. There was a time when half this town would have been to the funeral parlor. The old editor could say more in one little paragraphic than the jughead we got there now can say on the whole editorial page, so-called. The governor and Supreme Court and everybody else paid attention to what he had to say. I'm going back there and write the goddam governor's name."

He went, his long overcoat flapping at his shins. It was winter. The telegraph editor, whom we called the Bishop, and I followed him. He drove a top-heavy Packard that he had bought secondhand. If a policeman had stopped him we could have fixed the ticket at headquarters. The streets were practically empty.

The funeral home door was unlocked. We went in. Nobody seemed to be on duty there. The first thing I did was to apply a copyreader's gum eraser to some of the city editor's penciled scrawlings on the guest book.

The old editor's coffin was in a sort of alcove, perhaps a family room. The city editor flopped his 240 or so pounds into a chair there. "This is one hell of a wake," he said. He still wore his overcoat. It was cold inside as well as out.

After humoring the city editor for ten minutes or so, we tried to coax him out. He wouldn't budge. We told him his wife—he had a fairly new one—would be worried about him. "Hell with that," he said.

Then we told him he might be intruding if not actually trespassing.

That set him off. He reviewed again the old editor's accomplishments and once more deplored the civic community's infidelity. "And besides," he said, "if nobody sits up with him, some goddam Duke University student from New Jersey is liable to come along and steal the body and sell it to the medical school for thirty dollars."

The Bishop and I decided that if we went out the door, as if leaving for good, maybe the city editor would come along. So we did. We stood down the porch aways in the darkness. A milkman had left two quarts of milk at the steps.

The door, which we had slammed behind us, creaked open. The city editor peered through the opening, cautiously. He came a few steps onto the porch, looking all about him but not seeing us. Then he turned to go inside again.

The Bishop grabbed him, pushed him aside, pressed the latch on the door, and pulled the door shut. The city editor tried the knob frantically, then rammed his bulk against the door. It didn't give. "Goddam you both," he snarled. "Now you've gone and screwed things up good." He had turned mean. "That was the best idea I've had in a month. I was fixing to take the body and sell it to the medical school for thirty dollars."

He swayed a little, steadied himself, and took a tentative step. Then he stuffed a milk bottle into each of his overcoat pockets, gingerly descended the steps, and staggered to his big old Packard.

There was a newsroom joke about the Packard. It was that the city editor hadn't got a standard $2.50 raise since he first parked it near enough the office for the publisher to see it.

13 Our Worst War Town

A reason I stayed at the *Durham Morning Herald* so long was that I became night managing editor and made more money, as little as it was, than I could persuade another newspaper to pay me. In mid-1941, however, the Norfolk *Virginian-Pilot* indicated an interest in me. I had two friends from college days who were happy there.

The year was running out when the *Pilot* called me to the job I had accepted a month earlier. By then Frances was expecting a child at any time. I asked for a delay in reporting to work. Well, but don't wait too long, came the reply. The Japanese had attacked Pearl Harbor a few days before. In the world's largest naval center things were popping.

Frances's doctor decided the baby wasn't due for another two weeks. One of her sisters agreed to stay with her if I went immediately to Norfolk. I had little choice. The *Herald* had hired two men—a state editor and a Sunday editor—to take over my routine, and I was fast becoming surplus.

I saw one more edition of the *Herald* to press, put on my hat and coat, and drove through the night to Norfolk. Upon showing up for work at the *Pilot* next afternoon, I was given a message to call Frances at Duke Hospital. We were parents of a little girl.

I met Frances Fulton Mason II a week later.

During the following months I met numerous other young people. The first of them was a fourteen-year-old boy named Leonidas.

Norfolk had become the nation's favorite example of wartime horrors. *Collier's* magazine started a journalistic trend with an article by Walter Davenport about the city's shortage of housing and abundance of sin. *Architectural Forum* accused the Navy of failing initially to include housing in its Norfolk-base expansion plans, Washington red tape of snarling catch-up efforts, and local real estate interests of resisting adequate construction out of a fear, based on memories of the post-World War I exodus, of a future housing oversupply. *American Mercury* called Norfolk, with considerable detail, "Our Worst War Town." *Business Week* got into the act. So did the experimental New York newspaper *PM*. A reporter from the Baltimore *Sun* who came down to explore the shame, unable to find public lodging for even a night, slept on a sofa in the apartment I had been lucky enough to snare for my family on "Newspaper Row," a block of old West Freemason Street at the harbor. When his piece appeared, the *Pilot's* editorial page sighed wearily, "The *Sun* Also Rises"; the editors felt that their old friend up the Chesapeake Bay had strayed farther from home than necessary to exploit a scandal.

Although I had joined the *Pilot* as state editor, I quickly was shifted to the city staff as a general-assignment reporter specializing in wartime problems—labor, agriculture, commerce, and crime as well as housing. The first story I wrote was about Leonidas.

The boy lived with his parents and grandmother in a three-room apartment partitioned in what had been the open attic of a frame house in East Ghent, a run-down residential district near the heart of the city. Bricks from a chimney had fallen during the night through the roof and upon his narrow bed. Leonidas had escaped by being absent.

"He was spending the night with a little friend," his grandmother explained as I examined the bricks and the hole they had made. Both parents were working, the father in the Norfolk Navy Yard, the mother at a restaurant. Leonidas was sulkily silent. A sallow youth with plastered-down yellow hair, he seemed to be abashed by the attention.

A *Pilot* photographer's picture of Leonidas standing at his brick-invaded bed appeared with my story in next morning's paper. I got on with more important things, such as the torpedoing of merchant ships by the German U-boats off Virginia Beach, the Navy's assignment of sailors to help harvest Princess Anne and Norfolk counties' truck and potato crops, sundry meanness in the beer halls, tattoo shops, and goat-nest hotels along neon-lit East Main Street, and the Office of Price Administration's investigations of ration ticket racketeering and grocery price gouging.

Then Detective Sergeant Phil Adams, head of the burglary squad, surprised me one evening at police headquarters by saying, "I've been looking for you to thank you for that tip." Adams was a debonair fellow who cultivated stool pigeons in the pawn shops and secondhand stores. I had no inkling of what he was talking about.

"That break-in tip," he said. "A little grocery store near Maury High School was burglarized a couple of times. We were pretty sure it was kids.

"Right after it was hit the second time you wrote that story about Leonidas missing a brick on his head by being out of his bed and spending the night with a little friend. Well, we got old Leonidas, and he took us to the little friend, and we found a closetful of loot in the little friend's house. You solved the case for us."

Norfolk was packed with the likes of old Leonidas. Judge Herbert G. Cochran, a former Rhodes Scholar who in 1942 received 1,325 boys and girls in Juvenile and Domestic Relations Court, allowed me to sit in his courtroom for a week. That was long before the U.S. Supreme Court in *In Re Gault* (1967) extended due process to minors; adhering to the state-of-reform in his time, Judge Cochran conducted his court as a sociological clinic, usually in secrecy.

I began a report of my experience by summarizing six typical cases, including that of a sixteen-year-old Tennessee girl married to a seventeen-year-old sailor, gone to sea, who solicited a vice squad member and took him to a hotel where a sixteen-year-old boy was night clerk. "These," I wrote, "are among the youths adrift in Norfolk. You know a little about them, if you read the newspapers and magazines. They come from broken homes, from overcrowded flats, from families greedy for war money, from a past that somehow, somewhere, got fogged and twisted. They meet in smoke-dim dancehalls, they fling away in an evening in beer gardens and nip joints more money than their fathers earned in a week ten years ago, they make down-payments for automobiles in their parents' names and speed through the night on gasoline obtained in a manner puzzling to officials. Occasionally they steal and plunder and destroy."

A teenage girl destroyed herself.

She was one of two who came together to Norfolk searching for soldiers they hardly knew but had married. The soldiers had boarded a transport at the army terminals for overseas, they learned.

Well, life wasn't worth living, the girls agreed. They decided to drown themselves in the harbor. But first they would go to a USO dance across the Elizabeth River in Portsmouth. There they were pretty much the belles of the ball.

Returning to Norfolk on a late ferry, they were approached by three sailors who had danced with them. To the sailors' dismay, they told them to get lost.

In midstream, one girl jumped overboard. The other was about to follow when a sailor pulled her back. A Shore Patrolman took charge of her. An hour later I talked with her in a holding cell at Norfolk police headquarters.

She said double suicide was her friend's idea and she was just going along with it, not having known whether her friend was really serious. Was she glad to be alive? "I guess," she said, shrugging.

Next day the drowned girl washed ashore. Detective Sergeant

Leon Nowitzky, head of the homicide squad, sent the body to the morgue. There he escorted the other girl and made her look at what the crabs had left of her friend's face. "To teach her a lesson," he said.

Nowitzky was built like a beer barrel. He was about as unfeeling as he was strong. Yet even he was distressed by another war bride's death.

She was a Virginia mountain girl married to her high school sweetheart, a sailor. She left her parents' home to come with him to a tiny apartment in Brambleton, a Norfolk working-class community. On her first morning there she made coffee for her husband on the gas burner. He hurried off in the dawn to his destroyer and to sea. She went back to sleep without knowing how to turn the gas completely off. She never woke up.

Responding to such tragedies and widespread discomfort, a subcommittee of the House of Representatives Naval Affairs Committee came to Norfolk in March 1943 to investigate conditions. Representative Edouard V. M. Izac of California was chairman. Among the members was Representative Winder R. Harris, who until 1941 had been managing editor of the *Virginian-Pilot*. Knowing where all the political skeletons lay, he had wangled his way to Congress upon the resignation of Colgate W. Darden, of Norfolk, to become Governor of Virginia.

At a small dinner that Harris gave for the subcommittee I sat with a third member, Representative Margaret Chase Smith, of Maine. Like Harris, she was new in Congress and had entered it by appointment, for which she was apologetic. Her husband, Representative Clyde H. Smith, had intended to retire and open the way for her to run for election, she said. But he had died in office. (She would go to the Senate on her own in 1948. Winder Harris by then was a lobbyist for the shipbuilding industry. He didn't like being a Congressman after all.)

Mrs. Smith asked me what I knew about the women's quarters in the Norfolk jail. It came out later that New York City Parks Commissioner Robert Moses and a special committee had prepared for Secretary of the Navy Frank Knox a blistering report on Norfolk that bore down especially on the police policy of locking up runaway girls with venereally infected prostitutes.

I told Mrs. Smith I had never seen the women's quarters but was sure they were pretty bad from what a woman reporter, having connived with a court to spend a day and a night in jail, had written and expanded upon orally to some of us. "It can't be any place for a girl with any innocence left," I added. Norfolk hookers of about that period would be rated by a mariner in Richard Hughes's novel *In Hazard* but a notch above their Panama sisters, the worst of any port.

Mrs. Smith confided that she had arranged to visit the jail next day and agreed to tell me her impressions. The story I got was missed by reporters for the afternoon paper and wire services.

It was less than sensational, though. Overcrowding was dreadful, Mrs. Smith thought. There were too few beds and no sheets at all, just blankets. She was shocked at the youth of some of the girls; one was just fourteen. But conditions weren't quite as bad as she expected.

On returning to Washington, Mrs. Smith wrote me her thanks for some clippings I sent her, and invited me up for lunch. In Norfolk she had suggested that I apply for a Congressional press opening she anticipated.

Instead I applied at the Naval Officer Procurement Office in Richmond for a commission. I would soon be thirty-one.

14 The Guns of April

The Navy made me a lieutenant, junior grade, and sent me to sea as a watch and division officer in the Pacific amphibious force in time for the Philippines fighting and the Iwo Jima and Okinawa invasions. My ship, a newly commissioned attack cargo vessel designed to haul weapons for discharge onto beaches in coordination with troop landings there, fired her first shot in anger—well, in fretfulness—somewhere between San Francisco and Honolulu.

We traveled with a destroyer from Charleston to the Panama Canal. After passing through the canal and being welcomed into the Pacific Fleet, we headed without escort northwestward, sticking fairly close to land. Although we had shaken down in the Chesapeake Bay, our orders were to engage in further exercises and tests before reporting at Pearl Harbor to load equipment for Luzon. So we were in no great hurry.

Off California one evening we sighted a puzzling light on the horizon. As we approached it, it descended. We were within a mile of it when it dipped into the sea. Promptly we launched a landing craft and retrieved it. It turned out to be a Japanese fire balloon launched perhaps by a surfaced submarine hoping it would drift to the United States West Coast and cause mischief. Eventually it was sent from Pearl to the naval weapons-testing station in Maryland.

Next evening a larger and brighter light appeared. Our captain, a retread reservist from the First World War, who had been promoted to commander upon taking over the ship, ordered the crew to general quarters. My battle station was at a twin-mount forty-millimeter cannon at the stern. The ship's single five-inch dual-purpose gun, her heaviest weapon, was nearby.

The captain asked the gunnery officer if he could hit the target with the five-inch. The gunnery officer was a Detroit lawyer who had been in armed-guard duty—in charge of the naval gun crew on merchant ships. I can still hear his response over the intercom:

"Yes, sir!"

The captain commanded, "Fire one round!"

The particularly harsh crack of a five-inch gun tore the warm air. Skyward sped the shell. The only effect of its explosion two thousand yards up was to accentuate the great distance between it and the light. Our old man had ordered a shot fired at Venus.

And he had set the tone, more or less, of our ship's behavior throughout the twenty-two months I was aboard her.

As liquor had mocked law and order back in Sanford during the waning months of Prohibition, in our ship it intruded upon the 1862 congressional ban on the crew's grog and Secretary of the Navy Josephus Daniels's 1914 order applying the sponge to officers' country. Any of the thirty-eight commissioned officers could scrounge up a drink at any time. No day passed but what a glass was lifted in the quarters where the five warrant officers bunked. Among the 350 crewmen were secreted various and sometimes ingenious antidotes to thirst.

My favorite boatswain's mate of the watch was John O., a native of the North Carolina Outer Banks, who had been a deckhand on trawlers and a harbor dredge. He usually was prompt, efficient, and excellent company.

But he failed to show up for a midwatch. After ten minutes I sent the messenger for him. Straightaway he appeared, sheepish and apologetic. I told him there had been no problem.

But John O. kept saying how sorry he was. He didn't believe the messenger of the last watch had wakened him, he said. He always slept lightly when he was to have the duty; hell, just a little tap on the shoulder would get him going. He wasn't one of these feather merchants that had to be dumped out of the sack. The bos'un's mate was supposed to set an example for the rest of the watch, even the quartermaster, and he didn't want anybody to have cause to complain he was late relieving. Yackety-yackety-yack. He wouldn't shut up. Finally I realized he was drunk.

"What the hell you been drinking, John?" I asked. He grinned and moved away. From then until we were relieved at 0400 he was all business.

It was never easy to tell when John O. was in his cups. He could be soused and not show it. I sometimes wondered if his great strength contributed to his ability to absorb alcohol. He owned a suit of tailor-made whites that fit him so snugly he looked like a circus strong man in tights. His blouse was a sight to behold one dawn when he returned from a seventy-two-hour liberty in Panama, where the ship underwent boiler repairs, during which he and, I guess, a bedmate or two had been unable to force it up his broad back and over his befuddled head.

The source of John O.'s shipboard libation soon enough was exposed. The assistant first lieutenant, an ensign from Akron, chanced to notice water coming from a scupper in the hull. In his plumber's mind he traced the pipe to the ship's brig. Pretty certain that nobody was confined there, he went below to learn why a valve was open.

He found John O. running a still in the brig.

John O. was steaming the impurities from alcohol that the deck divisions used as a paint thinner. The ensign put him on report. The captain ordered him deck court-martialed. John O. asked me to be his counsel.

The deck court officer was the Detroit lawyer who fired at Venus. Through a plea bargain with him I got John O. off with a twenty-day loss of pay and twenty-day restriction to the ship. The machinist's mate who built the still promised to pay half the fine but never did. John O. in consequence became unhappy with the whole deal. He was lucky, though, to have kept his second-class petty officer's rating. My bargaining chips were evidence that a storekeeper had smuggled the alcohol aboard under circumstances embarrassing to the supply officer and that a seaman ladled it out without requiring a chit, in violation of regulations that the first lieutenant was supposed to enforce.

Our executive officer meanwhile presided over a wine mess that consisted of several cases of liquor purchased in Panama with funds provided by subscribing officers. It was illegal, as the exec must have known. He justified it as being like wine messes in the maritime service. He had been a mate in merchant ships for twelve years before entering the Navy as a lieutenant.

He told me why he had traded his master's ticket for two naval stripes. Early in the war he was in a merchantman that the Germans torpedoed off Cuba. The lifeboat he entered drifted for a week toward Guantanamo Bay. Sighting the U.S. naval base there, he and the other survivors rowed ashore.

The exec, then chief mate, was debriefed by a naval intelligence officer who assumed the survivors were Navy men. Set aright, he said, "Yes, I should have known you were merchant seamen. I saw you coming in, and you weren't rowing in cadence."

He decided right then and there, the exec said, to get proper.

Officers belonging to the wine mess could draw only one bottle at a time and only in liberty ports. At Ulithi a JG who had not joined applied for a bottle nonetheless. He had discovered that the going price on the beach for a cat's-eye shell was fifteen dollars or a fifth of whiskey. He didn't know that a couple of lens grinders in a repair ship in the anchorage, having little work to do, had cornered the cat's-eye market and jacked up the price beyond all reason. He knew, though, that the Panama liquor had cost only two or three dollars a fifth, and he thought he knew his rights.

The exec turned the JG down. Very well, said the JG, he would appeal through channels to the Secretary of the Navy.

Without another word, the exec brought out all the liquor, opened a porthole, and dropped it, bottle by bottle, into the harbor.

To deep-six the wine mess was one thing; to bring the wardroom into line with Old Man Daniels's notion of correct deportment was quite another. The ship's doctor, an overage and overweight lieutenant, was custodian of enough medicinal brandy and sick-bay alcohol to keep a fleet healthy. When he hopped into a landing craft for an afternoon's shore leave on some Pacific island, the two-ounce bottles of brandy in his pockets rattled like ten shots of anchor chain running through a hawspipe.

The doctor was from Boston and had played football at Boston College. His thick, wiry hair was turning gray. A badly broken nose made his upper lip seem puffed. Other than performing circumcisions on two officers from the Midwest and treating extreme cases of foot fungus, which the sailors called jungle rot, he practiced little medicine. The chief pharmacist's mate, who owned a village drugstore in Alabama, and a registered nurse, who would have been commissioned if he were a woman but being a man was merely a first class, ran the sick bay.

When I am reminded of the battle of Okinawa, I think also of the doctor's celebration of Patriots Day 1945. I had never heard of Patriots Day until then. It is a legal holiday in Massachusetts and Maine, commemorating the fighting at Lexington and Concord that followed by a day Paul Revere's famous ride of "the eighteenth of April in Seventy-five."

D-day at Okinawa was April 1, which was Easter that year. The American landing went smoothly. But on the fifth the Japanese stiffened and a two-week stalemate developed. It was broken on April 19, when the Seventh, Twenty-seventh, and Ninety-first Divisions of the United States Tenth Army mounted an artillery drive with the support of battleship and cruiser fire from the harbor. The enemy, four-and-a-half miles deep and spanning the island just north of Naha, the capital, fought back with well-directed artillery and mortar fire. When I got home at Christmastime I looked into the newspaper files to learn just what went on that night. The American bombardment was the heaviest of the entire war, in the European Theater of Operations as well as the Pacific.

Our ship was in Kerama Retto unloading ordnance for the Twenty-seventh Division—bulldozers, troop carriers, and various other vehicles to back up the tanks and field pieces that our boats had landed for earlier waves of troops. From there the action in the water and sky and ashore was brilliant and thunderous. Our deck crews worked at each of the five holds under a single bulb wrapped in red bunting. The glow from a burning ammunition dump on the beach and from ship gunnery flares might have provided us light enough if smoke hadn't wafted over us from the clouds of it being generated by landing craft to shield a neighboring line of OBBs—old battleships.

On our ship the doctor's celebration of Patriots Day added to the din.

Just before dinner he offered me a drink of "B & B"—medicinal brandy mixed with Benedictine from a bottle he had stashed away. As we sipped, he explained Patriots Day to me. He already was tipsy. After eating, I went back on deck to help with the offloading. When I next saw the doctor, about two hours later, he had run out of B & B and brought up his reserve—sick-bay alcohol. "Old Mamie Riley," he sang, "how do you do today?"

The executive officer had sent him from the wardroom to his

stateroom. But he had gone a deck below to the warrant officers' quarters. There he sat on a bamboo sofa that the boatswain had swiped at the Naval Supply Center in Norfolk and recited to the pay clerk, who also was from the Boston, a football game, play by play, that Boston College had won from somebody or another, maybe Pittsburgh, fifteen years before. The pay clerk lay on an upper bunk, half asleep. "I can see him so plainly, good old Babe," said the doctor. "*So goddam* plainly. Just lying there, turned over on his back, shoulders on the goal line, still holding the ball. I see him right now." Tears slid down his cheeks.

I had the deck then, and had looked into the warrants' quarters because a light showed there. The ship was supposed to be blacked out; the shrouded deck bulbs were an exception. I told the pay clerk to get the doctor back to his stateroom, and rejoined the junior officer and the rest of the watch on the bridge.

Upon being relieved at midnight, I went to the wardroom for coffee. The doctor was there. And he was a mess.

Besides sectional pride and dipsomania, now he suffered from hives. Itch had sent him to the shower for relief. He wore a towel around his thick middle and wooden clogs on his blotched feet. He lay on one of the wardroom tables and scraped his back on the green felt.

"Come on, Doc, get up," said the ship's single Marine officer, a first lieutenant with orders as transport quartermaster, or combat loading specialist, but who, lacking training, was treated as supercargo. The executive officer had placed him in charge of the doctor.

"It ain't fair, Doc," the Marine argued. He rubbed a shoulder. "You said I could lay a block on you if I let you lay one on me, and you already throwed yours. Now, dammit all, it's my turn, and you gotta let me. Get up off your big ass and I guarantee I'll put you back on it."

The Marine was from Missouri, a big-boned farm youth who had starred in football at a teacher's college and coached high school athletics before joining up. A lock of stringy yellow hair, always damp, lay on his forehead.

"All right then, you bastard," growled the doctor, getting up. He braced himself near the pantry door. A rash covered considerably more of him than the towel did. "Show me how you did it at Presbyterian Prep. Let me see what you taught them at Podunk High. I want to get a look at that mule-lot form."

With elbows out and forearms in and fists balled, the Marine came in low. He drove 215 pounds of beef at the doctor's stomach. But the blow was glancing; at the last split second the doctor turned with surprising agility and bumped against the wardroom's metal sideboard while shoving the Marine through the pantry door.

The coffee urn and a dozen cups and saucers fell from the sideboard onto the deck. So did the recognition officer's slide projector and a record player that the boat ensigns had acquired in Honolulu, along with all the records except the Andrews Sisters singing "Rum and Coca-Cola," which the chief engineer kept locked in his stateroom safe. The crash was echoed by the clang of pots and pans that the Marine knocked from the pantry shelves.

Within seconds the captain's orderly, a skinny seaman wearing whites and a webbed belt, stuck his head in the door, looking frightened. The captain's cabin was directly above the wardroom. "Captain said what was that," he peeped. The doctor lay on the wardroom table again, panting. The Marine sat on the deck with his pants leg pulled over his knee, which was bleeding. The boy kept his eyes off them.

"Tell him the doctor dropped a cup of coffee," I said. The captain wouldn't do anything about the doctor. For one thing, he wanted the doctor to cadge him a Purple Heart for a scratch on the head he got ducking under the flying bridge chart table when he thought he heard shrapnel. And the doctor, responding to boredom, could always hassle him about such safety factors as how the booms were cradled and the boats gripped down and the beans cooked. Besides that, the captain knew the doctor had noised it around the wardroom that he intended to cite him for a medical survey based on an unbearable personality. All the captain would do about the doctor was tell the executive officer to make him study navigation, and nothing would come of that. I didn't mind sending the captain an impertinent reply by his messenger because I was going back on deck to help with the unloading and he could never tell, from however the boy described me, that I was the one.

"Slide, Kelly, slide," the doctor sang in a rasping voice as I left the wardroom, "Casey's at the bat, / Old Mamie Riley, / Where did you get that hat?"

15 Port in a Storm

I must confess that the war suspended for most of its duration the thoughts I had entertained since my bachelor party of swearing off Demon Rum. During the June 1945 typhoon I revived them.

By then our ship had crossed the equator six times and experienced a great variety of weather. I became chilled in the Solomon Islands when caught in a squall while attempting to free a landing craft from a coral reef. Heat down there normally was so consistent that much of our crew slept on deck. The Pacific could be as smooth as Scott's Pond back at Hawfields. On occasion we followed the bubbly track of a jeep carrier for two days before sighting her. I have good cause to recall a March night between Espiritu Santo, where we combat-loaded, and Okinawa, where a gale and ten-foot seas delayed offloading, when the air was refreshingly cool but absolutely still.

The prospect of invasion made the captain nervous. He took to sleeping on a wing of the bridge in a bed—a rack, the sailors called its type—that he had a shipfitter weld to the ship's side.

During the captain's slumber on my watch one night the engineering duty officer asked for permission to blow tubes. The standing order for the officer of the deck in such a case was to put the ship athwart the wind so the soot would be blown over a side and not mess up the weather decks. But I could find no breeze. The engineer became impatient as I moved the ship a point or two from one heading to another. At last I told him to blow. Soot and grime went straight up and came straight down. The captain under his white

U.S. Navy blanket took on the look of a coal pile. Next morning he threatened to take me off watch, which would have suited me; I was weary of the one-on-two-off schedule that two other lieutenants and I had been standing since the ship joined an invasion convoy. But there was no qualified replacement.

From Okinawa our convoy traveled southward to Ulithi. From there we steamed alone up to Guam to pick up supplies. We went down to Manus in the Admiralties, and were back in the Marianas when weather from the June typhoon, centered back toward Okinawa, made us roll and pitch. That was the storm that knocked off the *Pittsburgh*'s bow and shortened the flight decks of three aircraft carriers.

We dropped anchor on the lee side of Saipan, where we found lots of company. Although a rough sea was running and the ship was on a twenty-four-hour sailing alert, some of us took a landing craft to the officers club. We left the ship in midafternoon and were due back at 1800—at 6 P.M.

The club was serving martinis in dixie cups. On finishing my last one I never tasted liquor again.

I talked with a destroyer escort skipper I recognized as a high school basketball player in Durham when I was on the *Herald* there. He was ten years younger than I and ranked me by half a stripe. Also, I met a B-29 pilot who had just come back from a raid on Tokyo. There wasn't much left there to bomb, he said. I told him about the kamikazes in Karama Retto, half-trained pilots half-standing in half-stripped Zeros so they could see from their downward angle whatever ship they chose to ram; as many as seven had picked our transport area during the late afternoons.

I began to feel depressed and went outside. An old islander was working in the club's bright flower garden, squatting, and I watched him, squatting too. Soon my knees hurt.

Then I started walking to the landing where our boat waited. It was hard going. I came to a baseball field where a blue- and a red-uniformed team were playing. I sat down in the sand and watched. I tried to sort our underemployed American flyers, Japanese suicide flights, flowers at the club and my mother's garden, a two-base hit and a throwing error, twenty-four-year-old DE captains and a twenty-four-hour sailing alert, and a two-four out on a fizzled sacrifice attempt. At some point I decided not to return to the ship.

That turned out to be a short day. I woke up in the Sick Officers Quarters of a Navy hospital in a palm grove. A lieutenant commander doctor came into my room as I demanded my clothes from a startled pharmacist's mate second. He got me two poached eggs and bacon and coffee, and casually asked me questions about the ship and my job while I wolfed down the best breakfast I had eaten in months.

Then he fetched my khakis. The shirt was torn. And he gave me my identification card, which I didn't know had been taken. "You were a little agitated," he said. "The duty medical officer gave you a shot." I made no comment.

He said if I was ready to go I could catch a ride in a hospital jeep that would stop at the fleet landing. I thanked him, trying not to be too profuse.

At the landing I boarded an LCM taxi with twenty or so sailors. I told the coxswain where to take me but wasn't at all sure the ship was still there. Nevertheless, I sat with my back against the wheelhouse, where the pounding wasn't too bad, and fell asleep before he shoved off.

When the cox'n roused me, I was the only passenger left. I couldn't figure where we were in relation to where the ship had been anchored. The cox'n complained that he was overdue at the landing. But I made him keep cruising about, looking.

I became panicky. If the ship had sailed, I told myself, I would be court-martialed for desertion. I might be broken to apprentice seaman and dishonorably discharged if not sent to prison in Portsmouth, New Hampshire. Fran's daddy was going to be disgraced, I kept thinking. My daughter Fran was three and a half years old, and I hadn't seen her since she was two. I should have stayed home and waited to be drafted, I reflected. Why the hell hadn't somebody from the ship stopped me when I left the officer's club?

"That your bow number?" the cox'n asked me. It was indeed. The ship lay just ahead. I almost laughed.

The cox'n approached our accommodation ladder as he was

supposed to, against the sea. But when he slowed down near it, his bow fell away. The water was rough. Again he tried, again his bow sheered off.

LCM stands for landing craft, mechanized. The World War II version was fifty feet long and weighed twenty-two tons. It had a great bow ramp and an equally high wheel platform aft. Unlike the several varieties of smaller landing craft, it had two shafts.

The LCM taxi I rode had no crewman except the coxswain. Sailor passengers usually received a line when necessary for a landing. I wasn't about to fool with that.

"I tell you what," I told the cox'n, standing with him up at the wheel. "Come downwind with your engines backing just enough for you to steer. When you pass the ladder I'll jump onto it and you keep going. Otherwise we'll be here all day." It was about 0900.

So that's what the cox'n did, defying everything he had learned from *The Bluejackets' Manual*. It worked perfectly. I stepped lightly onto the ladder and hurried up it.

My roommate, the recognition officer, had the deck. Up until the time the ship's doctor and the Marine officer broke his slide projector playing football in the wardroom his job had been to teach the crew how to distinguish, by silhouettes, enemy from friendly aircraft. He would enliven training sessions by inserting a slide showing a naked girl among his Bettys, Zeros, Hellcats, Corsairs, and whatnot. Now, having no projector for his slide show, he was full-time mess treasurer. He stood only in-port deck watches, and felt put upon at that.

"Anybody looking for me?" I asked.

"I am," my roommate replied. "This is supposed to be your watch." Usually he was jovial, the most popular member of the wardroom. Now he was on the surly side.

"Stay put until I can change shirts," I said. "I'll be right back to relieve you."

I was unbuttoning my ripped shirt when the captain's messenger knocked on the bulkhead and parted the stateroom curtains. "Captain wants to see you in his stateroom immediately," he said.

Well. I figured I was going to catch it, after all. No officer assigned to that ship ever before had been unaccounted for when the executive officer made his eight o'clock report to the captain. There would be a penalty for unauthorized absence under any circumstance and no doubt a double penalty for being away all night during an emergency stop and twenty-four-hour sailing alert. I could see disaster staring at me.

The captain glared as I stood helplessly before him. He was forty-six years old, mostly bald, purple-faced, and pot-bellied. The ship's doctor wasn't far wrong when he said the captain had an unbearable personality. He was petty and mean-spirited.

"Mister," he rasped, his thin lips trembling with rage, "who was that goddam cox'n that made a Chinese landing on my ship?"

16 Go-Getter

Our ship was in San Francisco for repairs when the U.S. Army Air Force nuked Hiroshima and Nagasaki on August 6 and 9, 1945, and Japan surrendered on the fourteenth. I was appalled by the bombings, and remain so. On the fifteenth we sailed for Pearl Harbor, where we loaded supplies for occupation forces in Sasebo, which was to have been our invasion point.

From Sasebo we returned to Pearl, then headed to Norfolk for dry-docking. Ships were stacked on the Pacific side of the Panama Canal, and we had to wait several days for our turn at passage. Some sort of political trouble sizzled on the Colon side, and the captain forbade liberty. He went ashore, however, and about half the crew followed, sliding down a hawser from the stern to the concrete pier. Discipline was becoming lax.

Up the coast the weather was lovely, although it was December. Crewmen worked in shirtsleeves as I stood the deck watch off Savannah. With the arrival of peace, the watch list had been expanded from three officers to seven. When I next took the deck I found myself, from midnight to 0400, in a snowstorm off North Carolina.

The last bearing I ever took for the U.S. Navy was on Currituck light.

We reached Norfolk a week before Christmastime. I had enough points for release, and was paid off at Camp Shelton, a part of the Little Creek amphibious complex near the city. Then I went to the railroad station to take a train to Raleigh, where Frances and Fran, now nearly four years old, were living with Frances's sister and the sister's husband and two children.

At the station I bumped into a police detective called Jonesey, a member of the homicide squad. We greeted each other warmly. Although he wore plain clothes, Jonesey fit the police stereotype to the extent that he was so flatfooted he seemed to limp. He had on, as nearly always, a broad-brimmed hat. If for some reason he removed it at headquarters, another cop would yell, "Put on that hat or I'll arrest you for indecent exposure!" Jonesey was as bald as an onion.

I asked him how things were on the force and who had my old job as *Virginian-Pilot* police reporter. The reporter, he replied, was a nice fellow but still somewhat green. "He's no go-getter like you," he said.

I was thirty-three years old then, and forty years have passed, and that is the only time anybody ever called me a go-getter. Although I worked hard enough, and for it drew a pay envelope or check every week for forty-five years, except when I was in the Navy and was paid by the month, and was invited back to every newspaper job I ever left, I never had the drive and ambition that I've seen in a lot of people. For one thing, a certain shyness always dogged me. I couldn't have made it as a salesman or promoter of any sort; I probably earned a living the only way I could have.

If I struck a policeman as being a go-getter, it was because covering police was the most fun I ever had. I saw and did plenty of things I did not enjoy. But that part I quickly forgot.

The Norfolk police beat included headquarters and three precinct offices. First Precinct occupied most of the bottom floor of the four-story headquarters building. I would start my rounds there. One night I arrived just as a drunk merchant seaman was being booked. The turnkey searched him before leading him back to the lockup.

When he ran his hands under the drunk's peacoat, a squirrel bit him. "One time it was a pet white rat," said the turnkey, shaking blood from a finger. "I hate the sons of bitches."

Police worked in three eight-hour shifts, which they rotated. When I came upon a turnkey known as Goo-Goo, I automatically gave him a quarter to spare him from shaking me down. With the money thus cadged he bought cigarettes for the women in the lockup. Before handing over a pack he would require the recipient to open her blouse and wiggle.

Goo-Goo was silver-haired, pink-cheeked, pop-eyed, and raspy voiced. He wore a derby hat and spats to work, and did not remove the spats upon changing into his uniform. I remarked to the desk sergeant that I was surprised some female prisoner didn't raise a fuss about Goo-Goo's little calls when she went into police court. He looked at me in surprise. "Hell," he said, "they look forward to Goo-Goo's visits. All the girls are crazy over old Goo-Goo."

When I wasn't busy with a story I was likely to ride in Car Seventeen, an unmarked police cruiser manned by two plainclothes-men on emergency alert. We spent a lot of time eating in all-night cafes on mean streets, where the pig knuckles and spareribs were pretty good and the charges were a business write-off. There the cops checked mug shots with the proprietor and spoke with stool pigeons. And there, when they left, numbers writers and pimps went back to work.

We were sitting outside such a joint one stormy night, assaying the street scene before going in, when a regular police car pulled alongside. The uniformed driver rolled down his window and casually said, "Race you to Ward's Corner." Without responding, our driver turned the ignition key and hit the accelerator and siren button. The next three miles were a horror. Both cars rocketed, swerved, skidded, and screamed, ignoring traffic lights and rules. I was too frightened to look half the time. At Ward's Corner, an outlying shopping and business area, they broke off and went their separate peace-keeping ways.

On another night, in a semirural district, an explosion came from an automobile that chanced to be just ahead of Car Seventeen. Both plainclothesmen drew their pistols and the driver, spontaneously putting on the siren, put on speed for a chase. But the automobile up front immediately stopped and two young men tumbled out, hands raised.

They were badly frightened and just as puzzled. Where the noise had come from they had no idea.

Then someone noticed a red fluid seeping from the back of the automobile. At the policemen's order, the motorists opened the trunk. A demijohn of tomato wine, what we used to call monkey rum, had exploded. It belonged, as did the automobile, to the driver's father-in-law.

The cops laughed and left. Homemade wine wasn't their line of work.

Car Seventeen's equipment included a hand spotlight plugged into the cigarette lighter. The two cops liked to throw its beam onto a dark alley or parked car where a streetwalker had taken her pickup. Unlike Norfolk's notorious vice squad prowling hotel corridors, they weren't interested in arrests, only in voyeurism. On a street beside a field where a carnival was playing they flushed two Navy men from the back seat of a car, an enlisted man and an ensign. They told the ensign, who owned the car, to get going but held the sailor—all Norfolk cops called all sailors "goatheads"—long enough to give him a talking to. "You ought to be ashamed of yourself," one said, his voice full of indignation, "exposing yourself like that, right on a public street and practically under a streetlight at that, where anybody's liable to see you. You're a disgrace, that's what you are, a goddam disgrace to the service. *And with a commissioned officer!*"

Early in the war a passerby came upon a half-clothed sailor lying dead on the cobblestones of an alley beside the shabby old Victoria Hotel on East Main Street, where Lafayette once stopped. I went into the hotel with the Car Seventeen partners and Sergeant Leon Nowitzky, head of the homicide squad. A Navy Shore Patrol detail arrived just behind us, led by the Marine lieutenant colonel who commanded the permanent Shore Patrol company occupying a building near police headquarters. Sergeant Nowitzky figured, from where the man lay, that he had gone through a half-open window at the top of a narrow stairway connecting each floor to the hotel kitchen, no longer in use. "Accidental death," he ruled in the name of Dr. C. D. J. McDonald, the coroner, who wasn't there. Sailors occupied every room of the hotel that night. The police were happy to turn the rest of the case over to the Shore Patrol, who locked the door when we left. I never did learn what was going on at the Victoria.

Fights were commonplace in the East Main Street beer taverns. After the cops and Shore Patrol broke up a fairly bloody one, a girl ran up to a policeman holding an ear in a napkin. He gave it to a Shore Patrolman, who drove with it onto a ferry and across the harbor to Portsmouth and the naval hospital there, where its lawful owner had arrived in a paddy wagon a while earlier. Surgeons sewed it back in place.

Nerve center at police headquarters was on the top floor, where the telephone switchboard and radio transmitter, as well as the detective complaint desk, were located. All sorts of calls came there. On a bitter wintry night one reported that a cow was knocking down tombstones in the Old St. Pauls churchyard, a couple of blocks away.

A squad car was sent to investigate. Its driver and a foot patrolman chased the cow through the shopping district, where she broke a plate-glass window upon sideswiping it when cutting a corner too sharply, and to the waterfront. Backed up there, the cow went overboard and headed to sea. A Coast Guard picket cutter that drew less water than she prodded her with a boat hook back to the pier, where policemen put a line on her neck and hauled her ashore with a tow-truck crane.

The cow was traced to a packing plant in Brambleton, half a dozen miles away. The packer claimed that the cops' rough handling cost him about one hundred pounds of beefsteak.

A motorist who parked a newly polished automobile in front of a ship chandler's on Water Street called headquarters for protection from a billy goat. Seeing his reflection in the car's shiny door, the goat rammed it with his horns, then stepped back and surveyed the result; the distorted image evidently displeased him, for he struck again, harder than before, creating a major job for a body shop. The investigating policeman determined that the billy belonged to a little black boy who lived nearby. He declared it to be a civil case.

The headquarters telephone switchboard operator was a civilian employee, unlike his companion at the radio dispatcher's console, who wore a uniform. Mike Gattis was one of the three operators. He looked like a banker: elderly, dignified, and neatly groomed. No bank board, however, would have tolerated the black, crooked Italian cigars that he fancied.

As I got out of the elevator up there to review the records one evening, Mike was talking excitedly to George Anderson, the dispatcher. "First he coldcocked him with a chair," Mike said. "Knocked the pure shit out of him. Ker-blam! But the guy got up and staggered to this cabinet and pulled out a shotgun. But before the guy could get it to his shoulder our boy nailed him with a piece of two-by-four and flattened hell out of him. Then he dragged his ass to the window and throwed him out, through the glass and everything. Right onto the goddam street . . ."

I hurried to the dispatcher's console. "What happened, Mike?" I blurted. "What's all this about?"

"Oh," said Mike, "I was telling George here about this Alan Ladd pictureshow I saw this afternoon." Mike was a movie nut.

Crip Kirby was another telephone operator. I hesitated to call him Crip at first, although I'd know other Crips from the time I was in grade school with a lame boy who got about in a billygoat wagon, but everyone else did and it was clear he didn't mind. He was a hunchback, a gnomelike little man with a terrible temper and a caustic tongue.

Hard luck followed him like the rain cloud over that Al Capp cartoon character. I remember a Christmas Eve when his sorry son-in-law got drunk and blew the money he was supposed to spend on presents for the children, and the only gift that came to Crip's daughter's house was a tan blanket Crip bought at Kresge's. On top of that Crip had the duty on Christmas Day.

The police chief, Joe Lindsay, thought of Crip while drinking Christmas eggnog and called him at the headquarters switchboard.

"This is the Chief," he said joyfully. "Merry Christmas, Crip! A Merry Christmas to you, Crip old boy!"

Crip was unmoved. "It may be Merry Christmas where you are, Chief," he growled, "but you don't smell no ham cooking here, do you?"

Lindsay was a former precinct captain, the son of a tugboat master. Several years later he left the force in disgrace, I'm sorry to say, after a blue-ribbon grand jury issued a report linking him with numbers racketeers and the town's foremost madam.

His downfall came about in an unusual way. He, Public Safety Director Calvin Dalby, and Detective Captain Fred Watson went out of town for a day. Bubba Staylor, a detective sergeant invariably described in the press as "clean-cut," seized the opportunity to summon twelve policemen to the third base bleachers of the Norfolk Tars baseball park, where he briefed them for a gambling raid he would lead. He chose the bleachers because none of the cops could get to a telephone there and also because he knew the territory, having played third base for the Tars, a New York Yankees farm team, before pinning on a badge.

The raid turned up policy sheets and bookmaking paraphernalia and, lo and behold, a list of policemen's names, presumably a payoff roll. Only the chief was much damaged, however, and he might have weathered the scandal if a search warrant hadn't shown his lock box to be stuffed with one- and five-dollar bills, mostly ones.

Lindsay was succeeded by a recently retired Marine regimental commander, a hero of Guadalcanal, decorated and tombstoned to brigadier general: Amor Leroy Sims. Chief Sims wore on his sleeves the four gold stripes of his office and on his shoulders the silver star of his military rank, a one-grade mismatch. And he carried a swagger stick. He chanced to be passing the detective complaint desk the night a Marine corporal staggered in to report the theft of his car radio while he and his girlfriend were in a beer tavern. The corporal's tie was loose, his shirttail was out, and his collar was smeared with lipstick. "Marine!" Sims shouted. Without turning his head, the corporal jerked to attention. "Two-block that field scarf!" Sims commanded. The corporal fixed his tie, tucked in his shirt, braced

his shoulders, completed his business briskly, and marched out
without a question or backward glance, hup-two, hup-two . . .

Now the train that would take me to Raleigh reached the station,
half an hour late. My old friend Jonesey and I had been talking a
good forty-five minutes, about how Norfolk and its police force had
fared during the war. I shook hands with him and told him good-
bye and asked him to remember me to everybody at headquarters.
I was beginning to feel like a civilian again.

17 Hugging the Black Buoys

Going back to work was difficult. Two friends in Mebane, my
hometown, proposed to back me in a second weekly newspaper
there, but I thought they overestimated its chances of success. One
of them, a lawyer with business connections, said I would find all
sorts of investment opportunities if I made the move. I thought:
investment with what?

I toyed with the idea of applying for GI benefits and going to
law school to complete the study I had begun with Ashley Seawell's
books in Sanford thirteen years earlier. The knowledge and degree
would be useful in editorial work, I believed.

Before my terminal leave ran out, though, I went back to Norfolk
and the *Virginian-Pilot*.

Throughout the manpower shortage, the *Pilot* news staff regularly
had worked overtime. Some of the older members were unhappy at
losing the extra income with the return of veterans and a five-day
week. Younger wartime replacements fretted over the exposure of
their inadequacies. I, meanwhile, was assigned to a routine I did
not like—swing editor: filling in for various departmental editors
on their nights off.

I missed the Navy. I had immersed myself in it, its lore as well as
workings, out of duty and interest and also because I always had

felt that a journalist should understand the distinguishing character-istics of his community—tobacco in Sanford, for example, and tobacco and education in Durham, and government and politics in Raleigh, and naval and maritime affairs in Norfolk. I began to submit editorials on naval topics to Louis Jaffe, the *Pilot*'s editor.

When I left the Navy early in 1946 all officers were advised: "You are automatically a part of the Naval Reserve and can participate in various schedules of Naval Reserve activity as you wish and your other pursuits permit. A sound, progressive system of promotion for reserve officers will be established. Do not resign your commission . . ."

I remembered that two years later when I chanced to learn from an item on a bulletin board at the Norfolk Naval Station that a destroyer division going to Bermuda at Eastertime would entertain applications from reservists wishing to engage in two weeks of training. Bermuda struck my fancy. The island should be especially pleasant in the spring, I thought. I put in for orders.

They quickly came, assigning me to a *Gearing*-class destroyer departing the Norfolk destroyer-submarine piers 4 April 1948, at 0800. I got out my uniforms and packed a bag.

April 4 was a Sunday. I reported aboard the ship an hour before sailing time. The officer of the deck sent my gear below and ushered me to the wardroom. There I met the skipper, who was finishing his breakfast.

"Where are you from?" he asked. "Kansas? Iowa?"

Oh, no, I said; Norfolk. "I rode out here on a streetcar," I added.

"That certainly makes you different," the captain replied, amused. "The average reservist we get is a farm boy from the corn belt who wants to see the ocean again. What do you do in Norfolk?"

"I'm with the *Virginian-Pilot*," I said.

"The hell you are," he responded.

At that moment the watch messenger appeared and told the captain that the officer of the deck reported the ship was ready to get underway. The captain excused himself and left.

I went onto the weather deck to watch. The division commodore, a captain in rank, was in our ship, so she was the first to leave the piers. A harbor tug backed her out and turned her about. The three other ships followed under their own steam.

I had never been aboard a destroyer before. With her sleek compactness, low freeboard, powerful engines, and two screws she was vastly different in appearance and quickness from the high-sided, single-screw, merchant-type bucket I had sailed. I went up to the bridge for a closer look.

The captain greeted me with a half-salute. "Won't you take her out, Mr. Mason," he said. Not asked; said.

I couldn't believe it. Although the tug had cast off, we hadn't reached the channel. And we were in the busiest part of Hampton Roads. Our three companions were in our wake. But of course I answered, "Aye, aye, sir."

The executive officer of a destroyer is also the navigator. A chief quartermaster usually does the plotting, however, and such was the case in our ship. I asked the chief to point out our position on the chart, and felt an impulse to take his hand.

Instead, I told the helmsman to hold his course to the first black buoy and be prepared to come right there. At the buoy I gave him a course that would keep us just inside the black buoy line. Outward we steamed at two-thirds speed.

A ferry from Hampton to Willoughby Spit was about to cross our bow, ignoring our right of way. Rather than hassle it, I ordered our speed reduced to one-third.

Capital ships have speed cones in their halyards, to be raised and lowered to indicate speed changes. I knew about them, but only in the deep recesses of my mind; they hadn't existed in the amphibious force.

The destroyer just behind us nearly ran us down before our captain suggested, very diplomatically, that I lower the cones.

Farther down the channel I noticed, with some alarm, that the Virginia Pilots Association boat, a former yacht, was maneuvering inside the channel. I had been aboard her for lunch several times—a sumptuous meal, incidentally, followed by a little nap—and figured that one of the apprentices had the deck for ship-handling practice. He could damn well keep out of our way, I decided, and held course.

The pilot boat's capers seemed to agitate the commodore. He stood on the starboard wing of the bridge, careful not to interfere but very much there just the same. The captain said something to him that I could not hear. It seemed to pacify him.

The pilot boat returned to her mooring buoy, on the shore side of the channel. I gave our helmsman the course to the sea buoy. When we reached it the regular watch came up to relieve the special sea detail, including me. I told the captain I believed I could find my stateroom. The supply officer had put me in the only space available, in the bow, known as the "swamps." I stretched out on the bunk, so glad to be there that I didn't mind the pitch at all.

Only one other reservist was along. He had been the captain's roommate at the Naval Academy and, like him, was a commander. But he had resigned his commission long before the war and had gone into business. Right after Pearl Harbor he had returned to active duty, and during the next four years had held three sea commands, the last one a *Fletcher*-class destroyer. The cruise was strictly a matter of pleasure for him.

It was for me too, but in a different way. The ship's communications officer was behind in paper work, so the captain excused him from deck duty and gave me his place in rotation. We rendezvoused with a submarine and, with the rest of the division, played antisubmarine warfare games the rest of the week. The hide-and-seek was great fun. We engaged in man-overboard drills. When it came my turn to attempt a rescue, I twisted the destroyer about by putting over the wheel and backing one engine while going forward on the other, kicking up such a swirl that the dummy washed aboard. I felt like Horatio Hornblower.

Then we went into Hamilton. A civilian pilot came aboard and guided us through the narrow, twisting, white-water channel. I watched in fascination from the weather deck, just under the bridge.

I was still there when, the ship moored, the captain came down. "I looked for you," he said. "I imagined you would be interested in that channel."

"I was interested, all right," I replied. "But I didn't want to take a chance on your telling me to take the deck in a millrace like that. I had enough trouble getting through the last channel."

"Trouble?" asked the captain. "What do you mean, 'trouble getting through the last channel'?"

"Well," I explained, "I live in Norfolk, of course. And I've fished in and about the harbor a good bit, and sailed there a little. But I don't really know the channel. I'd never paid it much attention before."

The captain looked stunned. "Good God!" he said. "Didn't you tell me you were a *Virginia pilot*?"

A Postscript

Chatting at a party with Captain Gilven Slonim, USN, when I was managing editor of the morning newspaper in Norfolk, I told him the story of many years before when a commanding officer entrusted his destroyer to me under the mistaken impression that I was a Virginia pilot rather than a *Virginian-Pilot* newsman. Gil at that time was commodore of a destroyer division such as the one I had sailed with to Bermuda. He urged me to write a squib about my experience for the U.S. Naval Institute *Proceedings*, a prestigious professional journal read by most naval officers. "They'll pay you ten dollars for it," he said. "You can buy me a drink with the money."

Sea yarns are a popular feature of the *Proceedings*. Mine was published. I bought Gil a scotch and soda and sipped ginger ale. Toward the war's end I had become a teetotaler—a silent one, let me emphasize.

Some time later I was sitting with friends on the old deck, since removed, of the Princess Anne Country Club in Virginia Beach following dinner. We were joined by a party that included a Navy captain. With no knowledge that I had any connection with the *Pilot*, the captain told my story pretty much as it had appeared in the *Proceedings*. He had heard it, he said, from the destroyer skipper himself, who happened to be the admiral for whom he was working. I asked him the admiral's name. Wrong fellow.

In mid-1963, the year after I became editor of the *Pilot*, I was invited to attend the Fifteenth Annual Global Strategy Discussions at the Naval War College in Newport, Rhode Island, a week-long program climaxing a college term. There I learned that the "Virginia pilot" bit was told routinely to officers enrolled in a Newport naval school for prospective commanding officers of deep-draft vessels— naval aviators, for the most part, assigned to tankers, transports, and other auxiliary ships in preparation for aircraft carrier command. The moral of the story was, as I understood it: *Be damned certain you know who's running your ship.*

A dozen or so years later the commandant of the Armed Forces Staff College in Norfolk asked me to address his foreign officer students, who represented the various military branches of the NATO allies. At a luncheon following my talk I sat with the commandant, a naval rear admiral.

Before his selection for flag rank, he had commanded a Seventh Fleet cruiser. In her he had survived two mishaps, he reminisced, either of which might have cost him promotion from captain.

First, he had sliced twelve feet from a West Coast pier while docking his ship. I can't remember what he said the extenuating circumstances were.

Then, a day or so at sea, two stowaways had turned up in the crew's quarters, women wearing sailor dungarees. Fleet headquarters at Pearl Harbor had ordered him to turn about and deposit them ashore. His account was funny.

I responded with a recital of the time I took a destroyer out of Norfolk for a captain who misunderstood me to say I was a Virginia pilot when I identified myself as being from the *Virginian-Pilot*.

"I knew about that," the admiral said. "The public affairs officer here included it in some biographical data he wrote for me after I asked him to dig up something to use in introducing you. I left it out because I assumed it would embarrass you."

Why the admiral thought my little tiptoe through Hampton Roads would embarrass me when neither his sense of humor nor career had suffered from his two brushes with "Rocks and Shoals," as naval regulations are called, I had no idea. That was the second time I know of that available information was not used in introducing me.

I was scheduled to speak at a luncheon during a regional medical convention in Norfolk. Because a number of Navy doctors would attend, I put together some humorous as well as esoteric material I had picked up, as a spin-off to sea-warfare research, about Confederate States Navy surgeons. The program chairman's wife, a most proper lady, sent me a form on which to submit biographical material, such as place and date of birth, colleges attended, degrees held, honors received, military service, and decorations; the record would be useful to her husband, she noted, in presenting me.

Under decorations, I wrote: "Small anchor tattooed on left shoulder."

I'm sure the old girl thought I misunderstood the query.

18 Miss TV Tower 1949

Three years after returning to the *Virginian-Pilot* from service in World War II, I was still swing editor. I spent Friday afternoons editing copy for the Sunday edition before shifting that night to the city desk. Like sugar, tires, whiskey, and just about everything else, newsprint had been in short supply during the emergency. At least it was becoming adequate. But the *Pilot* had not restored its Sunday paper to full quality. The extra material needed to fill it was gathered, too much of it from the wires, by the day city editor. I reported weekly to him.

The day city editor, who had been an enlisted soldier in the First World War, entered the second one as a National Guard major and left it, without overseas duty because of a physical ailment, as a lieutenant colonel. He was addicted to war stories set in the Louisiana swamps. I was his captive audience on Friday afternoons.

One day he surprised me by asking, "How would you like to be Sunday editor of this newspaper?"

"I would like it fine," I promptly replied.

"How would you like to be Sunday editor of this newspaper working directly under the day city editor?" he further inquired.

Just as promptly I replied, "I wouldn't like it at all."

I suppose it was his turn to be surprised. There the matter rested.

But soon I had cause to suppose that the development of a Sunday feature section had been discussed in high places, with the city editor involved. Louis Jaffe, the editor, called me into his office. He offered me the Sunday editorship with independence from the newsroom but an obligation to advise with him and gear opinion articles to his policies. He stipulated that I include a book page containing a column of newly published poetry. Did I accept? Oh, boy, did I accept!

An office was cleared for me and three associates—Warner Twyford, a self-taught critic who was knowledgeable in art, music, and drama and wrote with a rare skill; Mary Eugenia Parke, a Radcliffe graduate who gradually took over the book page, freeing me to write as well as develop stories and commentary; and Frederick Sherman Holley, a Washington and Lee graduate who had studied fiction under Margaret Foley at Columbia University and was a competent poet. I never worked with an abler or more congenial staff.

To my wife Frances's delight, I had day hours. After a decade of night work and night sea watches I didn't adjust immediately to them, or to the switch from the noisy newsroom and its deadline environment. I was still finding my way into my new element on Christmas Eve, 1949.

After helping Frances put our daughter Fran's presents under the tree, I got to thinking about the city room and what was happening there. At about 8:15 I told Frances I believed I would check my office mail and be back soon. I walked into the chilly evening from our apartment near the old downtown produce piers on the Elizabeth River.

As I approached the building, Frank Blackford ran up from an alley leading to the pressroom and loading docks. Frank had worked on the *Washington Post* during the war and come to the *Pilot* at about the time I rejoined it. He and his wife Polly and their two little boys lived at Virginia Beach. They were our close friends.

The alley that Frank's feet pounded was one of the two behind the newspaper building. The other provided back-door access to WTAR radio station, which the newspaper corporation owned, just around the corner from us. WTAR was adding—with great apprehension—television, which would go on the air early in the new year. The station had just erected a 399-foot TV tower between the alleys, behind its building and also the newspaper plant.

"A woman's climbing the tower!" Frank shouted.

"Good Lord—who?" I asked. "Did you recognize her?"

"I didn't even see her," Frank said. "But she must have thought I did because she hollered, 'If you try to stop me, I'll jump!' I was about to get in my car, fixing to go home."

"Let's go back there and have a good look," I suggested.

"Listen," said Frank, "when I was on the *Post* I covered a man threatening to jump off a ledge about ten stories high, and he ended up splattering himself on me, and ever since I've been allergic to this kind of stuff. Besides, I came on early to work till eight, and it's already past that, and I told Polly I'd be home before now to help with the tree and the kids' toys. And this goddam female nut could keep me here all night."

I told Frank to get going and I'd take over the story. And that's what happened. He folded his great bulk into his Volkswagen bug and took off in a roar for the seafront cottage he and Polly recently had built.

By the time I'd checked in with the desk and picked up a notepad and hurried to the tower, a fire department truck and two police motorcycles were parked under it. A taxi driver had spotted the woman about a third of the way up the tower, briefly silhouetted just above the surrounding rooftops and barely within the streetlights' range, upon stopping in the WTAR-side alley at Buddy's place, and had called the police on Buddy's phone. Buddy was a bootlegger. He operated out of a one-room, stove-heated, cinderblock shack squatting on the strip of city property that accommodated the alley, which technically was a street. His late hours captured a printer and pressmen clientele and appealed to the floating trade.

The motorcycle cops were Patrolmen P. L. Huddleston and Robert

C. Wash. They wore the familiar winter gear of their work—belted peacoats, leather leggings and gauntlets, and heavy shoes. The temperature was thirty-seven degrees. A brisk wind blew from the north.

Huddleston removed his gun from his belt, hung a manila line there, and started up the tower ladder. He was big—well over six feet and maybe 225 pounds. Before joining the force he had worked as a hoisting engineer. Wash, of somewhat slighter build, followed him.

Huddleston trapped the woman 330 feet up, where the steel pyramid peaked, the ladder ended, and a sixty-nine foot ladder began. She screamed that she would jump if he touched her. Huddleston told her that all he wanted to do was help. He chatted on, very calmly, about how pretty the city looked from so high, about how nice it would be to go down to get warm. At length she whimpered.

Huddleston coaxed her onto his shoulders, and felt her relax. He looped his line under her arms and fastened it to his middle. Then he squeezed with her past Wash, who had come as far as possible too, and gave him the line's free end to tend. Down they started. It was slow going. Wash would snub the line to succeeding rungs as Huddleston descended below him.

The woman seemed to be unconscious. But soon she stiffened and began to cry. She wanted her baby, she sobbed; when she lost her baby, she said, she lost everything. Huddleston took off his gloves and put them on her frigid hands. Again she went limp.

Below a crowd of perhaps fifty had gathered. Several held portable radios, which lately had come on the market, that blared Christmas music. A drunk mounted the tower ladder, only to be hauled down by a policeman who had arrived with an ambulance unit.

The fire truck sprouted a one-hundred-foot ladder, and two firemen went to its top to relieve Huddleston of his burden and Wash of his line. But the woman was still lashed to Huddleston's shoulders when he stepped from the aerial ladder onto the truck bed.

She wore thin black slacks and a light tweed jacket. The jacket had slipped up, exposing half her naked back. Her feet were bare too; the drunk who had attacked the tower found her slippers on the ground and stuffed them in his pockets. She was slim and auburn-haired. The cuffs of Huddleston's gloves came nearly to her elbows. Her face was blue from the cold. She was moaning. The police ambulance whisked her to a hospital.

Members of the crowd picked up Huddleston and wobbled about with him, like some irregular football team saluting its coach in victory. Wash leaned against the ladder truck, shaking violently. Huddleston freed himself and straddled his motorcycle. He too was shaking. "Gotta go," he said. "It's Christmas Eve and I'm off at midnight." It was ten o'clock. The rescue had taken one and one-half hours.

I made the 11 P.M. deadline for the first edition with a column-long story. With the help of the obit writer and a rim man who had joined me under the tower early on, plus several telephone calls, I patched my piece extensively for the final. The woman, I learned, had a one-room apartment in Ocean View, half a dozen miles from the TV tower. She had come in a taxi from an Ocean View tavern to Buddy's place, but that driver had left without seeing whether she went in or what else she did. He told the police she had talked all the way into town about losing her baby and needing her husband. The police meanwhile traced her to Parkersberg, West Virginia, where her parents said she was twenty-five years old, single when she left home not long before, and in any event childless. Head-quarters intended to book her for disturbing the peace and possibly trespassing. Our news editor spread my story and two pictures, one showing Huddleston coming down the tower with the woman and the other showing him on the crowd's shoulders, across half the front page.

Polly Blackford gave me a coffee cup that holds a full pint for relieving Frank to come home early. It wasn't the only prize I collected for that night's work. The *Virginian-Pilot*'s publisher paid me a bonus.

He was Colonel Sam Slover, a formidable figure. He owned most of WTAR as well as the *Pilot* and its afternoon sister, the *Ledger-Dispatch* (now *Ledger-Star*), and major chunks of the *Petersburg*

Progress-Index and the two Richmond papers, the *Times-Dispatch* and *News Leader*. He was scared to death about WTAR's investment in television. Television was new, and nobody knew whether it would succeed.

The Colonel was getting along in years. I wouldn't bet he had read the *Pilot* next morning when he began a round of Christmas parties in his Old Norfolk neighborhood of big houses. But everybody else had read it. Everywhere he went somebody would approach him, eggnog cup in hand, and elaborately accuse him of staging the TV tower-climbing stunt to draw attention to his television operation. He enjoyed the kidding no end. He was puzzled that some of his neighbors seemed to know me, because he certainly didn't.

Next day he sent for me. He told me what a splendid article I had written, then reached, as if impulsively, into his pocket and handed me a bill. I think it was ten dollars. I know I was embarrassed.

Norfolk's infamous vice squad was embarrassed also—by the attention that my story brought to Buddy's bootlegging shop. Package sales are a state monopoly under Virginia's Alcoholic Beverage Control laws, which strictly limit hours; liquor-by-the-drink in 1949 was a long way from legalization. The vice squad forced Buddy to dismantle his shack. He seemed to vanish.

But the next summer Fred Holley came upon Buddy in a booth at the California Fruit and Confectionary, a Norfolk waterfront beer bar. Fred was a police reporter before hooking up with me in the Sunday office, and had known him as a police character. Buddy was with a woman and another couple. Fred and Buddy passed a few pleasantries. Then Buddy said, nodding toward the woman beside him, "Don't you remember Miss TV Tower 1949?"

She grinned cheerfully. She was small, copper-haired, and pretty.

Fred was both surprised and delighted. He soon managed to draw Buddy aside. "I'd lost track of her," he said. "I assumed she was in jail."

"Oh, hell, no," said Buddy. "Think back that when she appeared in Police Court the judge ordered a psychiatric examination of her and had her sent to the happy farm in Williamsburg. Okay? Well, the shrink said she had this insecurity problem that made her unable to cope with Christmas, being so far from home and all, plus one or two other little matters, so she wasn't responsible for what she did Christmas Eve, which was to try to attract a lot of attention to herself. I think the judge read the medical report and decided to hell with it—no harm had been done anyway. She's a real sweet kid."

Fred said he was glad to hear the case turned out so well.

"And you know what caused the insecurity?" Buddy asked. "Flat chest. Her tits ain't no bigger than this." He held up a thumb and first two fingers, pressed together.

"Well, I know medical science is advancing all the time," Fred said, "but how did the analyst establish that?"

"They gave her this physical along with the mental examination at Williamsburg," Buddy explained. "And when she had to undress a flounder fell out of her bra."

I hear from Fred now and then. He is on the *Los Angeles Times* desk staff and sometimes teaches poetry in the Cal State University system. He wrote the *Times'* outstanding style book, which the New American Library brought out in a paperback edition in 1981. His father was an Anglican priest and assistant headmaster of a Canadian boys' school.

"I'm not sure that flounder in Miss TV Tower 1949's bra was all that significant," Fred mused after telling me of his conversation with Buddy in the Norfolk waterfront tavern. "She was living in Ocean View, after all, and fishermen are forever hauling their nets loaded with flounders on the beach there. Flounders of all sizes. A plenitude of flounders. Why, it wouldn't surprise me one bit if all the girls at Ocean View wear flounders the way other girls wear foam-rubber cups."

19 Admiral Battleship

During my tenure as Sunday editor of the *Virginian-Pilot* in Norfolk, 1949-1952, I was forever receiving a manuscript, usually badly typed, linking some long-ago community figure or ancestor with lore and legend or, occasionally, possible fact. The author usually was an amateur historian, book club secretary, retired English teacher, or former regent of a Daughters of the American Revolution chapter. Personal recollections ran through the lot.

I was wary of all. They made me think of advice I heard from James Street and O. J. Coffin.

Street lived in retirement in Chapel Hill. I met him at a writers' conference at Nags Head, a North Carolina beach resort below Norfolk. Ridiculing a newly published Civil War novel by a writer who drew heavily on family sources, he said, "A grandmother's knee is a fine place for a boy to lay his head but a damned poor place for him to learn history."

Coffin was my journalism professor at Carolina. After wading through a student's interview with some old codger he snorted, "Nostalgia ain't necessarily humor."

Then there came to my desk one day, unsolicited and unannounced, a perfectly typed manuscript from a professional writer, a woman of advanced years living in New York, describing Norfolk as it had appeared to her as a child in a Navy family in the nineteenth century. She was Virginia Watson, a retired editor at *Harper's*, both the magazine and book-publishing branches. Her father had been commanding officer of the old barracks ship *Franklin*, tied up at the Norfolk Navy Yard, and later, as a very junior captain, of a collier engaged in the Spanish-American War: proud to have a seagoing command but a mite embarrassed that his ship was a floating coal yard. Her mother had been active in Norfolk's social life. The daughter remembered names and places and events.

I published the piece and, in a letter of appreciation accompanying a check to the author, suggested that she expand into a second article a paragraph she had written about a pleasant hotel where her family had leased an apartment. It chanced that the hotel, having fallen on hard times, was about to be razed. That led to further correspondence and finally the article I wanted.

Meanwhile, Miss Watson's original story especially delighted some Old Norfolk residents—ladies, for the most part, guarding the cotillions, charities, and cemeteries—who had known, or had heard their parents speak of, the Watsons. Among them was the Baroness de Lustrac, who, before her marriage to a French artillery officer she had met abroad, was Helen Reed, daughter of Mr. and Mrs. Fergus Reed. Mr. Reed had been a wealthy and generous cotton shipper. A Norfolk park is named for him.

The Baroness telephoned me one day to say that Miss Watson was to visit her and wished to meet me. Would I come to a little party she was giving for her house guest? Of course I would.

The de Lustracs lived in the old Reed home, which sat in a cluster of big houses near a tidal stream, linked with the inner harbor. I arrived at the party exactly on time. So did twenty or so women of the town's—not the city's now, but the town's—matriarchy. Among them I remember Mrs. Robert Tunstall, an accomplished poet who once confided to me that she jilted a third baseman in the Kitty League upon marrying a decoration of the Norfolk bar; Mrs. Thomas Willcox, whose son and daughter were friends of ours; Mrs. Arthur Stansbury, mother of the *Pilot*'s society editor; Mrs. John R. Curd, widow of a celebrated Confederate boy gunner; and Mrs. Robert W. Hughes, Jr., whose husband's father, a federal judge, in his salad days had shot, in an affair of honor, a young editorialist home from the Civil War named William E. Cameron, who survived to become Governor of the Commonwealth and editor of my newspaper.

"This won't do, having just one boy among all us girls," cried one of the matrons. "Isabelle, you must fetch Frank. I know he's sitting in you-all's house not doing one single thing."

So Isabelle brought Frank from next door to the de Lustrac parlor. She was Isabelle Truxtun Brumby, great-granddaughter of Commodore Thomas Truxtun of *Constellation* fame. He was Admiral Frank Hardeman Brumby, USN (Ret.). Although I had not met him I had seen him often, usually on Sunday morning at the

California Fruit and Confectionary, a neighborhood tavern, winding his way past the naval ratings and merchant seamen drinking beer, to pick up a copy of the *New York Times*, which was my mission too. To reach the California, as everyone called the joint, the Admiral had to cross a bridge; I lived on the side of his destination, on a street often called Newspaper Row, where century-old townhouses had been cut into apartments now sheltering, along with an architect, a couple of lawyers, several teachers, and sundry others, a fair portion of the Norfolk press's staff members.

Admiral Brumby was seventy-five years old and had been retired since well before World War II. He had become pretty much a recluse—a tall, thin, bald old gentleman, a bit uncertain of step but still properly erect. I knew he had been commandant of the Norfolk Naval Yard and assumed that most of his career had been in engineering. There I was wrong.

The Baroness placed Miss Watson and me on a sun porch off the parlor, where we might talk. She seated Admiral Brumby with us. A butler serving mulled wine included us in his rounds.

Miss Watson was as lovely and witty as her prose. Seldom have I been so captivated by a person. She told me how tiny the *Harper's* staff had been when she joined it, of the writers she had worked with, of how wonderful New York had seemed to a girl with literary ambitions just out of college, and of course of her Navy childhood. I caught her up on city and naval matters that seemed to interest her, and related some of my experiences in book reviewing, and supplied what information I could when she inquired about this or that of the old biddies among us. We became casual and jolly.

We neglected Admiral Brumby. The butler did not. Every time the butler came near, the Admiral snagged a cup of mulled wine from his tray.

At length Miss Watson and I paused. Admiral Brumby seemed to be dozing. But the butler approached again, and he extended a skinny arm.

To make belated conversation with the Admiral, I said, "Sir, it must be distressing to you that the Navy's only remaining battleship is out there in the Hampton Flats mud."

The USS *Missouri* had gone aground several days before, early on January 17, 1950. I had learned of her embarrassment within an hour, while still abed. Our daughter was in a school car pool that included a little girl whose father, a Coast Guard officer, was captain of the port. Usually, I suppose, the captain had his own transportation, but when alerted at about dawn that the battleship was in trouble he had hurried off in the family automobile. His wife, who was taking the children that week, called my wife and asked her to substitute. When I discovered what was going on, I called the newspaper to hire a launch and get a photographer to the grounding scene. I figured the Navy would hook enough tugs to the Big Mo to pull her off on the next tide and would deny that anything unusual had happened. My haste was unneeded. The ship stayed where she was exactly two weeks.

"Bottleship, sor?" inquired the Admiral. "Did you say bottleship?"

"Yes, sir," I replied. "I said it must pain you that the *Missouri* is aground and having a hard time getting off."

The Admiral sat up. Fury flowed into his face and reddened it. "Why, sor," he thundered, "it's a disgrace—a shameful and unmitigated disgrace! Do you hear me, sor? It's a goddam disgrace to the United States Navy, if the ladies will pardon me for saying so!"

He stood. There meanwhile was a great flurry in the parlor. "What's the matter with Frank?" one of the women called. "What in the world has got into Frank?"

Admiral Brumby slammed a fist onto the little table that held his collection of empty wine cups. They bounced and rattled.

"Why, sor," he shouted, louder than before, "if I hod commond of that ship—ond I remind you, sor, I have commonded bottleships—ond I hod in my compony one quartermoster who couldn't negotiate that chonnel, why, sor, I would disrate him—I would disrate the goddam lubber!"

Oh, well, it was about time for me to go anyway. I said good-bye to Miss Watson, made my manners to the Baroness, and returned to the office. The first thing I did there was look up Admiral Brumby in the files.

He had commanded battleships, all right—the *Kansas* from 1920 to 1922 and the *New Mexico* from 1924 to 1926. As Commander, Battleship Division One, he had flown his two-star flag in the *Texas* in the early thirties, and, several years and two more stars later, had commanded the Battle Force of the U.S. Fleet aboard the *California*. Among the Old Navy's battleship admirals, Admiral Brumby was Four-Star Admiral Battleship himself.

He died, God rest him, six months after I sat with him that pleasant January afternoon.

Fourteen years later, in June 1964, the Navy launched the USS *Brumby*, a frigate honoring him and his uncle, Lieutenant Thomas M. Brumby, USN, aide and confidant to Admiral George Dewey, who was with him in the *Olympia* during the Battle of Manila Bay. Both Brumbys were born in Georgia and both had graduated from the U.S. Naval Academy. USS *Brumby* was sponsored by Admiral Brumby's twin granddaughters.

A few years ago Doris Betts, the novelist and short-story writer who made feminine history by being chosen chairman of the faculty at the University of North Carolina in 1981, wrote me that her son David was a lieutenant on the *Brumby*. I replied with this advice for David:

Don't ever, goddamit, run her aground!

20 Flight and Fancy

A *Virginian-Pilot* claim to fame is that it alone learned on December 17, 1903, that Wilbur and Orville Wright during the morning had flown an engine-powered airplane at Kitty Hawk and that, although five other newspapers among a dozen solicited bought the story from a *Pilot* reporter, only it featured the news on its front page. The *Pilot*'s account was wildly off mark. Nevertheless, it was reprinted in *A Treasury of Great Reporting*, which Simon and Schuster published in 1949, with this notation, "The only newspaper in America to give the flight serious coverage was the Norfolk *Virginian-Pilot*."

The year after *Great Reporting* appeared, the *Atlantic* serialized "Miracle at Kitty Hawk," a collection of the Wright brothers' letters edited by Fred C. Kelly, the Wright biographer. Some of the letters charmingly described Kitty Hawk and neighboring communities in the *Virginian-Pilot*'s circulation territory.

I wrote Kelly in Kensington, Maryland, requesting permission to develop an article for the *Pilot*, of which I was Sunday editor, from the letters. As innocently as a child petitioning Santa Claus, I explained to him the *Pilot*'s connection with the First Flight and said that Harry P. Moore, the nineteen-year-old cub reporter who got the flight tip and marketed the story to noncompetitive papers, was on the local staff yet; that Alfred W. Drinkwater, the telegrapher who tapped out the message in which the Wrights served history by telling their father how far and how long they had flown, was a friend of the newspaper; and that Johnny Moore, the last surviving First Flight witness, sometimes guided me on fishing trips in the lower Currituck Sound.

Kelly replied immediately. He was preparing to syndicate some of the letters, he said, and asked me to wait for the package. Alf Drinkwater, he pointedly added, had nothing to do with the Wright telegram, and Orville Wright had been dubious of Harry Moore's reporting.

I knew vaguely that the *Pilot* had exaggerated the flight's distance and poorly described the plane. I knew also that Harry Moore cherished the newsroom's impression that after nearly forty-seven years he was still protecting, for reasons not clear, a mysterious source of information. I knew further that Keville Glennan, wealthy and retired, who put together the flight story and wrote its headlines, claimed a greater share in the accomplishment than Moore would acknowledge.

But I had felt no inclination to dig into the matter. Fred Kelly's letter got me going. My first step was to read his 1943 biography, *The Wright Brothers*.

Soon I realized that Drinkwater, who had long since traded his telegrapher's key for a real estate broker's license in Manteo, near Kitty Hawk, indeed had fudged his way into the First Flight lore, although he began in good faith. He had considerable knowledge about Kitty Hawk and the rest of the Carolina Outer Banks, and was a garrulous and picturesque man, and seemed to have shored up his fame, when it might have waned, to please beach tourists and newspaper feature writers as much as himself.

In 1908, five years after the First Flight, the Wright brothers returned to Kitty Hawk to test an advanced airplane. The world had paid so little attention to their 1903 hop-skip-and-jump that their second Kitty Hawk experiments became confused with the original. Among differences was that several experienced reporters witnessed the 1908 flights—from the tops of pine trees, mostly, although Wilbur Wright later would insist that they would have been welcome in camp.

Among them was Bruce Salley, a Norfolk free lance reporting for the *New York Herald*. Alf Drinkwater handled his stories at the Manteo telegraph office and kept the copy. It became his ticket to celebrity. I saw the crumpled, hand-scrawled pages in a display of Outer Banks artifacts in the Museum of Natural History in Raleigh in 1935, when I was a reporter for the Raleigh *Times*.

Fred Kelly's 1943 biography punctured Drinkwater's bubble. He went into decline. But soon he bounced back with an ingenious tale.

It just so happened, Drinkwater said in newspaper interviews, that when the Wright brothers at about 3 P.M. on December 17, 1903, gave Joseph J. Doshier, the U.S. Weather Bureau Station operator at Kitty Hawk, a telegram informing their father in Dayton, Ohio, that they had flown four times, the longest flight lasting fifty-nine seconds and covering 852 feet, the telegraph line was down between there and Currituck Inlet, forty miles up the coast; and it chanced also that old Drink was on temporary duty just then at Currituck Inlet telegraphing daily reports to the Navy in Norfolk of a tug's efforts to salvage the submarine *Moccasin*, which had run aground while being towed, in tandem with the *Scorpion*, toward Chesapeake Bay. To get his message out, Drinkwater now said,

Doshier had to telephone it to him at Currituck, and he tapped it to the Norfolk weather station for relay into the Western Union system and on to Dayton.

Kelly was familiar with Drinkwater's revisionist history. In his Wright brothers biography he insisted that "Doshier got an almost instantaneous connection with Norfolk," where Charles C. Grant manned the key. In a letter to me, encouraging me to sift the facts from the accumulation of First Flight reporting fiction, he said, "Within a second or two after he clicked the instrument, Doshier got a response from Norfolk. There was no telephoning or telegraphing to Drinkwater or anybody else at any intermediate point. Grant wanted to know if it would be all right to give the news to a newspaper friend, but the Wrights said no . . ."

Kelly accepted, as I had in my first letter to him, the popular assumption that Harry Moore was the newspaper friend to whom Grant went ahead and gave the news. But I collected persuasive evidence that the friend in fact was Edward O. Dean, a young man from South Carolina who would go from the *Pilot* to the *New York Times*. He hurried with his meager information to Keville Glennan, his city editor.

Glennan, twenty-three years old and not long home from Georgetown University, was intelligent, informed, and resourceful. He had followed with great interest Professor Samuel P. Langley's flight attempts on the Potomac River nine days earlier. Also, he knew the Wrights were on the Carolina Outer Banks and what they were about. Two U.S. Life Saving men he had met while covering shipwrecks between Capes Hatteras and Henry had told him and he put in a call to them at Kitty Hawk hoping to learn details of that morning's doings.

It was then about 5 P.M. Two hours later, as Glennan worked on Dean's tip, Harry Moore came in with a fist full of notes. "You heard about those fellows flying?" he asked Glennan. As much office boy as reporter, he had been in the newspaper's business office, a block away, taking late want-ads and subscription orders.

Although the *Virginian*, which Keville Glennan's father had owned, and the *Daily Pilot* had merged into the *Virginian-Pilot* five years before, the paper was under two roofs in 1903. The business office was in the *Pilot*'s old building, the news and mechanical departments in the *Virginian*'s. The buildings had different telephone numbers. Glennan had no doubt that one of the Life Savers, responding to his call, had been connected to the *Pilot* building telephone and told Moore what he had to tell.

Moore always denied it. But over the years he wrote conflicting versions of what successive newsroom editors believed to have been his scoop, the first in 1928, on the First Flight's twenty-fifth anniversary. He had been keeping tabs on the Wright brothers for more than three months, he said then, having heard a beachcomber describe "two loonies" and their flying contraption while sitting in a Norfolk restaurant "one September morning in 1903." But twenty-one years later he stretched the period to "almost three years" and told of spying during one of them on the Wright camp. In one account he had telegrapher Charles Grant delivering to his home a wire from a Life Saver describing the First Flight, in another he had an unidentified person telephoning him at the office. Moore was a worthy citizen and a fine companion. He also was a relic of when exactitude was not a newspaper priority and a little journalistic swaggering was acceptable, especially when details didn't seem to matter much. He was before his time in recognizing the entertainment possibilities of a newspaper.

So instead of a pleasant article reflecting the Wright brothers' appreciation of landscapes and seascapes in the Kitty Hawk vicinity, I wrote one untangling the *Pilot*'s First Flight coverage. No one else at the newspaper was aware of how much a mess it had made, during nearly half a century, of its most notable achievement, and I thought I owed it to us all to place in our files, for the sake of history, a detailed correction. In some of its First Flight anniversary features and Alfred W. Drinkwater interviews, the *Pilot* was even less faithful to the truth than Keville Glennan had been that night when, drawing on uncertain reports, background knowledge, and youthful imagination, he wrote about a flying machine "soaring for three miles . . . and gracefully descending to the earth again" instead of sputtering in the air for less than a minute and casting its shadow on less than 1,000 feet of sand before darting downward and breaking its forward rudder.

Fred Kelly helped me. We exchanged a dozen letters and notes as I checked my findings against his recollections of what Orville Wright had told him during his *The Wright Brothers* researches. He usually wrote on postal cards. In September 1950 he stopped off to see me as he traveled from Maryland to Kitty Hawk. I arranged to meet him at the pier upon his arrival aboard the overnight steamer from Washington. "You'll have no trouble recognizing me as I have a droopy face remindful of an old bloodhound, and I'll have a nice looking lady and two small children at my heels," he wrote.

I had no trouble at all; Kelly, then sixty-eight, an old newspaper hand as well as author of thirteen books, was a careful reporter. I dropped his pretty wife and their lively children at my apartment near the harbor to be entertained by Frances and our eight-year-old daughter Fran, and took him to the Glennan residence in a fashionable neighborhood along the Lafayette River.

Keville Glennan was seventy. He had dropped out of Georgetown University and passed up an appointment to the Naval Academy to join the Army as a private at the outbreak of the Spanish-American War, then come home from basic camp with a lame arm to work for the *Virginian-Pilot*. He left the paper in time, despite his inherited stock in it, to be a foreign correspondent for a newspaper syndicate, work in the Hearst chain, and be assistant managing editor of the *Washington Post*. He came back to Norfolk as managing editor.

At the *Pilot* he was remembered for pouring water on patrons of the opera house across the street who ventured into the newspaper alley to relieve themselves during intermission and for running his yacht so far out onto an Albemarle Sound sandbar that he and several guests had gone through a whole case of liquor when the Coast Guard at last pulled her off.

He and Kelly hit it off. Although a stickler for facts when he wrote, Kelly fibbed his way into the Wright phase of his career. An editor at *Collier's* magazine, knowing him as a Washington columnist—he claimed to be the first syndicated one—from Dayton catering to Ohio papers, asked him if he remembered the Wright boys. Kelly replied that he ought to, he had grown up with them—slept in their bed and worn their clothes. On being commissioned then to do an updated Wright profile, he sought out Orville and introduced himself; he never met Wilbur, who had died in 1912.

He told me that in his younger days, when unpacking his clothes in a ship bound for Europe, he accepted a drink with a stranger across the passageway and kept drinking in the stateroom the entire voyage, never glimpsing the ocean. He sent his friends Groundhog Day greetings. Charging Quentin Reynolds with cribbing from his Wright biography for a youth book, he also sent them a pamphlet with his lines in one column and Reynold's rewrites of them in an opposite column, which he labeled "The Art of Plagiarism." I asked him what he heard from that and he said, "Oh, Quint's not a bad fellow."

As a result of his Norfolk visit, Kelly inserted into the book version of *Miracle at Kitty Hawk*, which came out in 1951, two paragraphs crediting Glennan and Ed Dean as well as Harry Moore with breaking the First Flight story and concluding: "Though the account published was fantastically inaccurate, one must credit Glennan and . . . the *Virginian-Pilot* . . . with recognizing how important the news was and giving it a headline clear across the front page."

Also in 1951, I paid another visit to Johnny Moore, the fishing guide who at age seventeen helped the Wright brothers launch their airplane.

William Courtenay, O.B.E., M.M., aviation writer and war correspondent for the London *Daily Graphic*, was in Norfolk to speak at the Armed Forces Staff College on close air support for ground troops he lately had observed in Korea. He had learned to fly in 1917 as a member of the Royal Flying Corps before it became the Royal Air Force, and was proposing to the Royal Aero Club in England that it sponsor a delegation to Kitty Hawk for the First Flight's 50th anniversary in 1953. He wished to see the site before returning to London. Somebody at the staff college told me I was the person to escort him there.

I was happy to comply. On our drive down to the Outer Banks

he read Fred Kelly's *The Wright Brothers* but put the book away long enough to tell us about a U.S. Air Force survival manual he had come upon while on assignment in Alaska.

"It advised," he said, "that we should not eat the liver of a Kodiak bear. Now consider my proposition. One is five-foot-four and approaching the Kodiak bear, who is twelve-foot-two-and-one-half. There is no place to run to. The question, then, is this: who is likely to eat whose liv-ah?"

After Courtenay had viewed the splendid Wright Memorial and examined the marked area of the First Flight, we rode on to Collington Island in search of Johnny Moore. I found him tying up his skiff in a ditch. He wore tennis shoes, oilskin overalls, and a baseball cap.

Courtenay was overwhelmed to stand before Moore, weatherbeaten and gnarled, and to realize that he beheld in this rustic figure one who had seen a very great thing. "Now tell me," he urged, "please think carefully and tell me exactly how Wilbur and Orville Wright reacted to their marvelous feat. What did they do? What did they say? Precisely what did you see and hear?"

Johnny Moore beamed. In a sing-song voice he recited to one more city sucker for country-fried history:

"Well, suh. Well, now. Ol' Orville Wright, he jumped straight up, clicked his eels together three times, come down flatfooted as a mallard duck, and he whooped and hollered—said, 'Wilbur, 'fore God, we'll never have to hit another lick of work as long as we live!' "

William Courtenay, O.B.E., M.M., was stunned. He had traveled far and seen a lot, but he had never come before upon the likes of old Johnny Moore.

21 Small-Town Editor

Early in 1952 W. E. Horner, publisher of the *Sanford Herald*, offered to sell me, on easy terms, a tenth of his paper if I would come back and edit it. It was still a semiweekly. Since the mid-thirties, when the venerable weekly Sanford *Express* perished, it had feasted on an exclusive territory. But serious competition had become a threat. To head it off, Mr. Horner announced that the *Herald* would become an afternoon daily—a bold decision and, as things turned out, a wise one.

All my life, I reflected, I had heard people say that if only they had done this or that at a time long past they would be living on Easy Street today. Now it's my turn to seize or lose forever an opportunity to advance the capitalistic system and do a little something for my pocketbook, I told myself, and I might as well take a whack at it. So I accepted.

As a daily, the *Herald* would need additional equipment, including rotary presses to replace the flatbed, and a lot more space. Mr. Horner chose to build a new plant rather than expand the little structure into which the paper had moved fifteen years before from its original basement quarters.

Bad weather delayed the extensive grading that the building site required. A national steel strike held up construction. There were other complications.

Meanwhile, in Norfolk I found time to contract for the features, such as comics and columns, that the *Herald* should add, and to study some small afternoon papers' methods and schedules. I visited the papers in Suffolk, Hopewell, and Martinsville, all in Virginia, and in Elizabeth City and Kinston, in eastern North Carolina. I knew someone at each stop, and all were generous with information and advice. No two papers operated alike; none seemed to me to be an ideal model.

At last, in September 1952, I moved my family to Sanford, which I had departed as a bachelor in September 1934. Norfolk had been our home for nearly eleven years. I was forty.

The *Herald*'s new building had superior production arrangements. The printing, stereotyping, and press functions were coordinated in one great subbasement room, which opened onto a loading dock. There was ample space for newsprint storage.

If the editorial, advertising, and business departments were less efficiently arranged, I managed to cluster my little staff—two reporters and a women's editor—near the stairway leading down to the composing area. The women's editor was the society editor with whom I had worked nearly two decades earlier. Her job had changed little.

Only I among the people who produced the paper, from advertising director to printer's devil, had ever worked on a daily. I divided the news territory, including sports, between the reporters, supplied the women's editor with a syndicated gossip column to supplement her accounts of weddings and parties, and organized myself into a news editor, telegraph editor, city editor, editorial writer, and sometime reporter. The copy deadline was 1 P.M., press time half an hour later.

Sanford had grown into an industrial as well as marketing center, with a population of about 12,000. On the *Herald*'s first day as a daily, upon the tooting of a factory whistle at noon, the young woman who kept the books and minded the front counter hollered, "Dinner time!" There was a rush for the door.

When my news staff drifted back an hour later, I explained just why from then on the four of us would be courting stomach problems from brief and irregular lunch periods.

During the months I had contemplated getting out the *Herald* six times a week rather than its familiar two, I had not resolved how to handle the editorial page. I was mildly surprised that Mr. Horner, who had worked briefly on the news staff of the *Durham Morning Herald* before coming to Sanford in 1930, did not care to contribute to it. One of the reporters, a city boy and Harvard graduate, had written editorials for the semiweekly, but I found him to be unacquainted with local affairs and customs. I thought of relying heavily on thoughtfully clipped material, from books and magazines as well as other newspapers. But after a week or two I determined that if I could gather ideas while putting the paper together and spend no more than twenty minutes at lunch, I could write three editorials and edit the rest of the page during two afternoon hours and have time for what else there was to be done.

Much of what I wrote was unconventional. Although now and again I pointed-with-pride and viewed-with-alarm with the best of them, I also cranked out essays, book reviews, profiles, fables, and fantasy for the editorial double-column. Success was less than constant. I outraged the mayor, for instance, with a fictional piece about the accumulation of garbage on back porches and patios and in carports and lawns after he failed to make good a campaign promise to inaugurate a de luxe pickup service extending right to everybody's kitchen door. He complained that what I wrote was a plain goddam lie. My defense, that satire had been a legitimate form of criticism for as long as there had been commentary, got me nowhere.

In order to get a head start on the week's fattest papers, Thursday's and Friday's, I regularly worked Wednesday and Thursday nights. Most of those hours were spent editing "correspondence" from rural neighborhoods—chicken suppers, church notes, baby showers, birthday parties, home-demonstration club meetings, operations, piano recitals, family reunions. One wintry night I was turning out the lights to go home when Luman Moore, the *Herald*'s photographer-engraver, came in. He had been to the county jail for some reason or another and there had come upon a kid he believed would interest me. I went with Luman to see him.

He was a fifteen-year-old runaway from Pawtucket, Rhode Island, charged with burglary, a hanging offense under the old North Carolina code. Wet and cold and hungry, he had entered a residence by breaking a basement window, slipped into the kitchen, made himself a jelly sandwich, and was about to take a bite when a cruising policeman snared him. The county judge had no choice but to bind him over to higher court and the sheriff had no place to keep him but a jailhouse cell.

There was only so much to be said for the boy. He had left home because of trouble at school and hitched rides to Raleigh. There he had worked as pinboy in a bowling alley but, finding the pay inadequate, had taken to stealing—a camera, a coat, milk from porches, whatever he might use or sell. He was trying to beat his way to Florida when he became stranded in Sanford.

Nevertheless, his prospect of being held in jail three months until superior court met and then being tried as an adult for a felony distressed me. As late as it was, I went back to the office and wrote a part-report, part-feature, part-editorial about him for the next day's editorial page, which I decorated with his photograph. I called him the jelly-bread boy.

That rescued him. If that kid had been chewing on a chicken leg, a slice of ham, or a wedge of cheese when the cop nabbed him, he probably would be pulling time right now. But nobody can bear to see a child locked up for eating a jelly sandwich. I had half the town weeping, including all the ministers. The county judge sent for a Pawtucket priest and let the jelly-bread boy go home with him.

My piece won a state press association award. So did an editorial I wrote about scraps of string, ribbon, tinsel, and paper that my wife left under a card table she used for preparing Christmas presents for mailing—"The Christmas Table," I captioned it: not the dining table but the wrapping table. Oh, I was strong, I can tell you, on the pitiful, the homey, and the ludicrous.

I was strong, too, thanks to Luman, on news and feature pictures in the *Herald*. Luman was his own assignment editor half the time. He arranged with the sheriff's force, the police department, and the highway patrol to call him at any hour that news broke.

He was on the scene within minutes of a Saturday night two-car collision that killed seven persons, including five members of one family. The *Herald* had no Sunday edition. I spread a picture he took over the entire front page of Monday's paper, and used an open page three for the wreck story and the rest of the day's top news. Tabloids do that sort of thing routinely, but our full-size-page picture was spectacular enough to attract national journalistic attention.

Luman and I collaborated on a full-page picture-story on Sanford's slums—what would be known as, with the coming of the race revolution and its terminology, Sanford's ghetto. On a hill over-looking the downtown business district sat the sorriest shacks imaginable along unpaved streets remarkable for filth stagnating in ruts. Behind the shacks, amid rows of corn and tomatoes and beans and cabbage, protruded, inevitably, rickety privies: garden houses in fact as well as in the more delicate term.

A few days after the pictures and story appeared I was in my cubbyhole of an office typing away as usual when a pickup truck backed into the space between my window and the street. I found myself eyeball-to-eyeball with a poor little freemartin calf brought to town for slaughter. Soon the man who had parked the truck came in, scraping his feet. I recognized him—a former high school principal who farmed near Moncure, on the Raleigh road, and owned some of Sanford's prime slum property.

I had to clear space for him. A jolly but retarded man who carried a *Herald* route had left his canvas bag and jacket in my spare chair. Spread on the floor were several newspapers I had been examining for makeup. Further blocking the way was a huge collard plant a gardener had brought in for photographing. While I scrambled to receive my caller, the composing room apprentice intruded with a galley of twelve-point type, which he deposited on my already littered desk. "Charley," he announced—Charley was the foreman—"Charley, he said he didn't pull you a revised proof like you wanted because he ain't got time and for you to check the page corrections in type right away so he can make up the editorial page." As I read the uninked slugs sprinkled among blackened type my caller squatted.

"I saw that little picture piece you put in the paper," he said as I motioned for him to sit.

"Well, sir, I'm glad you did," I replied. "I would be mighty disappointed if you missed it."

My caller was grim. "You don't understand what you're fooling with," he said. "You don't understand the good of providing a roof for people that won't do a thing for themselves and wouldn't take decent care of a mansion in heaven if the Dear Lord Himself moved them into it and paid the rent."

"Whether I do or not," I answered, "I understand a little about building codes and minimum housing standards and public health laws—about the need for them when they either don't exist or are ignored. I have some knowledge, too, of where crime and meanness breed."

Now my caller glared at me. His eyes were as round and unblinking as the little freemartin calf's out there on the truck.

"Let me tell you something, Mason," my caller said, rising. His voice rose too. "What you ought to do is get into the real world—is to get *out of this ivory tower!*"

He left so brusquely that he knocked the paper carrier's coat off the copy hook where I had hung it.

22 Working Stiffs

Although Sanford in the fifties had more industrial plants than tobacco auction warehouses, and poultry was gaining on tobacco as a farm cash source, the downtown economy was still geared to the golden leaf. Farm debts to banks and suppliers came due at tobacco-marketing time, in the fall. And the semiweekly *Sanford Herald* chose that season for sending its annual subscription bills.

Most town subscribers to the paper paid a carrier ten cents a week for home delivery. But farmers and other residents of rural areas paid the office five dollars a year and received the paper by mail or motor carrier.

Upon going daily in September 1952 the *Herald* had a circulation of about 5,000, a respectable figure. But some townspeople told the carriers to stop delivery when the cost jumped from a dime to a quarter a week. And a lot of rural people balked at turning loose $12.50. Circulation plunged.

I had been told this would happen by newspaper friends in Martinsville, Virginia, where the daily was relatively new. Mr. Horner had been warned of it by North Carolina publishers who had made the conversion. Almost everybody took a morning paper from the nearest city; among them was fear that the local paper would lose its flavor as a daily. And expense of course was a factor.

Warned or not, Mr. Horner became alarmed when our press run slipped to 3,000 and the newly hired circulation manager, a former suburban district supervisor for the *Washington Post* unacquainted with country ways, failed to turn the trend. Both pressured me to jazz up the news content. I resisted passively.

The advertising department continued to meet its goals. It was headed by James R. McIver, whose family was among the early Highland settlers of the community and who, as I, had acquired part ownership of the paper. He kept a stable staff.

And the mechanical department made the transition from semi-weekly to daily with remarkable ease. All the printers and pressmen were local boys who had learned their skills at the *Herald*, and welcomed their suddenly increased responsibilities. They were a first-class lot, led by Charlie Fields, the foreman, and Russel Causey, who supervised page makeup.

But my news staff was numerically inadequate and wanting in useful experience. Also, it was, to my shame, underpaid. One of the two reporters left within a week of my arrival. During the next five years I would fill his spot six times. My other reporter, the young man from Harvard, put in for a week's vacation while we were moving from the old building to the new. I told him he would simply have to wait until we had the daily in stride. On occasion I was surprised to find him and the printer apprentice wrestling on the composing room's cement floor, both panting and near tears. When he departed the paper a couple of years later it was to write editorials for one of the larger state papers whose editor knew his affluent family.

Rather than try to sensationalize news, I concentrated on good coverage and bright writing. Among the first replacements I hired was a rotund, rumpled fellow who answered my want-ad in *Editor and Publisher*, a trade magazine. He was operating an outlying news bureau for the *Richmond Times-Dispatch*, and came by train for an interview. I hired him mainly on the strength of a copy of *Variety* protruding from his tweed-coat pocket.

He knew local government in and out, wrote simply and swiftly, and, being a bachelor without apparent interest in a social life, cared nothing about work hours. Should a news source, such as the city manager and sheriff, be out when he made his rounds, he would leave a long, thin, expensive cigar at his desk; invariably there would be a return call, probably before he returned to the office.

In time he asked for several days off so he could visit his father in Connecticut, promising to make up the time with extra work. I told him he had earned a vacation and to enjoy it. Two nights later he called me from someplace in Alabama, where he had wrecked his car. Why he told me he would travel north and then went south I still don't know.

A little later he told me he was getting married. Soon he was joined in his apartment by a woman older than he who brought along a sixteen-year-old son and an infant of about a month, also a boy. He claimed none of the three on his social security records. Eventually he and his household departed without leaving a forwarding address, to the distress of a stream of bill collectors.

I employed a quiet youth with a studious look who brought greetings from his uncle, whom I had known at Chapel Hill. He took a room over a dry cleaning shop about two blocks from the newspaper building and installed there a full-size refrigerator and a hotplate. Once I persuaded him he was writing for a small newspaper and not a little magazine, he did passably well. Then he quit.

His room was too hot, he said. It was impossible to sleep there.

I assured him we could find him more comfortable quarters.

No, he said, it was too late. He had formed a poor image of himself, living in what amounted to a garret, trying to cook but usually making a mess of his meals, and hacking out tripe for a bunch of nobodies to read; he had to go away and establish an identity and develop a purpose.

I asked to be remembered to his uncle.

A gangling lad I had known at the *Virginian-Pilot* when he ran copy there while attending the Norfolk Division of the College of William and Mary, now Old Dominion University, worked for me for a year or so. Returning then to Virginia, he took over a foundering weekly. To raise money, he printed his own. He got off with probation—better than another acquaintance of mine fared in a later period, a sports writer who collaborated with a commercial lithographer to produce twenty dollar bills and was promoted to editor-in-chief of a federal penitentiary news sheet.

A new graduate of Wake Forest University was showing promise on the *Herald* until he tried to write a story about a cloudburst that washed an automobile off a plank bridge and its occupants, a brother and sister, into a flash-flooded creek, where the boy held the girl with one hand and an overhanging tree limb with another for more than an hour, until a volunteer fire company rescued them. Try as he might, he couldn't put words on paper. I instructed him to tell me what happened and I would do the writing. He began calmly but grew excited and stammered. By then he was leaning over my typewriter. I made him move away and start again. That worked; his notes were in good order, and at last I had all I needed.

The personnel manager of the *Winston-Salem Journal and Sentinel* sent me a high school civics teacher who wished to be a reporter but lacked the experience required there. I made good use of him despite his devotion to an orderly work schedule, and suffered mixed feelings when he set about organizing the shop into the American Newspaper Guild. He had little luck then, but afterwards put a dent in a major newspaper chain's armor against collective bargaining.

My brother Marvin, who had followed our father to N.C. State and become like him a textile executive, recommended to me a neighbor's son just home from the Korean War, in which he had been an Army journalist. Upon my hiring him, he found an apartment ample for his mother-in-law as well as himself and his wife and child. He was affable and able. But he got drunk at a high school football game he was supposed to cover, stumbled onto the field and out the gate, and went home, where he took an armload of rifles from a closet and began firing over the neighborhood with a particularly high-powered one. The cops put him in jail.

Next morning, which was Saturday, Luman Moore, the *Herald* photographer, helped him talk his way out. He came to the newspaper plant to say good-bye. "I neglected to tell you," he apologized, "that I'm a gun nut."

That very afternoon Luther J. Carter parked a yellow Ford convertible near my window, strode into my office, introduced himself, and applied for a job.

He was from Charlotte, a graduate of a South Carolina prep school and Duke University, who had spent a year in Hawaii as a Marine Corps staff sergeant, toured Europe by motorcycle, and worked on an English-language newspaper in Morocco before coming home and hooking up with the paper in Concord, a medium-sized city in the Charlotte area. His Concord experience was unhappy. But he seemed to me to be young enough and intelligent enough to start anew, and I gladly took him on.

He was hardheaded. But he also was knowing and thorough, and accepted instruction. Despite his very proper upbringing and schooling, he could be unfeeling. He frightened the wits out of a draft-board clerk by staging a sit-down strike at her desk when she declined, on standing orders, to supply information he wanted. His approach to the rustic but savvy sheriff was patronizing. His displeasure was apparent when, during his first week in town, the pastor of the Steele Street Methodist Church called on him at his desk, at the request of his sainted mother; rising stiffly to acknowledge the divine's presence, he snagged his trousers on a copy hook and bellowed, "Goddam-it-to-hell!"

Twelve months to the day after his arrival he said to me, "Well, I've been here a year, so I'm going to the *Charlotte News*."

Was there a connection, I asked, between time and place?

Upon departing from the Concord paper, he then revealed, he had applied at the *News* for work. The editor there, whom I knew fairly well, hesitated to take a chance on him. But he promised that if he could get a job with me and hold it for a year he would hire him. Luther J. Carter had met the test.

"Don't go to Charlotte," I urged him. "You've got too much family there. Besides, Charlotte is a traveling salesman's town and you'll get bored. If you're bound to leave, I can get you a job in a place that's a lot more fun—in Norfolk."

He took me up. His success on the *Virginian-Pilot* met my expectations. After a decade there he joined *Science* magazine, became its senior writer, and wrote several books on conservation.

Another of my *Herald* associates became city editor of the *Pilot*, but was longer getting to Norfolk. He was Bill McAllister, a high school student and my stringer in Pittsboro, a county-seat village seventeen miles from Sanford, halfway to Chapel Hill. I wrote him a letter of encouragement, and he responded enthusiastically. After earning two degrees at the University of North Carolina, working for a while at the *News and Observer* in Raleigh and for the *Wall Street Journal* in its San Francisco bureau, he became a fine investigative reporter at the *Pilot* before moving up to the city desk. From Norfolk he eventually went to the *Washington Post* as Virginia editor.

But my brightest *Herald* staff member was a young woman.

About a year after my return to Sanford, an old friend who read books, Rebecca Lawrence Benson, brought me a copy of *Mademoiselle* magazine that featured winners of its annual college fiction contest. A five hundred dollar prize went to Doris Waugh, a sophomore at Woman's College, now the University of North Carolina at Greensboro, for a short story, "Mr. Shawn and Father Scott."

A year later I read, on the basis of its good reviews, *The Gentle Insurrection*, a collection of short stories by Doris Betts. Included was "Mr. Shawn and Father Scott," which I remembered from *Mademoiselle*. Miss Waugh, I realized, had become Mrs. Betts.

By and by a postal card from Doris Betts reached my desk. She was living in Chapel Hill, where her husband, Lowry Betts, was a law student. Proposing to write a series of North Carolina profiles, she was canvassing the state's editors for interest. I replied that she could count me in.

Soon after that my wife Frances and I went to Chapel Hill. There I telephoned Doris that we would like to stop at her house on our way home. She replied that she would be pleased to meet us. It was evening when we knocked on her door.

Doris and Lowry were living in the old Veterans Village, a

collection of prefabricated houses put up ten years earlier for married students back from World War II. Lowry was out of town for the night, and Doris was holding the fort. She had two small children, LewEllyn and David, and two large dogs, Aaron and Moses.

Doris said Lowry was finishing law school and looking for a job, and she would like to do part-time newspaper work wherever they landed. She was a clerk-typist just then.

Back in Sanford, I mentioned Lowry to a lawyer friend. There chanced to be an opening at his firm.

So pretty soon the Betts family moved to Sanford—Doris, Lowry, LewEllyn, David, and Moses. Aaron didn't make it.

Doris came to work with me at the *Herald*. It wasn't much of a job, reading proof, rewriting phoned-in stuff, helping out. But it was the only part-time work we had.

That was 1956. I had been working on newspapers for twenty-two years, and had taught a good many young people something about the trade. But I didn't teach Doris Betts anything. I didn't try to. I was afraid that if I knocked much journalese into her head, I would damage her as a creative writer.

I recall a piece she did about a session of county court. She began with the first case and went down the docket, ending with the last case, giving each the same space and emphasis. I was tempted to take it to her and say, "Look, little sister, this ain't the way we do it. We decide what's most important, or most interesting, and write it first, maybe in some detail, and then we judge what should follow, and in what order, and . . ." But I didn't do it.

Once she turned in an account of a testimonial dinner for the mayor, who was in political trouble. She made the setting grand, the speeches wonderful, the food delicious. I wanted to say, "Now, honey, what we have here is a bunch of ward heelers who were probably drunk by the time you got there. They don't talk like this. Didn't anything funny happen? Can't we humanize this a little?" But I didn't. Hell, I thought, I'll let it go as is; and for this once I'll print something in the paper that His Honor the Mayor—who was a fish dealer—won't take exception to.

I didn't want to take a chance on messing up Doris's style.

And a little later I'd be glad I didn't. For she would write, unassigned and on her own, something that was lovely.

She went home to Statesville, over toward the mountains, for a brief visit, to a funeral I think. And she wrote an essay about it, in the form of a letter to David, her little boy, so David would know about a kinsman he never saw.

In that piece she had people sitting on a porch. One old boy's rocker was turned upside down, so that he sat where his back should have been with his back against the seat. People don't sit like that in a parlor or hotel lobby or on a country club veranda. But they may sit that way under the shed of a tobacco barn, or on the narrow porch of a shotgun house in a mill village, or in the shade of a pin oak tree in a lawn swept bare with a switch broom where geraniums bloom in a circle of whitewashed rock.

Usually, it seemed to me in 1956, and seems to me now, you have to go away and become old and tired and return to where you started before you take note of someone sitting in a chair turned on its back. To a young person who hasn't traveled far, sitting like that— and living the way that portends, and being a part of a place and a time and a fashion—is just a cranky way for a person to behave.

But here, I pondered, is Doris Betts, who is barely in her twenties and looks to be eighteen, with just two years of college behind her, in bobby socks and saddle shoes and pleated skirt, hunched there with ankle on knee, scribbling away in a notebook when she's caught up with reading proof—or else bouncing about, bouncing and scooting, up the stairs and down, here and there, always bouncing and scooting, and forever scribbling; well, here's Doris Betts, who strikes me as a child, and yet sees far beyond what the eye beholds and understands a damn' sight more than she ever learned in a library or a classroom.

Putnam brought out Doris's first novel, *Tall Houses in Winter*, while she and I were working together. She has published five books since then, for a total of seven, and is working on two more. She'll never write anything that surprises me. I've known how she can write for more than thirty years, since reading her first published short story.

But I didn't know that Doris, without bothering about a degree despite more study, would become a marvelous teacher, an adored teacher, and a capable university administrator as well. I didn't have any idea that she would advance from a part-time instructorship in creative writing, commuting from Sanford to Chapel Hill, to an Alumni Distinguished Professorship of English and, for a three-year term, chairman of the faculty at the University of North Carolina, and the most quoted and most photographed member of the Chapel Hill campus.

I've forgotten what the *Herald* paid her. It was probably the minimum wage. But this I remember: she was just as cute as a speckled pup.

23 Courthoused

By the mid-fifties the *Sanford Herald* was going great guns. It recovered the 2,000-plus subscribers it had lost upon going from semiweekly to daily in September 1952—and raising its prices 250 percent—and inched past its former total of 5,000. The circulation manager, who had come from the *Washington Post*, where he was a suburban district supervisor, was replaced by a local boy recently out of the Army who knew nothing about reader preferences according to age and income or about multiple-readership trends but understood the community and its habits as well as how to deliver a paper and to count and tell time and to profit from mistakes.

Although I had lived in Raleigh and Durham for eight years and in Norfolk for eleven before returning to Sanford as editor, I remembered much about the town and its people. I insisted that the *Herald*'s two reporters write the news objectively. On the editorial page and in signed articles, however, I did not hesitate to proceed from a point of view and to be informal and sometimes personal.

Sanford and Lee County presented classical examples of what H.

L. Mencken called "ruling-class" government. Ernest L. Fields, who operated an old-fashioned ice-and-coal business and, as an icehouse spin-off, sold fish, was mayor of Sanford. He was known as Fish Fields. J. T. Ledwell, chairman of the board of county commissioners, was a retired flour salesman of advanced years and populist leanings. Both were unlettered, high-handed, and capable of hardness; neither knew nor cared much about the niceties of the democratic system—which hardly distinguished them among North Carolina semirural public servants. The seven-member town board of aldermen and five-member county commission were composed mostly of small merchants, working men, and farmers. As almost every voter in the county was a registered Democrat, so were all the officeholders, elected and appointed.

North Carolina's lower court system back then was so curious a patchwork that it was on the verge of legislative reform. Mayor Fields had judicial as well as executive and legislative authority. Once a week he conducted mayor's court, with the legal credentials of a magistrate or justice of the peace, at city hall, usually in secrecy. There was a general impression that his office-courtroom was a clearing house for his friends and friends of his friends who found themselves mildly messed up with the law.

Armed with an opinion by the state attorney general that mayor's courts were open to the public, I showed up at one, notebook in hand. His Honor threw me out. "Go make your molehills out of mountains somewheres else," he enjoined me. "Go be a thorn in somebody else's saddle."

Delighted with his language if not his ruling, I quoted the mayor studiously in a story about the encounter. Also, I began to report precisely what he said at aldermen's meetings, which were held at night, making it convenient for me to attend. Among utterances I recall was a question he directed to a neatly dressed young man who requested the removal of some trash or maybe the installation of a street light, whom he thought he recognized as the son of a woman whose small restaurant served country food: "Ain't you the boy I ate hoghead at his mama's?"

A Fields admirer sent word that he intended to beat me up if I continued to embarrass the mayor. I didn't believe him; people who are going to poke someone, I knew, like people who are going to sue, as I would learn, don't issue a warning, they just act. And anyway, I already had stopped, out of both conscience and weariness of the game.

Mayor Fields was a politician within yet beyond the Southern stereotype described by political scientists. He was as committed to racial segregation as any other vote-getter. Yet Sanford's large black community was his political base. In 1954, during congressional debate over a bill to remove Southern bars to black voting, he paid Negroes fifty cents—or gave them, in the local lore, a sack of fish—to register. They bought twenty-five-pound blocks of ice from him in the summer and hundred-pound bags of coal from him in the winter, maybe on credit. They bought croakers from him for about what he paid. He treated them well, and was accessible to them, and they trusted him—the dignified pastor of the Northern Presbyterian Church and the school principal and the undertaker as well as the masses.

That was the year of the U.S. Supreme Court's *Brown* decision, outlawing segregation of public schools. I wrote editorials advocating calm acceptance of the judgment without resort to legislative legerdemain or judicial filibustering; defiance would be expensive, divisive, and futile, I argued. Nobody paid me much mind; Earl Warren's court and its sociological notions seemed remote from Sanford and the tobacco fields beyond it.

Even after the court's "all-deliberate-speed" implementing order of 1955, and with it the spread across the South of resistance measures and movements, I encountered no significant criticism of my stand. I was, after all, no outside agitator, but one of the neighbors' children with solid Confederate certification. And what I wrote was pretty much what the morning papers that reached Sanford, the Raleigh *News and Observer*, the *Greensboro Daily News*, and the *Charlotte Observer*, were saying. Integration was discussed infrequently about town.

Then the Patriots of North Carolina, Inc., the state's version of white citizens councils, came into being. Its leaders for the most part were elderly. They revived the racist politics they had practiced as young men, early in the century, when the Democratic party broke the Republican-Populist-Negro hold on the state by wooing back the Populists and then proceeding to disenfranchise the blacks, and when the Republican party, in apology for its Reconstruction past, pronounced itself "lily-white."

Among the Patriots' leaders was E. L. Gavin, a Sanford old-line Republican who had been a U.S. district attorney during the Hoover administration. He advocated not only continued segregation of schools but segregation of tax monies financing schools as well, with whites paying for their children's education and blacks for theirs. That was old hat in North Carolina; half a century earlier, in the Democratic "redemption" period, the state's beloved "education governor," Charles B. Aycock, lacking a veto, had threatened to resign if the legislature embraced such foolishness.

I hooted editorially at the Gavin proposal and reviewed its shabby history.

Nobody was really ugly to me, but I began to receive some flak. Letters-to-the-editor came addressed to the "Herald-Enterprise," the *Enterprise* having been a pre-Depression Negro weekly. A county school board member denounced me for scorning a much-published article by a New Jersey black advising Southern teachers of his race to cherish the status quo. Meanwhile, life in Sanford went its way as though the Supreme Court never had strayed from *Plessy*.

It chanced that in that time the board of county commissioners split over a farm program, with the county farm agent caught in the middle. The *Herald* received a letter signed "Charles Simpson" complaining that a three-member faction led by Chairman Ledwell had schemed at secret meetings warranting a grand jury investigation. The writer cited instances, places, and "hand-picked comedians." I printed his charges in the letters column on the editorial page.

But Charles Simpson, as it turned out, was not the letter's author. While embarrassed, I was not much perturbed. If the attack was harsh, I had read harsher, and if I couldn't vouch for its source, that wasn't the first unverified letter ever to appear in a newspaper. Also,

I had no doubt that the author knew what he was writing about, and I was pretty sure of where he got his information.

Nevertheless, four of the five commissioners hired E. L. Gavin as counsel—on a contingent-fee basis, I suppose—and sued the *Herald* for libel, asking for $50,000 each. Although the U.S. Supreme Court's landmark libel judgment, *New York Times Company v. Sullivan* (1964) was a long way off, North Carolina courts had held that public officials were fair game for robust criticism. In a preposterous maneuver to escape vulnerability, the four petitioned the court as individuals, suing separately, rather than as public officials, although at issue was their official conduct.

W. E. Horner, publisher of the *Herald*, delighted in his reputation as a tightwad. He lately had become enraged at me for refusing to read and initial instructions for turning uncanceled postal stamps into pennies that he wrote and circulated through the office—so enraged that he screamed and stomped. He saved string and wrote memos on the backs of used envelopes. But he took the commissioners' suit in good stride, as he did most matters involving substantial sums; he even bragged that the claims against us were the largest ever filed in Lee County Superior Court.

I went to Raleigh to engage William Lassiter, counsel for the North Carolina Press Association, to defend the *Herald*. He confirmed my beliefs that the commissioners had no grounds for recovery, but suggested that, for courtroom cosmetics, we employ a Sanford attorney as his associate, and suggested one who chanced to be among my closest friends.

But my friend would have no part of the case. A sometime state legislator and county attorney, he had political connections with the plaintiffs. A lawyer who occasionally did legal work for the *Herald* agreed to appear with Mr. Lassiter if we would employ also an elderly member of the local bar who, if not very busy, was very highly regarded for his good humor and decency and hence would provide him insulation against the unpopularity of his clients. I felt like a leper.

While absorbed with the "Chuck Simpson case," as it had come to be known, I picked up a telephone that was ringing on an unattended desk in the office's news corner and heard a sweet little voice inquire, "Is this the newspaper up there in Sanford?" I answered yes'm, this was the editor.

"Well," said the caller, "I just wanted you to know I've decided to courthouse Joe Ledwell."

She meant J. T. Ledwell, chairman of the board of county commissioners. Please go on, I urged, all ears.

I learned that the caller was a maiden schoolteacher in a coastal South Carolina village who had developed an acquaintance with Mr. Ledwell during his traveling-salesman days. He had been down there fishing the week before, and had telephoned her, wishing to come to her house, but she had told him no, she didn't think he should, it wouldn't be convenient for her. But he had come anyway, and had banged on her door and, when she refused to open it, had torn the screen and otherwise made himself a nuisance. She had sworn out a warrant against him for breaking-and-entering, and the case was to be heard by a justice of the peace next Thursday at 2 P.M. She just thought the Sanford newspaper might like to know about it.

She thought right. On Thursday at 2 P.M. a *Herald* reporter was in a South Carolina jaypee court. So were J. T. Ledwell and half the Sanford bar.

Not much came of the affair. The Ledwell defense team got the trial postponed, and in time it evaporated. Even so, there was enough on record to enliven the *Herald*'s front page next day and to cast some doubt on the $50,000 tag Mr. Ledwell had placed on his integrity and good name.

Turn about being fair play, I took no particular umbrage when pretty soon a deputy sheriff served me with a subpoena to appear before a Lee County grand jury that was investigating the Chuck Simpson case for the possibility of criminal libel. During the twenty years I had been trying to educate myself in libel law I never had heard of criminal libel. Mr. Lassiter in Raleigh told me, when I called him for advice, that it was companion to the old strictures on bull-baiting, lewd and lascivious behavior, and spitting on the sidewalk, and was seldom employed.

Under the North Carolina system, grand juries have eighteen members and meet at the start of a criminal court term. A bill of indictment may be returned by twelve of them. Usually the district attorney—he was called solicitor then—meets with the grand jury, but he was absent the day of my appointment. The foreman advised me that anything I said might be used against me later. I promised to be candid. Meanwhile, I looked at those eighteen faces, most of them sunburned from just above the eyebrows to well below the chin, and recognized but one: the pallid features of a young man engaged in a family business whom I sometimes saw at parties. I was happy to see him.

But he turned out to be the most hostile of the hostile lot. "Trying to make trouble, weren't you?" he kept asking. It was a long and monotonous inquisition.

Returning to the office well past 5 P.M., I telephoned Jack Hooks, the solicitor, at his hotel. His home and office were two counties over. The clerk said Mr. Hooks did not wish to be disturbed before dinner.

I went to his room and knocked. I kept knocking until he appeared, stuffing his shirt into his trousers and looking annoyed.

I blurted that I was perfectly willing to be tried for anything he accused me of but I didn't like being harassed by his grand jury and wanted no more of it. He was puzzled and upset. I told him what there was to tell. He knew none of it; evidently his local part-time assistant had handled my subpoena. Jack was very nice to me, and I apologized for my intrusion.

And that was the last of that.

Reminiscing twenty-five years later about the Chuck Simpson case, J. R. McIver, the *Herald* part-owner who had risen from advertising director to assistant publisher, wrote: "The lawsuits caused us a lot of trouble and expense but amounted to nothing in the long run. The commissioners, one by one, withdrew their suits and paid the court costs. But Bob Mason's goof had served politics!"

I won't argue the point. What the lawsuits cost us was $2,729.74. The trouble was real, but eased by comedy. I can't assess the political consequences.

For by 1961, when the last commissioner took down his case, eighteen months after the first, I had been back in Norfolk for four years. If that sounds like a long time for a civil suit to have gone untried, it was possible then, and may be yet, in North Carolina to keep one dangling fifteen years. Not recovery from the *Herald*, but inconvenience to it, was the commissioners' objective. In Norfolk I would become involved, over two decades, in a fair number of other newspaper lawsuits, among them one that the *Virginian-Pilot* won before the U.S. Supreme Court. In none of them was law so totally lacking for the plaintiff as in the Chuck Simpson fiasco.

I had not expected to leave Sanford. While I was there the *Greensboro Daily News* asked me to join its editorial page staff and the *Charlotte Observer* offered me its news editorship. I was tempted by neither. Then there arrived out of a clear sky an invitation to become an associate editor of the *Virginian-Pilot* under Lenoir Chambers.

Out of affection for the paper and Mr. Chambers, I agreed to discuss the proposition. But I was too confined at the *Herald* to travel all the way to Norfolk, so I proposed to Mr. Chambers that I meet him halfway, on a Sunday. We agreed on the Ricks Hotel in Rocky Mount, North Carolina. There we had lunch and a splendid afternoon.

That led to a second meeting, this one in Durham at dinner in midweek, with Frank Batten, publisher of the *Virginian-Pilot*, joining Mr. Chambers and me. I had not met Frank, who was just twenty-nine years old; he had been a student at Culver Military Academy, the University of Virginia, and the Harvard School of Business during my Norfolk stints. I took an immediate liking to him. And I began to reflect, as the three of us talked and laughed, on the pleasures and rewards of working with excellent companions on a good newspaper.

In a postscript chapter of *Salt Water & Printers Ink*, Lenoir Chambers's history of the *Virginian-Pilot*'s first hundred years (1865-1965), there appears this sentence: "Robert Mason, an old newspaper hand who was held in high esteem by associates, was prevailed upon to give up part-ownership of the Sanford, N.C., *Herald* and become successively associate editor, managing editor, and editor of *The Virginian-Pilot*, succeeding Chambers."

My wife wept. She dearly loved Sanford. Our sixteen-year-old daughter Fran was ready to shove off. She thought that growing and marketing tobacco, which she heard about at school all the time, was tacky.

24 The Jaffe Influence

Lenoir Chambers was sixty-five years old and in his eighth year as editor of the *Virginian-Pilot* when I became one of his two associates in October of 1957. He had come from the *Greensboro Daily News* (now *News & Record*) to the Norfolk morning paper in 1929 as associate editor under Louis Isaac Jaffe. Six years prior to Mr. Jaffe's death in 1950 he was appointed editor of the *Pilot's* afternoon sister, the Norfolk *Ledger-Dispatch* (now *Ledger-Star*). He returned to the *Pilot* to succeed Mr. Jaffe.

He was glad to be back. He had inherited Douglas Gordon's command of the *Ledger* in 1944 to the bitter disappointment of Gordon's long-suffering associate, Joseph A. Leslie, Jr., who stayed on. Mr. Gordon had studied law at the University of Virginia and practiced it in Richmond, his home city. He broke into print as occasional drama critic and book reviewer for the Richmond *Times-Dispatch*. His elegant writing led him into the *T-D* editor's chair. Col. Samuel L. Slover, who, operating from Norfolk, in those days owned both the *T-D* and *Ledger* and also the Portsmouth *Star* and most of the *Petersburg Progress-Index*, brought him to Norfolk in 1922.

Mr. Gordon suffered from asthma, which he treated with whiskey, and weak eyes, which he favored by typing on pale green paper. He cared little about news and followed it casually, even into World War II. Battles interested him mainly for any Virginia connection he might discover among the generals and admirals who waged them. He left the more current stuff to Joe Leslie; "Give Joe a copy of the Sunday *New York Times*," he would say, airily, "and he can grind out editorials for a week."

Mr. Chambers did not lift the *Ledger* much above its old stodginess. The Gordon past and Leslie presence seemed to burden his spirit. Upon his departure, the modest but souring Mr. Leslie, an editor at last, soon found in the *Ledger* city room a kindred soul and with him hacked away. Back on the *Pilot*, Mr. Chambers settled down with a history and a ghost to his liking.

Exactly who had the good sense to seek out Louis Jaffe and make him editor of the *Virginian-Pilot*, I never learned. Jaffe was born in Detroit, grew up in Durham, and in 1911 graduated Phi Beta Kappa from Trinity College, later Duke University, where he edited the campus newspaper and magazine. After a brief hitch with the *Durham Sun* he joined the *Richmond Times-Dispatch* as a reporter and advanced to assistant city editor.

The First World War took him to France as a lieutenant. After the Armistice he shipped into the Red Cross, which sent him to the Balkans to survey its relief activities there. He was working for the Red Cross news service in Paris in 1919 when the *Pilot*'s publisher, Col. Lucien D. Starke, Jr., called him to succeed as editor former Governor William E. Cameron, who was retiring at age seventy-seven. The colonel's experiences were in law and business. He is bound to have relied on someone else's appreciation of Jaffe's editorial potential.

As his first associate, Jaffe selected John Newton Aiken, a *Ledger-Dispatch* reporter he had known at Trinity and in the Army. He made arrangements with Stringfellow Barr, a history professor at the University of Virginia and later president of St. John's College in Annapolis, to contribute editorials, and with H. L. Mencken to carry on the *Pilot* editorial page his Baltimore *Sun* political fulmi-nations. Aiken's departure to Baltimore, where he became editor of the *Evening Sun*, opened the way for Chambers's arrival at the *Pilot*.

Louis Jaffe had a passion for social justice. He received the 1928

Pulitzer Prize for distinguished editorial writing for "An Unspeakable Act of Savagery." In later years the editorial's caption was well remembered by Mr. Jaffe's admirers, but among them there was confusion as to its contents. One impression was that it deplored a particularly abhorrent lynching along the Virginia-Kentucky border, where liquor-making and religious snake-chunking also were problems. "Lynching goes unpunished in Virginia," he wrote, "because, deny it as one will, it commands a certain social sanction. An unwritten code is involved to give the color of social necessity to a crime which is plainly destructive of guarantees which have been regarded as inviolate in Anglo-Saxon thinking and jurisprudence since Runnymede." Whites lynched blacks. "To the *Virginian-Pilot*," Mr. Jaffe concluded, "it seems more and more clear that there will be no adequate grappling of this form of savagery until the punishment of lynchers is made a primary obligation of the State, and legislation is enacted to that end." City police chiefs and county sheriffs were disinclined to track down lynch-mob members.

A more general impression was that Mr. Jaffe had been awarded the Pulitzer Prize in recognition of his angry reaction to the September 1926 kidnapping by the Ku Klux Klan of the Rev. Vincent D. Warren, a cheerful and cherubic Catholic priest, in old Princess Anne County, now Virginia Beach. A band of robed and masked men forced the priest from his automobile into theirs, drove him through much of the night over dirt roads in a swampy area, and stopped at last at the edge of thick woods. There they questioned him hatefully about his Norfolk parish's work with black children, threatened to burn him, and toward morning released him, with a fine sense of irony, near a country church, Nimmo Methodist. He was unharmed but exhausted. A Princess Anne grand jury pondered the evidence but concluded nothing of consequence. No arrest was made.

"It is a stultification to pretend that the abductors were innocent of the Klan gospel and had no connection with Kluxery," Mr. Jaffe said in the *Pilot*. "All the facts point the other way. There will be a gain all round in frankly recognizing the facts. These are that Kluxery has treated this community to a brazen, contemptible, and high-handed piece of violence, and that the authorities sworn to enforce and preserve the peace are to an alarming degree indifferent to it."

Mr. Jaffe's Pulitzer Prize in fact was ascribed to an editorial he published on June 22, 1928, the day after eight armed thugs yanked a black man from a Houston hospital cot, where he was being treated for a stomach wound taken in a shootout with a detective he killed, and strung him on a tree just outside the city. The Democratic National Convention was assembling in Houston, an astonishing choice because of its Southern location and the prospect that Al Smith, of New York's sidewalks, would be nominated for President. Reporters from all over the nation and some foreign capitals were in the city. And Houston was trying to present to them and the world its best face and manners.

Every newspaper in the land must have editorialized on the year's most conspicuous lynching. It is difficult to believe that Louis Jaffe's comment was so outstanding as to merit the most prestigious of journalism awards. A clue to its selection is in a far paragraph:

"The year that saw four months pass without a single lynching now has accumulated five of them. Five lynchings in six months represent a proportional reduction in savagery from last year's record of sixteen lynchings in twelve months, but the year is only half gone and no one may be too confident. We have come a long way from the dark days of 1892 when America celebrated the 400th year of its discovery with 255 lynchings, but we have not yet arrived at that social abhorrence of this crime that must precede its practical extinction . . ."

With help from Monroe Nathan Work, a sociological researcher at Tuskegee Institute, Mr. Jaffe put together a thick file on lynchings and kept it current. He carefully examined each new lynching for its horrors and implications. He campaigned doggedly for greater state attention to lynchings. In a letter to Columbia University supporting the Jaffe nomination for a Pulitzer, Governor Harry F. Byrd wrote: "Mr. Jaffe's editorials over a long period in advocacy of making the punishment of lynchers a state responsibility, supplemented by his personal representations to me, had more than any other single outside urging in convincing me that I should make one of my major recommendations the passage of a drastic anti-lynching law providing that lynching be made a state offense." Virginia has recorded no lynching since that law's enactment. John Hohenberg indicated in *The Pulitzer Prize Story* (1959) that Mr. Jaffe was recognized for his Virginia crusade as well as his Houston reflections.

Louis Jaffe was a short, compact man who wore, according to the season, a sweater under floppy jacket, a linen suit, and a wide-brimmed hat, felt or Panama. His approach was direct and a little frightening. A longtime Norfolk legislator and councilman marveled that when he answered his office telephone and heard "This is Jaffe," whatever information the editor wanted invariably vanished from his mind. Yet Mr. Jaffe could be sentimental. A piece he wrote about a little magnolia tree that pressed its way between bricks in a pavement, in which he drew upon Genesis 1 and Deuteronomy 20, was recalled as often as his lashings against the rope, the poll tax, and the courthouse fee system.

He acquired substantial stock in the *Virginian-Pilot*, and after the paper's merger with the *Ledger-Dispatch* became wealthy. Although his responsibilities were confined to the editorial page, his influence extended into the *Pilot's* news department and the corporate board room. His commitment to newspaper work was so profound that he turned down appeals to write books and magazine articles. Several cabinets of his correspondence with fellow editors, public officials, university associations, and foundation figures are in the Alderman Library at the University of Virginia. Even so, Lenoir Chambers, his close friend and successor as editor, remembered a blustery evening when, after a long day's work together, they walked to the parking lot beyond the pressroom loading docks and saw a stack of papers blown off them, whereupon Mr. Jaffe, crippled by arthritis and failing, pointed a gnarled finger at the flying sheets and said, "That is what we write for—the wind. The wind. What we wrote yesterday is wasting down this alley, and what we wrote today will follow it tomorrow." He laughed, but not in mirth.

Two Jaffe colleagues agreed that "after he had gone over the copy of an associate editor with a black pencil, a rewritten editorial might emerge. He would never tolerate shoddiness. The subject had to be absorbed, the attitude toward it had to be made clear, and the conclusion had to be the point." The Jaffe editorial formula is contained in that admiring comment. I doubt, nevertheless, that he routinely performed journalistic wonders with a copy pencil.

He knew as well as any editor that the way to produce an editorial is to write it well, not refine it from flawed copy. Most of his associates during the thirty years of his editorship were as skilled with words, sentences, and paragraphs as he; among the relatively few of them were, besides Aiken and Chambers, Jack Schaefer, author of *Shane* and other Western novels, and Alonzo T. Dill, a competent historian who wrote *Governor Tryon and His Palace*, a fine account of a turbulent time in North Carolina as well as of its colonial capital, and biographies of Virginia signers of the Declaration of Independence, sponsored by the Virginia Bicentennial Commission.

During Mr. Jaffe's latter years, when I was the *Pilot's* Sunday editor by his nomination, I submitted a good many editorials to him, usually on naval or maritime topics, which it seemed to me his page neglected. His way was to glance over my piece, tell me that surely I could do better, and give it back to me. And my way became to return with it to my desk on the floor below, get on with my regular work, and in time deliver it upstairs again, maybe retyped and maybe not. After reading it then, Mr. Jaffe would say, "That's much better; fine." Like most newspaper writers of my experience who had spent little time on newsroom desks, he was impatient with what another hand produced.

For a dozen years Louis Jaffe and Lenoir Chambers manned the *Pilot's* editorial page essentially together. When one was away for a few days or on vacation, the other would recruit a newsroom substitute or else call upon Professor Stringfellow Barr at the University of Virginia or Professor Phillips Russell at the University of North Carolina and get out the page. Though they differed vastly in personalities, they thought and wrote alike.

So no seam was created in the *Pilot* editorial page by the death of Mr. Jaffe and the return from the *Ledger* of Mr. Chambers.

25 Lenoir Chambers

The terms of my return to the *Virginian-Pilot* in late 1957 were to write editorials for Lenoir Chambers, the editor, for five years and then replace him upon his retirement at age seventy. As editor, my duties and responsibilities would be limited to the editorial page, following a tradition at the Norfolk morning paper going back as far as anybody could remember.

I greatly admired Mr. Chambers. He had been a three-letter athlete—football, basketball, and tennis—and Phi Beta Kappa student at Chapel Hill, an English master for two years at Woodberry Forest School in Virginia, which he had attended, a graduate student in journalism at Columbia University, and a combat infantry lieutenant in the first World War. Although he was aristocratic by birth, appearance, and attitude, and was courtly to a fault, blending into a clubroom like walnut and leather, he could be affable, entertaining, and even boisterous among close friends. I never knew anyone to enjoy a drink of liquor more than he.

When I entered the three-office editorial suite on the floor above the *Pilot* newsroom, which I thought to be unfortunately remote, Mr. Chambers was completing a two-volume biography of Stonewall Jackson for William Morrow and Company, the New York publishing house, on which he had been working during vacations, over weekends, and at night for twelve years. A Morrow editor from Norfolk, Helen Brinkley King, had approached him about a book, and he had suggested writing one on the war he had experienced, but Frances Phillips, Morrow's chief editor, had ruled that the Civil War was a better topic. Many years later, going through the Chambers papers at the Wilson Library in Chapel Hill, I realized from his letters home during his army days that he had intended to draw upon them for a book. For his Jackson work he had to start from scratch. When he finished, he knew more about Jackson than anyone else had ever discovered.

His ideas of honor and deportment went straight back to Jackson's time. He was contemptuous of two men his age, an editor and a physician, who had not repaid him $40 borrowed separately by each long before—by the editor when a young reporter needing funds to move to a bigger paper than the one where they worked, and by the physician, like him at the time a collegian, to pay his bills at a mountain resort where they were playing in a tennis tournament. Nor would he forgive, after thirty years, a neighbor who had tapped his white-jacketed shoulder at a German Club spring ball and informed him, no doubt in embarrassment and reluctantly, that he was out of uniform and should go home and change into tails. He was genuinely shocked at the coarseness of President Truman's note that time to the *Washington Post* music critic who was underwhelmed by daughter Margaret's singing voice. Although he swore robustly, and in no way was a prude, he did not care for gossip, unsavory comment, or off-color jokes. Rather than criticize an associate's work he found unacceptable, he was likely to put it aside, upside down, and leave it so unless questioned, which would be awkward; his distaste for office confrontation I came to understand but not to cultivate. Should his watch be off time as much as a minute a month, or if its minute hand were not on the dot when its second sweep reached twelve, he would send it to a jeweler's; yet he cared nothing for the mechanics of putting out a paper and agreed readily, although mystified by my concern, when I volunteered to modernize his editorial page's design and routinely supervise its composition.

It was necessary for him to stand at his morning editorial conferences to face his two associates over the many layers of newspapers, magazines, books, and typewritten pages stacked on his desk, most of the lot opened and heavily marked with a pencil. Having worked through the evening before on his book and stayed abed that morning as long as possible, he was apt to need some filling-in on the news, but would not say so. So the sessions would be long and maybe tedious.

Wearing flannels or tweeds, with carelessly knotted striped tie flowing from buttoned collar, he would stride and flex his knees, and now and then turn and gaze from a window over roof tops and trees to the harbor, where the masts, superstructures, and stacks of passing ships appeared: a scene for a poet, he once remarked. He wore half-rimmed glasses and had lost most of his hair, which in his youth was blond, but had kept most of his athletic trim—had kept, too, the thin moustache grown when he was a company commander in France. He had a habit of tracing with forefinger the lines he read aloud, in emphatic tones, in developing a position on an event or issue, and of pointing professorially to the one or other of us before him whom he questioned and counseled. He might tell an Old Jack story, for which he would apologize; he had come to think of his literary subject as personal.

Mr. Chambers's book came out at the close of 1959. It was nominated for the Pulitzer Prize in biography. Also nominated for a Pulitzer Prize that year were his editorials opposing Virginia's "massive resistance" to public school desegregation. The Pulitzer for distinguished editorial writing he won.

Virginia appeared to be ready for the U.S. Supreme Court's *Brown* decision when it was announced May 17, 1954. Governor Thomas B. Stanley reacted calmly. The *Virginian-Pilot*'s comment set the tone it would follow for six hard years: that "intelligence and wisdom" should guide the Commonwealth's "earnest and honest search for sound action" to meet the racial change.

But by late 1955, six months following the Supreme Court's implementing order, Virginia's climate had changed drastically. Senator Harry F. Byrd and his long-dominant political "Organization," which drew its inspiration and strength from agricultural Southside Virginia, turned Governor Stanley's ruddy face against the prospect of even token race-mixing. A study commission appointed by the governor recommended a hokus-pokus pupil-assignment plan and a constitutional amendment facilitating state tuition grants to students attending private schools. Also, a Virginia white citizens council that took its name from the inscription on a Confederate monument in a country courthouse lawn, "Defenders of State Sovereignty and Individual Liberties," commenced to move and shake.

The *Pilot* objected to the commission's plan for the damage it might do Virginia's constitutionally mandated "efficient system of public free schools throughout the state" and for channeling public funds into private hands. But when it was put before the voters in a referendum they approved it two-to-one.

Soon enough the returns became academic. For Senator Byrd decided the commission hadn't gone far enough. He dictated to Governor Stanley a policy, which the General Assembly rubber stamped, under which the governor would close any white school to which a black child was assigned and deny it state funds; while the governor might in time return the school to its petitioning district authority, the funds cut-off would stick.

Again the *Pilot* protested. And it was appalled when in September 1958 three Norfolk high schools and three junior highs with a total enrollment of 10,000, under a federal court order to accept seventeen black pupils applying for admission, were padlocked by the state, along with schools in Charlottesville, seat of the University of Virginia, and obscure Warren County. "There is no moral justification for this harsh punishment of the state's largest city," wrote Mr. Chambers. "Surely there is greater wisdom in Virginia than this would imply."

Among the editors of Virginia's major newspapers, Mr. Chambers stood alone. The Richmond papers, with a better geographical base for governmental clout than Norfolk provided—Johnathan Daniels, the Raleigh editor and author, called Norfolk the "Hong Kong of the Albemarle," Albemarle being the neighboring North Carolina coastal region—sounded like a Southside barber lecturing his Saturday-afternoon customers. The two Roanoke papers went along with massive resistance, and those in Lynchburg warmed up to it after a brief period of skepticism. Closer to Norfolk, the Petersburg and Newport News press echoed the Richmond press. The little afternoon paper in Charlottesville was idiotic too.

Down the hall and around the corner from Mr. Chamber's *Pilot* office, and out of his shadow, Joe Leslie followed the Byrd line in the Norfolk *Ledger-Dispatch*. He was a son-in-law of E. B. "Ebbie" Combs, the "genteel boss" of the Byrd Organization (as J. Harvie Wilkinson III called him in *Harry Byrd*, a political biography), and believed as devoutly in the infallibility of Virginia's leadership as he did in the purity of the Baptist faith. He wrote evenly and politely, but he made no sense. Unless the "harshness of the court decision" was ameliorated, he argued, many areas of Virginia would abandon their schools; and when the state did to them what he had feared they would do to themselves, he placed the blame "squarely on the federal machinery and those who have set the court machinery in action."

Although the Norfolk school board's members were appointed by the segregationist city council, which Mayor W. Fred Duckworth dominated, a majority of them deplored the school closings. The teachers' union, the Norfolk Education Association, demanded reopening and cooperated with "tutoring groups of locked-out pupils" that met in churches, synagogues, civic club buildings, and private homes. Most tutors, however, charged their young clients $10 each while receiving their contractual teacher salaries.

A three-judge federal court and the Virginia Supreme Court in almost simultaneous decisions in January 1959 knocked out massive resistance. The Duckworth city council meanwhile tried to extend it by denying local funds to all forty-two schools in the Norfolk district. But time ran out on all the diehards.

So did Governor Lindsay Almond, the Claghorn with flowing white mane who had followed Governor Stanley into the Capitol Square mansion by vowing to give up his right arm before permitting a black child to sit in a schoolroom with a white one. As dexterous as ever, he summoned the General Assembly into special session and surrendered to the inevitable, laying out a course much like the one recommended by the study commission that Senator Byrd overruled.

Throughout that year of Norfolk's high school blackout, I contributed to the consistency and continuity of the Chambers editorial staff's stand for compliance with the Supreme Court's order, taking up where I had left off in Sanford. We explored the various state and federal court decisions and legislative actions bearing on "Topic A," as Mr. Chambers called the school issue, and deplored racist politics. Basically, though, the Chambers plea was for sanity, decency, and human dignity.

Mr. Chambers had no identity with black causes. Whereas his predecessor and close friend, Louis Jaffe, had known intimately most of the local, state, and national leaders of black organizations and movements, and was a founder of the black college that became Norfolk State University, Mr. Chambers was no social activist. He was uncomfortable with the fevered integrationists and anti-Byrd zealots who cheered him.

My daughter Fran, who on arriving from Sanford had entered Maury High School for the 1958 spring term, was among the 10,000 Norfolk pupils locked out the following fall. She went with me to the federal court building to hear the judge's order that triggered the school shutdown. There I chanced to chat with a junior member of the NAACP Legal Defense and Education Fund team of lawyers that won the case. He said anxiously that he had been unable to buy that day's *New York Times*, which carried the text of a relevant court judgment that his senior colleagues wanted. I invited him to come to the *Pilot* editorial offices later and borrow the copy there.

Mr. Chambers was holding his editorial conference when the young black man, neatly dressed for the courtroom, barged in without knocking. "Counsel wants the *Times* now!" he exploded. I found the paper; he grabbed it and departed, running. To my explanation of what was going on, Mr. Chambers scowled and snapped, "That man has no manners."

Returning to my typewriter, I thought: Well, damn, this office has been fighting since 1954 in behalf of a court order to end school segregation and permit Negro children to grow up with whites and share their advantages, including their contacts and institutions and culture. Now here comes a prime example of what the judgment would correct, over a long period of time, if given a little good will and half a chance, and the lesson is completely lost upon our editor, the lesson being that a black education, from the first grade through professional school, being *black*, falls short of polite white people's expectations. Where the hell was this man expected to learn Virginia Club niceties?

But I kept my tongue. If, I reflected, Mr. Chambers was isolated by birth, upbringing, and experiences from the masses, white and black, it was all the more to his credit that he was committed absolutely to democracy and its laws. The only blacks of his acquaintance were servants. He didn't even know the printers and security guards and cleaning people he saw every day; he wasn't acquainted with three-fourths of the news staff. He wouldn't have been caught dead across the street at Freddie Chinchilla's Jefferson Ward Democratic Club, the illegal saloon where Mr. Jaffe occasionally had joined some of us at lunch. That was the Chambers way, and it was innate. Order guided him in all things. Massive resistance disgusted him for its sham, its illogic, and its hatefulness.

He became so committed to his campaign against it that he seemed to be reluctant to accept its close. In any event, he was terribly suspicious of the surrender message that Governor Almond delivered on January 28, 1959, to the special legislature. "The governor," he complained, "held his recommendations within strict limits. They deal principally, as expected, with changes in the compulsory attendance laws and with ways of enlarging the tuition payment system. In both respects the governor is moving in the effort to take care of parents who won't send their children to mixed classes. Both proposals have dangers and uncertainties . . ."

But next day he conceded that Governor Almond's "position . . . commands respect" and "lifts him to a level far above men who would care less about the strict constitutionality and legality of a blocking device just so it would block for a time. He is now in a sound position of leadership in great difficulties and, no doubt, facing many temptations to play a lesser role. . . . Such a demonstration commands respect and justifies support."

And support it received, although by a narrow legislative margin and without the blessing of Senator Byrd, who had stopped answering the governor's telephone calls.

Once the schools reopened under the state's new "freedom-of-choice" laws in February, Norfolk turned from the bitter squabbling over them and got on with better things. It never was a Little Rock or even a Charlotte, where ugliness accompanied classroom integration; indeed, the Virginia Conference of the NAACP chose it for a testing place largely because race relations there were far advanced when *Brown* was handed down. Much of its official intransigence grew from Mayor Duckworth's commitment to Byrd policies and the taste he developed, uncharacteristically, for lionization; the Defenders and neo-Kluxers thought about as highly of him as they did of Jefferson Davis. Before Ford Motor Company transferred him from Memphis to manage its Norfolk assembly plant, he was an old North Carolina boy of mountain Republican stock, and in time he would refer to Norfolk's splendid Confederate soldier statue as a "glorified pigeon roost" and instruct the Norfolk Civil War Centennial Commission, which he appointed, not to expect any city money for celebrating "that mess a hundred years ago." But amid all the white-supremacy applause he came to feel omnipotent enough even to denounce some of the 100 members of an establishment business committee that, toward the end, pressured him to help reopen the schools, and to ignore unofficial warnings from the U.S. Navy that if Norfolk didn't shape up it would ship out.

The business people were old friends of Mr. Chambers. Their displeasure with massive resistance, however tardily generated, refutes a notion of later years that the editor suffered social slights, if not shunning, for his stand. He may have received a few telephone calls he didn't like, and encountered chill and lookaways here and there, but he encountered nothing that approached ostracism. Pleasure in his Pulitzer Prize far outweighed snide remarks that the hope of it was what had guided his pen all along.

A companion comment to the honor's belittlement pained me—that in supporting the court the *Pilot* had worked one side of the street while the *Ledger* hustled the other. The editorial differences were sincere, and the expression of them under one roof reflected journalistic freedom of a high order. But they invited skepticism just the same, and not all of it was contrived.

Massive resistance's advocates quickly became its apologists. It bought time for Virginia to dampen public anger, said legislators who had voted it into existence. "It threw up a bulwark that held fast against integration for three years," Joe Leslie wrote. "And this struggle served the highly important purpose . . . of demonstrating how serious is the issue of encroachment of federal powers on state sovereignty." Mayor Duckworth huffed that "nobody got hurt."

But some children got hurt; some of the 10,000 who were denied schooling for a year never returned to a classroom. And some others, including my daughter Fran, who graduated from Maury High School on schedule, thanks to tuition-group credits, and went on to Hollins College and a degree, were denied some of childhood's innocence and trust. I know that when Fran approached seventeen she had a lot less faith in her state and its high officials than I did when I buttoned on a pair of white flannel britches from Rosenbloom's, ten miles away in Burlington, to go with the blue coat from my Sunday suit, and fixed to get my high school diploma from Mr. Joe P. Moore, the pipe-smoking, bass-fishing, choir-singing, slightly stuttering superintendent of the Mebane Public Schools. My daughter thought the Maury class of '59's commencement was pretty much a farce.

26 Back in the Briarpatch

By the end of 1958, a year after starting, I had adjusted to writing editorials at the *Virginian-Pilot* with Lenoir Chambers, the editor, and William Shands Meacham, the other associate editor. Bill Meacham, from Petersburg, had studied at the College of William and Mary and New York University, where he also had lectured.

After reporting for the Norfolk *Ledger-Dispatch*, he had been editor of the Danville *Register*, the morning paper in Southside Virginia's principal tobacco and textile city, and associate editor of the *Richmond Times-Dispatch* under Virginius Dabney. In 1942 he had left journalism to become Virginia's first paroles commissioner by appointment of Governor Colgate W. Darden, Jr., and to engage subsequently in federal parole work. He had come to the *Pilot* in 1947, a few years after Mr. Chambers moved from it to the *Ledger*, to write for Louis Jaffe as editor.

A big, balding man with a reddish moustache, Bill had a genius for collecting for whatever he would write exactly enough information to do him, no more and no less. He rewrote some of the stuff he churned out for the *Pilot* into regional editorials for a Southern edition of the Sunday *New York Times*, and frequently contributed to "Topics of the Times," a *Times* editorial-page column of anonymous essays, and to sundry magazines and reviews. His vanity was enormous, and although Mr. Chambers took care not to prick it, tension between the two could be discomforting all round.

I got used to that, too. And then one day Frank Batten, the publisher, took me to lunch and asked me to be managing editor of the *Pilot*.

Frank was just thirty-two and had been in charge of Norfolk Newspapers, Inc., for three years. But he already was demonstrating some of the intelligence and drive that would make him one of the nation's foremost newspaper executives—chairman of Landmark Communications, Inc., embracing the papers in Greensboro, Roanoke, and twenty-five smaller communities as well as Norfolk, plus television stations in Los Angeles and San Jose; chairman of TeleCable Corp., with cable television franchises over much of the country; and president of the Newspaper Advertising Bureau and of the Associated Press.

With mixed feelings, I went back to the newsroom I had left six years before. I knew that most of my old colleagues would welcome me. But I knew too what needed to be done and that before it was accomplished there would be some scratching in my briarpatch.

The man I succeeded was an accomplished antiquary who viewed the *Pilot* as an extension of his early American furniture and book collections. Its ancient format and old ways gave the paper distinction and charm, he believed, and he clung stubbornly to them despite the publisher's urgings for change. Surveys indicated that newcomers found the paper to be too cluttered for quick perusal, and the newsroom methods were inefficient and costly.

They had a considerable history. For as long as I had known the *Pilot*, it had shown some museum tendencies. H. L. Mencken wrote in *Newspaper Days* that when he became Sunday editor of the Baltimore *Herald* in 1901, "One of its worst relics of a more innocent day was a full page of fraternal-order news—supplied by the secretaries of the various lodges, but so badly written that copy-reading it was a heavy chore. The theory in the office was that this balderdash made circulation—that all the joiners of the town searched it every Sunday morning for their names. This seemed to me to be bad reasoning, for any given joiner was bound to be disappointed nine Sundays out of ten. One Sunday I quietly dropped the page—and not a single protest came in."

Forty-one years later, when I first went to Norfolk, the *Virginian-Pilot* had exactly such a page. Copyreading the stuff that lodge secretaries sent in was such hard going that a Radcliffe graduate was assigned to it—Mary Eugenia Parke, whose humor and wit saw her through the ordeal and who fortunately was available to write a book column when the fraternal page, as it was known, at last perished from the newsprint shortage during World War II.

The *Pilot* also ran back then a Sunday page of social news from a dozen or so North Carolina villages in its circulation territory, and half a page each Saturday of sermon topics for next day's church services. This matter, like the fraternal-lodge flummery, was set in agate type—the smallest in the shop—that discouraged reading it even by those who were presumed to be interested. The war killed that too.

Nevertheless, long after my return to the paper from the Pacific Theater of Operations, the Rev. W. H. T. Squires, M.A., D.D., Litt. D., pastor of Knox Presbyterian Church, faithfully came to the *Pilot* office each Friday to deposit in the city desk copy basket the menu for what he would feed his flock come the Sabbath. Dr. Squires was author of *Unleashed at Long Last*, a history of Reconstruction in Virginia rivaling, as a classic example of the dynamics of tragedy, the Book of Job, but, I fear, not much more read than our phantom sermon-topics columns. A copy of his book I came upon at an estate sale in 1984, forty-five years after its publication, was in mint condition with many pages uncut.

A handful of staff holdovers from that fading era of journalism were still around when I became managing editor of the *Pilot* in January 1959. Dean among them was Frank Sullivan, the business editor.

He grew up in the West, and was a sergeant in the horse cavalry out there before breaking in as a reporter for the *Milwaukee Journal*. He came to Norfolk in the late twenties with intentions of boarding a ship for Europe, where a job awaited him on the Paris edition of the *New York Herald Tribune*. Being low on money, he went to work at the *Pilot* to earn enough for passage, but instead settled down.

When I met him in 1942, he was in his early forties, already white-haired, a bachelor, and fond of the bottle. He covered courts then. But he had been transferred to the business beat when I returned after the war. Also, he had married; he was sensitive about his meager schooling, and the affection with which he was tardily smitten was reinforced by a master's degree that went with its object. Out of habit and skill from his soldier days, he smoked cigarettes that he rolled from flaked tobacco and a brownish paper, which burned fitfully, throwing off sparks that peppered his shirt fronts and coat lapels with tiny burn holes. He came late to the office one night from the Chamber of Commerce's annual dinner and fumbled at writing a story, having overstayed the social hour. The night city editor, a martinet of unusual insensitivity to human frailties, kept shouting across the city room to him to get going, that he was holding up the local news page.

Frank got enough of it. He walked up to the city desk and delivered, during the next five minutes, as cogent and persuasive a summary of grievances against the night city editor's administrative shortcomings and excesses and personal despicableness as a professor of oratory might have put together after surveying the city staff for a consensus attitude. Then he tore up the page or two of copy he had managed to type, put on his hat and coat, and went out, staggering only a little.

Next day he apologized so profusely that the night city editor accepted it as a heartfelt tribute to his leadership and an endorsement of his personality, and became a worse tyrant than ever.

Another reporter of the old school, although relatively young, was George M. Kelley, Jr., the political writer. He grew up in China as a missionary's son, attended an English school there, graduated from Wake Forest College, now University, and served in Army intelligence during World War II. In fashionably tailored suits and trenchcoat with looped belt, he cut quite a figure at city hall. But as admired as he was there and in the newspaper building, he followed a code I no longer believed in—that a reporter's worth should be measured by the confidences he kept. He wrote with grace and authority, and he wrote quite a lot, but he didn't write half of what he knew.

The path he followed went a long way back at the *Pilot*, and had been deepened by G. Wright Lankford, who was the city hall man when I arrived. At a tender age he had taken the William Jennings Bryan oath, which was sponsored by such youth groups as the Christian Endeavor, the Baptist Young People's Union, the Young Men's Christian Association, and maybe the Boy Scouts. It was never to taste liquor. National Prohibition was new.

Married and twenty-nine years old, G. Wright had kept his vow, through the University of North Carolina and until he was established at work. Then one swallow of bootleg whiskey changed him from a teetotaler into an alcoholic. He took to gambling, and that led him into debt. His life fell apart.

At length Winder Harris, the *Pilot*'s crusty managing editor, gave him two weeks to sober up and straighten out.

G. Wright got a judge to commit him to the city prison farm, which had replaced the work house, and underwent a cold-turkey cure. He was so wretched for a week that he could barely function. But he managed to spend the next week chopping corn and digging drainage ditches and putting up fences, and his nerves calmed down and he slept nights and felt strength oozing back into his body. He asked Mr. Harris for two more weeks of rehabilitation, because he still had a ways to go and also because he liked the toil and sweat; and when he went back to work he was a new man.

But he was still an old-time reporter. I chanced to learn, during my early months at the paper, from a neighbor who was in the state legislature, that the city council then sitting had secretly voted back to office a city manager fired by a council majority subsequently ousted, and gave my information to G. Wright. "That was nearly a year ago," he said. He knew all about it; he had waited upon the former city manager, as Virginia politicians express it, meaning that he had borne the invitation—had been the messenger boy—for him to return to his high post, and had received and delivered his refusal. "But I never could get it to the place where I could write it," G. Wright said.

Toward the middle of the war, when the *Pilot* was understaffed and its work was onerous, he took to drinking again, and didn't live long; and that was a shame, because he was fiercely proud of that battle he won.

He was the second of the reporters who were at the *Pilot* when I got there who didn't make it into the postwar era. The first was William B. Southall, better known as Senator.

Virginius Dabney wrote in his memoirs, *Across the Years*, that when he was appointed chief editorial writer of the *Richmond Times-Dispatch* in 1934, Senator Southall was his only assistant: "an attractive man with a slight stutter who had been wounded with the U.S. Marines in Belleau Wood." He had left Hampden-Sydney College to enter the Marine Corps as a private. His wounds kept him in a Paris hospital for many months after the Armistice.

Southall, continued Dabney, who soon was advanced to editor, "was a fairly effective performer, but he was notoriously lazy. For example, when he arrived at the office in the morning, he would snap on the desk light and then depart for anywhere from a half-hour to an hour. He had a certain facility for turning out editorials, but not if they were on complex subjects requiring research. He seldom read anything but the Richmond papers and the *New York*

Times. We took a dozen of the better magazines, but if Southall ever looked at one of them, I never detected him in the act. Nor could I ever find that he was reading any book. In addition he annoyed me by throwing paper and other debris on the office floor, with the result that the area around his desk looked like the residue of a minor hurricane . . .”

So Senator Southall was demoted to the *Times-Dispatch* reportorial staff. In time he was cut adrift there. When I arrived at the *Virginian-Pilot* he was a member of its city room. Word of his death in 1944, following a wretched illness, reached me in the Pacific. I wrote back to the office that he was the only person of whose intolerance—he despised practically everything that didn't have a solid Richmond connection—I had been wholly tolerant.

His nickname came from his devotion to Senator Harry F. Byrd. At one point in his *Times-Dispatch* career he wrote a political column under the pseudonym Father Byrd, after Richmond's founder, William Byrd II. It pleased him that Senator Byrd called him Father Byrd.

On the *Pilot* he performed menial tasks for the most part, hacking out obituaries, lodge notices, and police news. The highlight of his Norfolk reporting was an interview with Major General John Archer Lejeune, who lived with his daughter there and whom he had followed in France. His protracted absences from the *Pilot* office were not in the morning but at night. He divided his time between his desk and a beer tavern a block away, which he could reach in half a minute by cutting through an alley.

He missed Richmond, and on his days off returned there to be with his wife, a public health nurse. Invariably he rode the Chesapeake & Ohio, delighting in the packet that ferried passengers across Hampton Roads between Norfolk and Newport News and furiously enduring the crowded, grimy cars of the hundred-mile rail trip. The Newport News train was beginning to move from the Richmond station when he got there one afternoon, and he yelled, "Stop the train! Stop the train! I'm Leon Henderson, and I've got to get aboard!" Somehow he made it. All the way back to Norfolk and at work that night he marveled at whom he had said he was: Leon

Henderson, of all persons, a colorful New Deal figure he in no way admired.

He was full of Richmond stories, most of them set in the newspaper offices, the Westmoreland Club, or Capitol Square. In them appeared various of the city's bluebloods, whom he regarded affectionately but irreverently. A typical Southall yarn was about a lawyer who in his old age, after many years of flunkeying for the Byrd Organization, was rewarded with appointment to the Richmond Court of Hustings bench. "But the sad thing w-w-was," Senator would say, "nobody called him j-j-judge. Nobody a-tall, not even in his court. It happened that as a young man working his way through law school at the University of Virginia he had played the p-p—dammit, the piano— in a Charlottesville sporting house, and everybody continued to address him as P-p-p-professor."

It might take Senator a good fifteen minutes to describe an after-work session he and LaMotte Blakely had shared, along with a jar of corn whiskey, with Douglas Gordon. Mr. Gordon was editor of the *Times-Dispatch* at the time, and Southall and Blakely were his associates. Spread before Mr. Gordon on his desk was that afternoon's editorial page of the rival *Richmond News Leader*. He read in mocking tones some pontification by Douglas Southall Freeman, the *News Leader* editor. "O, Lord, how can a man be so stupid!" he cried. He rendered a couple more sentences in the editorial and howled, "The damned ignoramus!" Farther down the column he interrupted his burlesque to assert, "Anybody who can swallow that ought to be locked up for his own safety!" Blakely meanwhile was fooling with a pistol he had found behind a tome on a book shelf. It went off— *k-blam!*—sounding like a field piece, and put a hole in the floor. Mr. Gordon stopped reading the Freeman editorial. Carefully he folded the page and carefully he put it away. "I'm glad," he solemnly told his fellow custodians of the *Times-Dispatch*'s conscience, "I'm glad the son-of-a-bitch is dead."

When Southall was at the *Pilot*, Mr. Gordon had become editor of the *Ledger-Dispatch*, with offices on the floor above. Mr. Gordon was ailing, and Joe Leslie, his only associate, was overburdened. After grinding out his nightly routine of obits, stabbings, shootings, and wrecks on the main highway to North Carolina for next morning's paper, Southall sometimes would turn out an editorial or two to be left on Joe Leslie's typewriter. In them he denounced draft-dodgers, black-market racketeers, Byrd Organization skeptics, Hollywood morals, North Carolina barbecue, and the Axis powers. He flung paper on the floor. He stomped cigarette butts. He belched beer fumes, swore, and approvingly reviewed his stuff aloud. He perused no magazines, consulted no books, and engaged in no research of any other sort. He did all deadlines violence. But he was among friends, and I hope he knew it.

27 New Broom

A rash of city-county mergers has spread across Tidewater Virginia in the past quarter-century. Princess Anne and Norfolk Counties, once notable for truck farms and fishing villages, have disappeared into Virginia Beach and Chesapeake. These sprawling new cities now abut the old municipalities of Norfolk and Portsmouth and also Suffolk, which lately has swallowed, like a menhaden consuming a bluefish, Nansemond County. The Norfolk-Portsmouth Metropolitan Area was credited with a population of 799,853 by the 1980 census. Across Hampton Roads harbor, beginning at the far shore seven miles from Norfolk, an additional 363,817 persons were counted for the Newport News–Hampton Metropolitan Area—but that might as well be in another world. Although two bridge-tunnels connect the areas, attitudes and habits of 300 years divide them.

The *Virginian-Pilot*, which traces its Norfolk ancestry to 1865, today lists all five South Tidewater cities in its masthead. It maintains substantial news, advertising, and circulation bureaus in the four beyond its headquarters office in Norfolk, and houses its giant offset presses in Virginia Beach. Tom Turcol, a member of the Chesapeake news staff, won the 1984 Pulitzer Prize for local reporting with a series of articles about a Chesapeake official's financial shenanigans. The Virginia Beach and Portsmouth news staffs rival Norfolk's in strength.

The merger trend began at about the time I became managing editor of the *Pilot* in 1959. Princess Anne County politicians sponsored consolidation with the resort community of Virginia Beach to break Norfolk's habit of annexing county territory. Under Virginia's peculiar system, counties and cities are wholly separate; while a city may bite into a county sharing its boundary, it is forbidden to nibble at another city.

Norfolk had about 300,000 residents when Virginia Beach was born again. No one doubted that Virginia Beach, a bedroom community sprouting shopping centers, soon would outgrow Norfolk in population. And when Chesapeake came along a little later, dismantling the Norfolk County government located in Portsmouth and creating a civic center in Great Bridge borough, until then a crossroads, it commenced to overtake Portsmouth's count of about 100,000.

How best to expand and coordinate the *Pilot*'s coverage of the developing metropolis with altered governments, and to protect its historic domination of the region, was a problem for me and my colleagues, and I'm sure it challenges our successors as the scene continues to unfold. Fortunately for me, the newspaper already was experienced in bureau operations in Portsmouth, Suffolk, and South Norfolk, a component of Chesapeake, and in part-run editions featuring local news and lesser-rate advertising, and in applying special attention to fashionable Virginia Beach and rambunctious Princess Anne. Unfortunately, neither the bureaus nor the Virginia Beach–Princess Anne effort would have merited many paragraphs in a journalism class primer. I had to undertake reforms as well as innovations.

The Suffolk and South Norfolk offices I inherited had one reporter each, both of them city room rejects. The Portsmouth bureau was manned by a city editor and several inexperienced reporters, who were heavily burdened by resentment among city officials and business leaders because the *Pilot*'s parent company, Norfolk-Portsmouth

Newspapers, Inc., had bought and immediately closed the afternoon Portsmouth *Star*, and by the short shrift the *Pilot* had given Portsmouth in a period that a lot of Portsmouth people thought had not ended.

I knew something about that period.

My first job at the *Pilot* upon entering its payroll in January 1942 was state editor. Although Norfolk and Portsmouth, each crowding a bank of the mile-wide Elizabeth River, ought to have been one community, the state editor handled Portsmouth news, along with the smattering of Suffolk stuff and the stringers'—correspondents'—letters from nearby Virginia and North Carolina towns and wire copy filed in Richmond and Raleigh. The South Norfolk items went, far more logically, to the *Pilot* city desk.

Mr. Trent presided over the three-man Portsmouth news staff. Whatever his first name was, I never heard it spoken or saw it written. To everybody he was Trent, that only: a small man with a limp who hissed out of one side of his mouth and lived alone in a Portsmouth walk-up hotel. He wrote some news and edited, more or less, and scratched out headlines for it all. One of his reporters was a rummy and the other spent more time selling Christmas specialties, pens and notebooks and ash trays and the like for business people to give their customers, than at gathering and writing news.

Newspapers and assorted junk were stacked high on Trent's desk and so close to his typewriter that he could move its carriage only about four inches, with the result that he wrote in narrow columns—an anticipation of the form that teletype copy would take during the brief period when wire services gauged it to the justified, twelve-em tape perforations for Linotype keyboards they also transmitted. Although he hacked out mostly tripe, he could rise to occasion, as he did the night a mid-Portsmouth theater blaze threatened an entire block; because of the lateness, he dictated a running account to me by telephone, blending each new lead into the last previous one.

Normally the Portsmouth file was fetched by copyboys in the Norfolk office who rode the intercity ferries, which long since have been replaced by twin tunnels. They brought, besides stuffed envelopes, whispered accounts of social carryings-on in the bureau's dimness. The second of the two scheduled news batches generally arrived so late that I had to railroad it—had to rush it unread, except for Trent's scanning, to the composing room. Precious little of it ever was lifted there from the Portsmouth edition into the final, although I nightly gave the news editor a list of what should be considered. The *Pilot* indeed treated Portsmouth as a third-rate colony, and it was a long time living down the evidence of it.

Had the *Pilot*'s desks been better organized, placing area news in the final would have been simpler than it was. The city, state, and telegraph desks operated independently and in some rivalry to fill the general news hole, each sending copy at its own pace to the composing room; there the printers put the type into chases—page forms—according to when it came up and how it fit, under the loose direction of the news editor. At the end of the work night, the news editor checked over and set aside surplus type for possible use in the next night's early edition. Only the editorial, women's, and sports departments filled allotted spaces, although the more important local news that didn't make the front page was displayed on the back page, which was called the dinky front; the longer pieces there were jumped—continued—to inside pages.

That's how things worked, as they had been working forever, when I took charge of the news operation as managing editor. The main difference between then and seventeen years earlier, when I first came to the *Pilot*, was that Duke Manning, having recently retired, no longer ran the telegraph desk, and John Combs, his assistant, had died. Two men less alike would be hard to imagine.

Adlai D. (Duke) Manning grew up in Anniston, Alabama, where his father was a judge, and attended a small preparatory school in upper Virginia that closed during the Depression. His right thumb was missing. Usually he claimed it was blown off by a hand grenade that exploded prematurely as he tossed it from a foxhole in the First World War, in which, according to that version, he was a captain. But he casually mentioned to me, while discussing printing equipment, that he lost it to a lead saw in a composing room.

He was a printer as well as copy editor, and held an International Typographical Union traveler's card that qualified him to work in any union shop where he might stop. Upon slugging up—hanging on a board a type slug bearing his name—he would be required to take, under the ITU's rules, any job under its jurisdiction that was available, from setting type to constructing advertisements to reading proof; and if the foreman did not need him for either machine or floor or proof room duty, then the chapel chairman, or union steward, was required to substitute him for any situation-holder, or regular employee, who within a stated period had worked overtime, until he had duplicated the overtime period. Either as a composing room sub or a newsroom copyreader, he had worked in most of the states and on every major newspaper in the country. He settled at long last on the *Virginian-Pilot*, he said, because it turned out to be the next best thing he knew to a government pension.

Duke never drove an automobile. When he traveled far, it was by train. As with Father Takakura, the German priest with a Japanese name in John Hersey's *Hiroshima: The Aftermath*, his favorite reading matter was timetables, a supply of which he carried in a coat pocket; he knew all the nation's rail lines, and what train would take you where and when it would arrive at and depart the station, and the relative quality of dining-car fare, and the price of tickets.

For several years he was slot man, or chief of the copy desk, at the *Chicago Tribune*. One of the rim men, or copyreaders, there was his brother Lou, who had attended Virginia Military Institute and also was a newspaper vagabond. Lou was at the *Pilot* when I wrote editorials but had shoved off when I moved downstairs. He told me he was on the desk rim at the *New York Times* when he heard of an opening on the *Boston Globe*, and after work one night took a train north to explore it. On the way up he drank a bottle of whiskey and went to sleep. When he arrived in Boston he did not remember leaving New York, and told a taxi driver to take him to Times Square. "Times Square, New York?" asked the cabbie. "Where else?" replied Lou. He went back to sleep. When the taxi stopped he owed the driver $50.

Duke's job as *Pilot* telegraph editor included making up the front page. From time to time he and the news editor would disagree on what story should get top play—should receive the biggest headlines on page one. If the news editor overruled him, Duke next day would buy newsstand copies of the Washington, Baltimore, and New York papers, which invariably featured the story he had wanted to streamer, and dump them on the news editor's desk without comment.

Only he called his assistant by his first name. To the rest of us his assistant was Mr. Combs.

As Duke was minus a thumb, Mr. Combs was minus a leg. As far as I know, he never explained the impairment. He was a graduate of Johns Hopkins University, a handsome, gray-haired, dignified man, and a soft-spoken one until aroused, when he could be a terror. There was a story, unverified but undoubted, that he had used a crutch to coldcock a superior at the *Philadelphia Inquirer*, where he had been real estate editor. He had worked also at the *Denver Post*, and kept in plastic covers a well-illustrated story from it describing a hike he had completed on crutches up Pikes Peak. But on a night when the elevator conked out he refused to climb the stairs from the newspaper lobby to the second floor, where the newsroom was located.

He applied great care and precision to the headlines he scribbled for the wire stories that Duke tossed across the desk to him. He was a nitpicker and forever checking a date or place against the library's files, reference books, and encyclopedias. At the approach of a deadline when Mr. Combs, with an unusually high stack of copy before him, stuck to his methodical pace, Duke in frustration grumbled, "Dammit, John, I don't need a cabinetmaker for this job—what I need is a carpenter!"

What the *Pilot* needed was an assembly line instead of a cluster of shops to craft its product. I set about to organize it on becoming managing editor.

To collect ideas, I spent about a month studying desk procedures at the *Charlotte Observer*, and *Richmond Times-Dispatch*, the *Washington Post* and *Star*, and the *New York Herald Tribune*. I called at the *Herald Tribune* when John Denton, in a bold effort to salvage the failing paper for its new owner, Jock Whitney, was applying makeup techniques he had developed at *Newsweek* magazine—

oversize pictures and liberal white space, or margins, labels instead of conventional headlines, and sports stories and offbeat features splashed on the front page.

In the end, I installed pretty much the system that I had used, in miniature, at the *Sanford Herald*.

28 Clean Sweep

Memories of the circulation plunge that accompanied the *Sanford Herald*'s necessarily abrupt change from semiweekly to daily afternoon newspaper in 1952 made me resolve to overhaul gradually the Norfolk *Virginian-Pilot* when I became its managing editor in 1959. But I had to start somewhere.

So right away I killed the back-page "dinky front," a relic from one-section newspaper times, and opened the first page of the second section for display, in succession, of North Carolina news, southeastern Virginia news, and metropolitan Norfolk news. While the *Pilot* already published editions for each of those areas, until then Norfolk news had been featured on the back page of the last section of each edition.

Some subscribers objected. Older readers in Norfolk missed the long-familiar back page's big headlines and, at its bottom, small advertisements in light type, although they still got the same fare in a different place. And older readers in outlying places missed the spritely written Norfolk stories.

Frank Batten, the publisher, pondered the complaints and kept his nerve. Some in his staff had qualms. These worsened with the arrival of summer and the annual migration of families who could afford it from Norfolk to the beaches, including beaches on the North Carolina Outer Banks. Norfolkians who expected to catch up on home news as they sipped coffee on their Nags Head verandas were appalled to discover in its stead stories under such North Carolina datelines as Manteo, Elizabeth City, Currituck, Hatteras, Rocky Mount, and Raleigh. They knew whom to call or write.

I got advice from the publisher's office that circulation was going to hell. But within a few weeks the tempest passed. The fact was that only about a dozen complaints had been received. I was reminded of something that NAACP leader Roy Wilkins lately had said in chiding the nation's press for its irresponsible handling of racial conflict—that a self-appointed black prophet could start a movement with a dollar's worth of telephone-booth calls to a newspaper city desk. A country club golfing foursome might accomplish as much by dialing a publisher's number on a locker-room extension phone.

To prepare for printing truly regional editions, with content tailored to each, I set up a single copy desk to process city, state, telegraph, and women's news, while leaving the editorial, sports, and Sunday departments to function separately. The news editor apportioned the paper's space among the departmental editors by distributing to them page dummies—typewriter-size sheets of paper scaled to a newspaper page—with advertising columns marked in. On these the various editors indicated to the slot man—the copy desk chief—how they wished their stories to be treated. This was standard operating procedure on most newspapers and in line with the system I had followed on the little *Sanford Herald*. It facilitated attractive makeup of inside pages as well as front, orderly flow of copy from the central desk to the composing room, and elimination of overset, or surplus type.

Over a period of months I chose a metro editor to coordinate city reporting with that by the nearby bureaus and authorized the state editor to organize two North Carolina bureaus and employ stringers—correspondents who were paid space rates for their production—in smaller communities. And I made changes and adjustments throughout the news department, in and out of Norfolk.

When I launched my experiments the *Pilot's* advertising, circulation, mechanical, and business departments were not only modern but far advanced. Frank Batten had established research, promotion, and personnel offices, which were unusual in the industry. The slow-paced and comfortable, but inefficient, methods of the news department could not have endured so long if some exceptionally able people had not made the most of them. The *Pilot* had a distinctive look, and excelled in local writing, and was respected for its accuracy if not its scope. I was determined to preserve its flavor. And I was grateful for the good assistance I found.

Sid Griffin, out of Wake Forest and Richmond Colleges, both universities now, was news editor. He and I had worked together in the Raleigh *Times* building, he in the Associated Press bureau there and I as telegraph editor. Leaving the *Virginian-Pilot*'s quality to others, he concentrated on getting it out—on pushing copy off typewriters, over desks, into type, and onto the presses. He was as persuasive in the mechanical departments as he was in the newsroom.

Ronald W. May, a reporter, felt the force of Sid's pressure from the time he came onto the local staff. As he dallied at deadlines, Sid got on him pretty hard. Wishing the news editor to realize that he wasn't exactly a cub, Ron gave him a copy of a book he had written with Jack Anderson, the Washington columnist, *McCarthy: the Man, the Senator, and the 'Ism'*. A book was the last thing in the world that would have impressed old Sid. "The only thing I want to see with your name on it," he told Ron, "is something written in twenty-five minutes."

Sid and I agreed on his assistant, Larry Hirsch, for the key job of slot man. Larry was from Oak Park, Illinois, and had been brought into the world by Ernest Hemingway's father, Dr. Clarence Hemingway, who practiced obstetrics there. World War II erupted at about the time Larry graduated in humanities at the University of Chicago. The combination of a faulty heart and pacifist tilt kept him out of uniform, but he came east to work in a Wilmington, North Carolina, shipyard. For a time he sailed as an engineering yeoman in merchantmen. After the Japanese surrender he went to work on the Wilmington *Star*—as an uncommon lot of other people over the years had done, including Murray Kempton and David Brinkley. He had stopped at the *Greensboro Daily News* before reaching Norfolk.

The copy desk opened in midafternoon with the arrival of an

early man who went through the stuff sent over by the women's department, saw the comics and other standing features to the back shops, and otherwise cleared the decks for the night's work. Larry and his three or four other rim assistants reported at 6 P.M.

Page by page, Larry saw the dummies filled out and dispatched through a pneumatic tube to the composing room. He wrote some of the headlines himself, especially clever ones for lighter stories, and tinkered with the others, fuming and snorting at imperfections. The last page he cleared was the front, which Sid or I had diagrammed.

The *Pilot* carried in those days a two-or-three-line syndicated feature, "Today's Chuckle," in a front-page ear, opposite the one with a brief weather forecast. Just before releasing the page Larry invariably would ask the early man, whose stint was ending, "Chuckle out?"

And the early man would answer, "Chuckle out!"

Joe Dunn, a bright young fellow from the University of Virginia who had passed up a *Time* magazine job to work for the *Pilot*, was the early man. Night after night he engaged in that little dialogue: "Chuckle out?" "Chuckle out!" It got on his mind. It entered his dreams.

At length he bought and modified a toy cannon that fired a little flag with "BANG!" printed on it. The next time Larry asked "Chuckle out?" he put the cannon on the desk, pulled the lanyard, and answered on a red banner protruding from the barrel, "CHUCKLE OUT!"

Larry only grunted. That wasn't response enough to suit Joe, who forthwith bought a parrot at a pet shop and was fairly advanced at teaching it to say "Chuckle out!" when he was promoted to chief of the Virginia Beach bureau, from which he would go still higher.

Larry played several musical instruments, favoring an old pump organ from a church that his pretty wife Mary, whom he had met in Wilmington, gave him. For "Per-Verse," a Sunday feature bearing a caricature of his bony, bent-nose, boxerlike face, he wrote sophisticated poetry. He painted too—"landscapes, seascapes, and escapes," he called his oils. They were oddly fusty.

His heart ailment persisted. A little while before he died Landmark

Communications, Inc., the new name for the *Pilot*'s expanding corporate parent, published a collection of his Sunday verse. The last reads:

Take Your Time

Time is the image of eternity.—Diogenes

Meet me at half past new moon,
Give or take a day or two,
But do not come with time
Chained to your wrist
Or umbilical to your vest,
Or with a sermon that sounds an alarm
On the sins of nonuniformity and unpunctuality.
I have geared more than half my life
To deadlines for the chronicling of the ephemeral,
And I have beaten the clock
More often than it has beaten me.
But it has more years to run than I,
And I am running down.
So meet me at half past new moon,
Give or take a day or two,
Or maybe three,
And I will show you
The pendulum of forever
And explain why there is no five-star final
Printed across the sky.

Having been introduced in 1958, "Per-Verse" was one of the few features to have been added to the Sunday paper since I resigned its editorship to go to Sanford in 1952. Its format had changed none. I borrowed Sid Griffin's new assistant, Will Winstead, and gave him the task of sprucing up the "Lighthouse," the Sunday section containing editorials, reviews, commentary, and essays. Will was a Wake Forest honors graduate who had edited a weekly newspaper in North Carolina and read copy at the *Richmond Times-Dispatch*. He knew printing and was an expert at makeup. Once he had given a new appearance to the "Lighthouse," I had him extend it through the rest of the paper, section by section. I didn't want to spook readers with sudden change.

His second stop was at the women's department. That term isn't used now; the women's section that contained fluff about parties, engagements, and weddings, mixed with cooking and other household advice, now is labeled "Style" or "Living" or "People," and concentrates on fashions, interviews, profiles, restorations, entertainment, and other lively matter, much of it meaty. The larger papers were just beginning to move in that direction back then.

A man lately had been made editor of the women's department. As far as I could tell, he wasn't exactly wedded to the job, and his principal achievement in it had been to appear on "What's My Line?," a popular Sunday night television show, and to stump Bennett Cerf and Dorothy Kilgallen and the other panelists, being tall and athletic-looking and in no way like somebody professionally concerned with debutante balls and D.A.R. pronouncements. In scouting about for a replacement for him I came upon a name over a series of women's articles in the *Washington Star* that rang a little bell.

The author, I discovered by inquiring at the *Star*, was a free lance with magazine experience and South Carolina low-country background living in Northern Virginia. The information confirmed my notion that she was a sister of a girl I had known at Chapel Hill— one of the 200 coeds, all juniors and seniors, in that innocent era. The sister I remembered mainly for having quit one spring Sunday night a party at a cabin on the Haw River, a dozen miles from the campus, that took a turn to her disliking, and for having walked home; by dawn, at her approach to Spencer Hall, the lone women's dormitory, she had worn out her shoes and come through a rain shower, and hence was barefoot and soaking wet when she saluted the house mother, stationed at a desk near the front door, by jiggling with her teeth a jonquil plucked from a yard at the edge of town that she carried in her mouth.

That was the younger sister. I invited the older one to come down from Alexandria and be interviewed for the *Pilot* women's editorship. She appeared in a conservative blue suit with lacy blouse and in hat and gloves, and chatted brightly, a little about her sister and their cousin in Congress but mostly about people and places unfamiliar to me. I could hardly get a word in edgewise. At length I told her she should see also the personnel director and leave references for him to pursue. She said she hadn't expected that. A bit huffily, she left.

She didn't much cotton to the personnel director, and became indignant at his mention that she should visit the company doctor for a health check as part of the interview. Several hours later at the hotel where we had arranged for her to stay she got into a ruckus with the night manager over his inability, or refusal, to fill her late order for another bottle of whiskey, and also ran up a $60 telephone bill with a call to Caracas, Venezuela.

I eventually hired a woman of about thirty-eight who had studied design at Carnegie Tech, now Carnegie-Mellon University, had a flair for style, and was striking-looking, animated, imaginative, and the mother of five; and, as a naval aviator's wife and wartime WAC officer, was far-traveled and worldly wise—but lacking in daily newspaper experience. She took to the city room like a swan to the marshes. And after a crash course in women's editing provided by the American Press Institute at Columbia University, she began leading her department into a new era.

Sports was the last department I approached. And I approached it reluctantly.

William Norment Cox had been sports editor of the *Virginian-Pilot* for more than thirty years. While born in West Norfolk, a Portsmouth suburb, he sprang from Highlanders in Robeson County, North Carolina, and had an address there when he attended Chapel Hill in the early twenties. A one-act play he wrote when a student, "Scuffletown Outlaws," about the Indian guerrillas who operated in Robeson during Reconstruction, was included in a Carolina Play-makers anthology. After graduating he went to New York to try his hand at the stage; an impression afterwards that he shared diggings in that period with Thomas Wolfe he did not discourage.

But fame and fortune eluded him, and he returned to North

Carolina and found a sports job on the *Durham Morning Herald*. From there he went to the *Greensboro Daily News*, and from there to the *Pilot*.

He was sports editor of the *Daily News* when I was in high school in Mebane, thirty-five miles down the Southern Railway tracks. My father received the *Daily News* by mail, and every afternoon on my way home from school I stopped at his office to read it. He recommended Bill Cox's column to me as an example of good writing, and I followed it studiously.

Bill's eccentricities stood out even at the *Pilot* when I arrived there. He wore a peacoat and watch cap in football press boxes and a farmer's straw hat at Norfolk Tars baseball games. When his wooden-trimmed station wagon, which the parking lot attendants called the "Termite Special," fell apart, he bought a rusty jeep.

He hated basketball, thought poorly of tennis, and barely tolerated golf. But he delighted in boxing and prodded the Virginia legislature into extending, in 1934, its legality beyond club rings to public arenas. In time he stopped attending all sports events except boxing, while allowing his two assistants to assign themselves to what they chose.

As a contribution to wartime conservation he wrote his column, *Breaks of the Game*, on the back of used paper, usually handouts—press agentry plugging products, events, and causes—that came in his mail. Having added little of late to his experiences, he drew deeply upon memory for comment, and frequently strayed into topics far removed from the playing fields of Williamsburg, Charlottesville, and the Norfolk Naval Operating Base and nearby Naval Air Station—the delights, for example, of a January dip in the surf at Ocean View, where he lived, the neglect of Erskine Caldwell in literary criticism, the inferior quality of reading matter in his dentist's office, and the relationship of Graeco-Roman wrestling to free-verse poetry. Hardly anyone noticed when a Linotype operator, setting type for a column in which Bill moved from the football season's opening to Wolfean reflections upon the joys of October in Old Catawba, copied the wrong side of a middle page and spliced into the graceful prose four paragraphs and an unfinished sentence that had something to do with Gaines dog food.

Those of us who subscribed to Bill's sports philosophy were outweighed by subscribers to the newspaper. His stuff went over poorly with the crowd at "Colonel" Polly Rozzano's Thirty-first Division Drum & Bugle Corps Club bar and at Gus Meloni's barbershop across from the Federal Building. The *Pilot's* circulation manager claimed that the sports section lost him more business than it got him.

And it was hard to dispute him. At the unfolding of the sixties, with the drying up of boxing in Norfolk, Bill shifted his attendance to the Wednesday night wrestling shows and went nowhere else, except maybe to an occasional midget-auto race. In his much-expanded staff there was confusion as to who was in charge of the assignment book and whose night it was to run the copy desk.

So I made Bill sports editor emeritus and reached up to the Baltimore *Sun* and plucked Ed Brandt, whose color coverage of the Colts I had admired, to take charge of the department. Ed was traveling with the Orioles when we made the deal, and I had to wait until the baseball season ended to install him as sports editor. The wait was worth it.

For Ed treated Bill with great respect and consideration, and Bill, now writing his column just three days a week and enjoying it, came to like and admire Ed. Much, much later I talked Ed into moving to the metro desk, which had run into trouble, and he gave the *Pilot* a second lift. He found time to write *The Last Voyage of USS Pueblo: The Exclusive Story Told by 15 Members of the Crew* and *When Hell Was in Session*, Rear Admiral (later U.S. Senator) Jeremiah A. Denton, Jr.'s account of his survival as prisoner of war in North Vietnam. When he returned to the *Sun* after my retirement, the *Pilot* lost a superior news executive.

Meanwhile, the Norfolk sporting community reacted to Bill Cox's semiretirement by giving him a testimonial dinner at the old Monticello Hotel. Both Ed Brandt and I attended it, with Ed sitting at the head table. Speaker-of-the-evening was Peahead Walker, former football coach at Wake Forest and assistant to Herman Hickman at Yale University and, at the time, head coach of the Montreal Alouettes of the Canadian Football League.

That was the first time I had seen Peahead since 1939, when he was at Wake Forest and I was at the *Durham Morning Herald*. I went with Oakey Mitchell, the *Herald* sports editor, to see Peahead's Demon Deacons at practice. Peahead trotted out a big freshman fullback named John Polanski for scrimmage against the varsity with the observation to Oakey that this-here boy was coming along pretty good and was probably just a little better, at that early stage of his development, than Bob O'Mara, the Duke University star of the season. "Where'd you find him?" Oakey asked, admiringly. "His daddy's a Baptist preacher down there in Gates County," Peahead drawled. Gates is a peanut-farming county.

When Polanski became a varsity standout a year later—freshmen couldn't play in those days—Oakey remembered Peahead's remark and called him "John the Baptist" in his column. Peahead made him stop, claiming then that the young man was thinking about studying for the Catholic priesthood when he returned to the steel-mill country he really had come from. Instead of a priest, Polanski became a Detroit Lions running back.

Oakey once called on Peahead at Pinetops, a farm town in eastern Carolina where he was employed for the summer as manager of a semipro baseball team made up mostly of college boys. A young lady sitting along the third base line attracted more attention, including that paid by the players, than activities on the field. "It was mostly from the way she put her feet up on the grandstand railing," Oakey told me later. After the game Oakey said something about her to Peahead. "Yeah," said Peahead, "she's from over at Conetoe and comes to about all our games. My third baseman's going with her. Ain't he brought her tits out pretty?"

The address that Peahead delivered at Bill Cox's testimonial dinner was in that vein. It was, in a manner of speaking, X-rated. Ed Brandt wrote in next morning's *Pilot* that it was well received.

29 On the Street

Journalism is reporting and the extension of it. No editor who fails to understand the methods and problems of reporting can do his paper much good. But it does not follow that good reporters invariably make good editors, or that the best editors were superior reporters; newspaper work is like baseball, in which some of the finest managers never made it to the major leagues as players, and superstar players rarely succeed as managers. Personality, preference, and judgment tend to separate persons who have acquired, one way or another, and from varying motivation, the basics of a common skill.

Even so, for too many years a reporter had to come off the street and onto a desk in order to move very far up a newspaper's payroll, whether he had supervisory inclinations or not. Nobody really gained in the process; chances were that a paper would trade a superior craftsman for an inferior administrator, and the guy would sour.

Out of appreciation of reporting, regret that I had thought it necessary to enter desk work at an early age to stay employed, and shame of the pittance we had paid reporters at the *Sanford Herald*, I was determined to lift reporting at the *Virginian-Pilot* into a rewarding career. I emphasized reporter pay in the news department's budget from the day in 1959 I became managing editor.

In building and maintaining a good local staff, I well knew, I would encounter frustrations. As the nation's newspapers go, the *Pilot* was in middle range. Bright young people it recruited or accepted from small papers would be tempted to try their increased experience and skills on the big-time press. The trend preceded my time and would outlast it. I remembered very well that Bynum Shaw and Glenn Kittler had come to the *Pilot* just as I was settling back into it after World War II naval service, had made themselves valuable, and had gone away. There had been others, but I had wished those two would stay.

I chanced to be helping on the city desk the day Bynum strolled in looking for a job. He had just been paid off as a cook on a merchant ship in the harbor, and wore a seaman's gray slops—a slight man with crinkley hair already a mite gray and with soft features and a shy manner. The city editor sent him, as a try-out, to South Norfolk to report a council meeting, and he forthwith raised the quality of reporting for that adjoining town.

Kittler—we never called him Glenn—was a different sort: slicked-back dark hair, horn-rimmed glasses, a touch of cynicism. He grew up in Chicago, was in the Army in Europe, worked out West as a publicist, and spent some time on a South Carolina weekly. He followed a couple of other newsmen from down there to the *Pilot*. He and Bynum Shaw had as much pure writing ability as anyone I ever knew.

Bynum moved up the Chesapeake Bay to the Baltimore *Sun*, where the command made the mistake of sticking him on the copy desk rim. He escaped by using his lunch hour to rewrite an obituary, routinely sent over by the city desk, into a journalistic gem; the subject was Robert Murray, a retired *Sun* city editor and former Norfolk police reporter, whose robust individualism had been overlooked through ineptitude or else sacrificed to a persuasion, for which there usually is merit, that newspapers make too much of their departed members. In any event, Bynum's piece earned him a writing assignment in the *Sun*'s Washington bureau. He became chief of its West German bureau, where he collected the material for two novels he wrote, *The Sound of Small Hammers* and *The Nazi Hunter*, and was back in Baltimore writing *Sun* editorials when he chose to return to Wake Forest University, his alma mater, to succeed his old mentor, Edgar E. Folk, as head of the journalism department. I once tried to lure him to the *Pilot* editorial page, without success.

Kittler left the *Pilot* for a public relations position in New York, but quit it to do free lancing. He sold to *Reader's Digest* and the *Saturday Evening Post*, and on a *Guideposts* assignment wrote an interview with Dr. Albert Schweitzer in French Equatorial Africa that earned him a bit of fame in the sectarian press. Also, he turned out a dozen books, most of them as a ghost writer or collaborator— with General Eisenhower's cook, for instance; perhaps the most solid of these was *Triumph: The Incredible Saga of the First Transatlantic*

Flight—the NC-4's three-leg crossing in 1919 from Long Island to Portugal after taking off with three other U.S. Navy seaplanes.

He usually wrote, he told me on a visit back to Norfolk, a first draft on yellow second sheets, which he edited by working from the last page to the first so as to stick strictly to the grammar, and speed-typed the result on white paper. But on one occasion, when pressed for time, he wrote an entire book in a single draft, using ink eraser to correct typing errors, and delivered the manuscript for publication unread. I don't claim that's the route to great literature. But I've seen the time a newspaper could benefit from such facility.

The first good reporter to leave the *Pilot* during my watch was Eugene Roberts, a Chapel Hill graduate who had worked in Goldsboro, one of the bigger towns in agricultural eastern North Carolina, where his father was a high school journalism teacher. Gene was cold-eyed, tenacious, and unerring. He was on the waterfront beat, and I had no doubt he could become the best maritime reporter on the East Coast. Then he got a call from the *News and Observer* in Raleigh.

"You can do better here than there," I told him.

"I know it," he replied. "But when I was a little boy in Goldsboro it was my ambition to cover politics for the *N&O*—that was the one thing I wanted to do more than anything else. I dreamed of it. I felt the same way when I was in college. And now I've got the chance, and I can't bear to think that what I wanted so much isn't worth it."

All right, I said, I could see he had to go and I wouldn't argue about it. "But you won't stay," I added.

He didn't stay even as long as I would have predicted. Pretty soon he was city editor of the *Detroit Free Press*, and then a war correspondent in Vietnam for the *New York Times*. The *Times* installed him as national editor after a couple of years, and he departed New York to become executive editor of the *Philadelphia Inquirer*.

James Harper, another Carolina graduate, whose family owned a weekly paper in Southport, North Carolina, on the coast, came to the *Pilot* from the Chicago news service, which provided police and other routine stuff for the newspapers there, happy to be near salt water again. His coverage of Norfolk courts earned him the admiration of judges. Like Gene Roberts, he went to the *Free Press*.

While at the *Times*, Gene recruited William K. Stevens, a West Virginia University graduate, from the *Pilot*. Luther Carter, the young man I had sent from Sanford to Norfolk, bade me good-bye and settled down with *Science* magazine in Washington, where he became senior writer. And Bill McAllister, whom I brought to the *Pilot* on the strength of his work for the *Sanford Herald* as its Pittsboro stringer, went off the San Francisco bureau of the *Wall Street Journal* and, after I had coaxed him back to Norfolk for a second hitch, eventually moved up to Washington as the *Post*'s Virginia editor.

Adam Clymer was attracted to the *Pilot* by its bold editorial support of the Supreme Court's school desegregation decision. A New Yorker, he had been president—editor—of the *Harvard Crimson* and in Africa on a Knox fellowship when he applied in Norfolk for a reporting spot. I took him to the editorial suite to meet Lenoir Chambers, who had just received the Pulitzer Prize for his school editorials. Mr. Chambers and I told him about the educational crisis and its aftereffects, and strayed into storytelling. As we talked and laughed, Clymer became bemused. "Do you suppose," he asked, "I'll be handicapped, working in Norfolk, for not speaking like a Southerner?"

He wasn't, as we managed despite our amusement, to assure him he wouldn't be. More than half the people in Norfolk, a world port with two international military commands, pronounce more as Clymer does than as I do. I doubt if he had taken on any Southern ways when a few years later he hooked up with the Baltimore *Sun*'s Washington bureau, from which he shifted to its Moscow bureau, then returned to Washington and joined the *New York Times* staff.

The upward mobility, if you'll pardon the expression, of some of the *Pilot*'s brightest and best, I consoled myself, amounted to an impressive endorsement of our hiring standards and training program. But I was inconsolable when Maggie went away.

Maggie was Margaret Ruffin Wilkins. She married a newsman

when both were young, and they had three daughters and a son. Her husband became tragically ill. She took his job, although she had no training for it, except maybe by osmosis, and did well enough to hold it and progress.

She was an absolute beauty—high cheekbones, delicate nose, big brown eyes, wavy brown hair, and slim and long-legged and graceful. She had grown up in Norfolk in fashion and comfort, a doctor's daughter, without much thought to managing finances and no particular gift for convention and order. Although her wages reached the top of the American Newspaper Guild scale, now and then her pantry would become bare and her furnace's fuel tanks dry. A relative sooner or later would bail her out, and she would pack her children into a failing automobile and rent a beach cottage for a vacation long enough to allow her to catch her breath and ponder the betrayals of a household budget.

Divorce became inevitable. It nevertheless crushed Maggie.

All sorts of suitors soon appeared. To avoid serious involvement with any, she vowed to date only foreign officers temporarily in port.

The first she went out with was a Royal Australian Navy lieutenant commander completing advanced missile study at a Norfolk Naval Station school. Within a few weeks she put the cover on her *Pilot* typewriter and emigrated to Melbourne, taking Gay, Missy, Kate, and Johnny. Her marriage there to Charles Falkiner, who had a wife and two daughters, was delayed until he could shape a course through Australia's rough divorce laws. In the meantime Maggie established the *Trading Post*, a magazine-type publication modeled after one she had read in Virginia Beach in which persons advertise any sort of item with a commitment to pay a percentage of the sale price if a buyer turns up. It was an instant success. Maggie set up two more *Trading Posts* in Melbourne, started and sold one in Sydney, and franchised still another in Brisbane. By the time she was wed again she had so much business going that Charles resigned from the Navy, which he had entered as a thirteen-year-old midshipman, to help her run it.

They contracted with a shipyard to build them a Chinese junk with a steel hull the thickness of a destroyer's, which they christened *Wan Fu*, and in her set sail for the United States, steering westward. In the crew were Margaret's two younger children, the older girls having returned to Virginia to enter the College of William and Mary, Charles's two, and a shared newcomer, little Charles, who was five. After a year at sea, counting a long stop at Capetown, they reached Norfolk on Christmas Eve 1977—eleven years after Maggie and her brood had left town.

They tied up *Wan Fu* at a Norfolk Yacht and Country Club pier and hit the sack, as sailors say, in the club's guest quarters. My wife Frances and I routed them out next morning and took them to our house, a few blocks away, for breakfast.

"How'd the voyage go, Maggie?" I asked.

"Well," she said, "I began to realize it wasn't going to be all lark the first night we were in a storm and I went up to relieve my husband of the watch and he put a harness on me and lashed me at the wheel and rushed off to our bunk."

A reporter with Old Norfolk connections about as solid as Maggie's didn't leave the *Pilot* because it didn't hire him in the first place, as much as he wanted it to. He was Bob Woodward, a hero of the *Washington Post*'s Watergate investigation.

When at the height of his fame Woodward told Frank Batten, the *Pilot*'s publisher, that right after finishing at Yale he practically got on his knees and begged for a job on his paper. He was from Illinois, but his mother had a lot of family in Norfolk. His great-grandmother, Stella Upshur, for many years wrote an advice column of the Dorothy Dix school under the pseudonym Beatrice Fairfax for the Norfolk *Ledger-Dispatch*. I don't think Bob ever got to me, or even past the personnel office. All I can say in defense of whoever sent him away is that the *Post* didn't take him either until he had acquired some experience on a little newspaper up in Maryland.

His great-grandmother's old paper, now the *Ledger-Star*, also passed up in that period a likely prospect—Tom Wicker.

It was looking for an editorial-page editor. Frank Batten sent an assistant to interview Tom at the Winston-Salem *Journal*, where he was covering city hall, writing editorials, and turning out novels under another name for the up-and-coming paperback trade. They had dinner in the old Robert E. Lee Hotel.

A former Richmond *Times-Dispatch* reporter who had hired out to the cigarette lobby and moved to Winston-Salem chanced to be in the dining room and overheard their conversation—which, according to him, consisted mostly of Tom giving the *Journal* hell for kowtowing to the city's powerful business establishment, including the R. J. Reynolds Tobacco Company. He felt constrained, in the light of who paid his salary, to report in detail this blasphemy to Tom's editor.

"So of course I had to fire Wicker," the editor told me a few weeks later when I saw him at a meeting of the American Society of Newspaper Editors in Washington. The *Ledger* meanwhile had chosen another man.

If Wicker was indiscreet, he was not inaccurate, and landed, after a brief spell as associate editor of the Nashville *Tenneseean*, in the *New York Times* Washington bureau, where in four years he succeeded Scotty Reston as chief, and then became a *Times* columnist and associate editor and, on the side, a television panelist and author using his own name.

If the *Virginian-Pilot* lost some good reporters and overlooked another, it also kept its share of them. One was Charlie Rodeffer.

He was born in the Virginia Valley and went to Bridgewater, a small college there operated by the Church of the Brethren, in which he was ordained as a youth. Early in his freshman year he discovered philosophy, which was taught only to upperclassmen, and began to read it. Soon the department bogged down; all the books on the subject had disappeared from the library.

Charlie had them. Although he had properly signed for the lot and renewed those that came due, he was asked to give them up. So he began to concentrate on mathematics. The degree he took in that led to an instructorship at Texas Tech University in Lubbock. During his two years there he married a departmental secretary from North Carolina.

The Depression caught them. Charlie tried to sell automobiles near his old home and then worked on a weekly newspaper while his wife taught school near hers. The marriage had pretty well come unraveled when I met Charlie.

He was teaching mathematics by day in a college-credit program that the Navy established in Norfolk soon after World War II and working nights at the *Pilot*. The Navy work ran out and he became, in his middle years, a full-time newsman: a bullfrog of a man, pop-eyed, wide-mouthed, and puff-throated, with his belt hitched so far under his top-heavy stomach that only about three inches of freeboard showed between it and where the inseams of his trousers met; he moved at a half-trot, which made him pant and grimace.

He had a great knack for turning a highly technical subject into an instructive and entertaining story. Lacking in him, though, was the gift of brevity. He missed all the deadlines one night, and was still pounding his typewriter when the last edition went to press. Everybody else left the office, and the news editor turned out the lights. Charlie responded with a terrible oath.

He was given to outbursts. Once he silenced a woman reporter who had been needling him by telling her, in gaudy language, how she made him homesick. And on occasion the whole newsroom was startled when, in the midst of writing and for no apparent reason, he turned his agonized face to the ceiling and bellowed: "Oh, if I could only get rid of this *goddam inferiority complex!*"

Also subject to occasional self-doubt was Warner Twyford, the *Pilot*'s versatile entertainment editor who had been my close associate in the Sunday office. In a review of a concert, play, or art show he might be devastating. But a performer's protest or a reader's rebuke would put him into a pout, and if charged with bias or incompetence he would become ill with despair.

Like most news people of the manual-typewriter age, he typed by his own system. Unlike most, he was extremely fast. Although he made revisions in every paragraph, some extensive, he could deliver a thoughtful column or searching review in half an hour. His construction was flawless.

He covered everything from the old Gaiety burlesque house to the fine Feldman string quartet and Norfolk symphony to traveling stage plays and operas—and also Clyde Beatty's circus, which he much admired. The directors of the Norfolk museum and little theater sought his advice, and a Virginia Beach dinner theater adopted his name.

Rose LaRose, the strip queen, always called him when she came to the Gaiety for an engagement. During my Sunday editorship he took me, at her invitation to bring a friend, to her hotel suite, where we stuffed ourselves on goulash that her mother cooked. Her mother, who was Hungarian, always traveled with her. After lunch we went with Rose to the Gaiety to see a carved horse from a carousel that Dudley Cooper, a Norfolk entrepreneur with a taste for the arts and a hunger for publicity, had given her upon disassembling the crumbling Ocean View amusement park, which he owned, to make way for a shopping center. Rose intended to use it in her act. She demonstrated to us how she intended to seat herself on it. "Just so," she said, assuming a sidesaddle pose. "From some angles one may look grotesque when one relies on a G-string."

Warner nodded in artistic agreement.

When we first met he lived in Newport News and commuted to work, riding the Hampton Roads ferries and Norfolk streetcars. That was his routine for many years, day after day after day. Then one morning he left his house key with the woman he had married when they were twenty or so, along with his large collection of books and records and everything else he owned except the clothes he wore and carried.

After the divorce, he married a girl as young as his first bride had been. In time he left again, taking with him only what he could not do without, and by then it was a habit. I had lost track of his marriages and living arrangements when he became ill. He died slowly, and left in his desk a thick diary in which he recorded many joys and no sorrows.

As Warner Twyford had lived for the present, George Tucker lived for the past. He believed the American Revolution was a mistake and counted himself a royalist.

George became a newspaper reporter in an odd way. While clerking in a Norfolk record shop, where he knew everybody and everything, especially the more malicious gossip, he wrote for the

Sunday *Virginian-Pilot* a fascinating account of Edgar Allan Poe's visit to Norfolk shortly before his death in Baltimore. Although somewhat elaborately phrased, it was researched in scholarly fashion and I was pleased to publish it. That was in 1949. George was forty: balding a bit, round-bellied, somewhat mincing, with horn-rim glasses set low on broad nose, forever yacking, devilishly merry.

He did several more Sunday pieces, some of which he illustrated with pen-and-ink sketches notable for swift strokes and elegant flourishes and curlicues. He became a newsroom habitué and city desk consultant, especially in genealogical matters. Eventually he was hired to write features and lend a hand on the obituary desk.

As if to reestablish himself further, he married a librarian of good lineage and joined the Catholic church, having earlier switched from Baptist to Episcopalian. He worked a late shift, and brought his dinner to the office. Unlike the copy desk hands who unwrapped sandwiches from paper bags and poured coffee from thermos bottles, he unloaded from a fair-size box a full-course meal that, with linen napkin spread upon knees, he ate from Spode china with Gorham silver.

More people than were there remembered the evening George pranced into the city room giggling over his discovery that a Williamsburg rake had stormed into the parish church, yanked the parson's wife from a pew he claimed to own but had neglected since being a sermon topic some time back, and thereby added outrage to the ignominy he had earned by living with a mistress. "This will set the town on its ear," he sputtered. Even the city editor was titillated. But he cooled down on learning the scandal occurred in 1696.

Among my early moves as managing editor was to set George to writing a column that we named, because his approach was from England and the sea, "Tidewater Landfalls." He preferred to write of colonial affairs and events, but occasionally broke the pattern with hilarious yarns set in the Berkley of his upbringing, a working-class community on the Elizabeth River, or the doings of Norfolk blades and dowagers of whispered pasts. Nobody had to tell me about the risks of corniness here. But nobody had to tell me, either, that George was wonderfully entertaining and that his way of matching writing style to period and of spicing a droll story with an astonishing phrase was no less than art. The newspaper published two collections of his stuff in book form, and the city's United States Bicentennial Commission commissioned him to write a book about the pre-Revolutionary borough. Following his retirement in 1975 he wrote *A Goodly Heritage: A History of Jane Austen's Family* and *Concerning Jane Austen: Some Biographical Aspects*, which were published in England, and contributed to *The Scribner Handbook of Jane Austen*. And after a lapse of ten years, at age of seventy-five, he revived his column for the Sunday edition of the *Virginian-Pilot & Ledger-Star*.

Among George's longtime friends were Frank Blackford, the reporter for whom I substituted in covering the Christmas Eve shenanigans of Miss TV Tower of 1949, and his artist wife Polly. Frances and I and our daughter Fran used to meet George at the Blackfords' beach home on Sunday afternoons and help them fix dinner for us all, including Fran and the two Blackford little boys. George, still a bachelor, always fixed the salad. And Frank without fail excused himself along about then to go into his bedroom, close the door, and watch Bulwinkle on his color television set, which was the first I ever saw.

Heywood Hale Broun, in Norfolk to telecast some event or another, was startled to see Frank, who seemed to be the specter of his father, Heywood Broun, the sports writer turned drama critic. Someone once wrote that Heywood Broun looked like an unmade bed. So did Frank: tall, heavy, and shaggy, with a nose that might have been borrowed from a Roman statue. He was in charge of the *Pilot*'s Virginia bureau—was, in truth, the bureau itself, although he frequently was assisted in covering the town and Princess Anne County by assignment reporters from the Norfolk city room. Eventually the town and county merged, and the Norfolk papers built a Virginia Beach branch that often was mistaken for their headquarters.

Frank was an authority on Southern writers and collected their works. He could cite Faulkner the way a barber at the Auditorium

Tonsorial Emporium in Norfolk could cite baseball rules. In Richmond, where he grew up, he had been among the young people who gathered at the feet of the aging Ellen Glasgow.

He attended Episcopal High School in Alexandria, of which his great-uncle Launcelot Minor Blackford had been headmaster. After sampling the wares at the University of Virginia, he took a job as bookkeeper for a Virginia Beach used-car dealer—thus rounding out an identity with three favored Virginia institutions: *the* High School, *the* University, and *the* Beach. However, upon learning from an aptitude test given him by a Norfolk Academy master that if he were a Dartmouth College freshman he would rank in mathematical skills among the bottom 10 percent of his class, he moved to Ocean City, Maryland, with the idea of writing a novel. To feed his family he sold some fiction to a newspaper syndicate, and that led him to a police reporter job on the *Washington Post*. From the *Post* he had come to the *Pilot*. He and Polly built their oceanfront house with his share of the money that Scribner's paid for the Civil War memoirs of his grandfather, Lieutenant Colonel William Willis Blackford, Confederate States Army, which it published as *War Years with Jeb Stuart*.

One of Frank's more memorable assignments was to cover a yacht's beaching off Sandbridge, just above the North Carolina line. Sandbridge today is another overcrowded beach resort on the Atlantic Ocean. Back then it was a fishing community with so few residents that invariably it was the first Virginia precinct to report election returns. Its only public telephone was in a combination grocery store-cafe-beer joint on a party line that linked most of the community.

Carolina Telephone Company serves that corner of Virginia. Frank had a hard time getting hooked into the Bell system and the Norfolk city room. Once he had succeeded and dictated a few paragraphs, he told the rewrite man to hold on while he organized his notes for the rest of the story; lest the operator claim the line meanwhile, he asked the nearest person, a bearded man drinking beer with a couple of buddies, all three wearing blue watchcaps and yellow oilskins, to read into the phone from a paperback he drew from his pocket. The book was *The Diaries of Franz Kafka*.

"If you don't know a word, just skip it and keep going," Frank instructed him. "The important thing is to keep this line busy till I can take over."

"Goddamit, mate," the fellow replied, "I'm literate. And, if you don't mind my saying so, I thought that was a piss-poor lead you just filed." He turned out to be a former Richmond ad-agency writer handling the Miller & Rhoads department store account, who had quit the rat race and signed aboard a trawler.

Frank said later he didn't think the lead was all that bad. I'd take his word. He was one of the better *Pilot* reporters who stayed.

30 The Ivory Tower

Lenoir Chambers retired January 1, 1962. He had been awarded an honorary doctor of laws by the University of North Carolina to go with his Pulitzer Prize and continued to be in demand as a speaker because of the critical success of his Stonewall Jackson biography. Frank Batten, the publisher, commissioned him to write a history of the *Virginian-Pilot* to mark its centennial year, 1965, which appeared as *Salt Water & Printers Ink*—two years late, alas, but a lasting history of Tidewater Virginia as well as of the newspaper.

Frank appointed me editor. I moved into Mr. Chambers's office while maintaining authority over the news department. My impulse was to keep a watchful eye on the editorial page while devoting most of my energies to the news product, which is how most editors-in-chief operate. But Mr. Chambers urged me to supervise the editorial page directly—he charged me, indeed, as old Presbyterian preachers back home in Orange Presbytery used to charge the young fellows fresh from the seminary, to keep the faith and defend the doctrine; he looked on me as being in the line of succession and wanted no intrusion in it. I took him seriously. I would write editorials daily, as it developed, for a total of twenty-three years, and only during my year with him did I write them under supervision. So I spent at least half of each day with the editorial staff, and I was forever aware of the long shadows of Lenoir Chambers and Louis Jaffe and Governor Cameron. But I wrote for myself and not for ghosts.

I agreed with Frank Batten that William Shands Meacham, who had been a *Pilot* associate editor for fifteen years and was approaching retirement age, should have the title of editorial-page editor, and made Sid Griffin night managing editor. Robert Collins Smith, who had taken my place in the editorial offices when I became managing editor, and was just back from Harvard University and a Neiman fellowship, was the third member of the editorial staff. I added a fourth, William Littleton Tazewell, who all his life had been Widdy.

Widdy also was fresh from Harvard, where he had been working on a doctorate in English in culmination of upwards of a decade of advanced study, some on scholarships—at the University of Virginia, where he edited the campus newspaper, the *Cavalier*, and stayed on for a master's, and at Indiana and Ohio State Universities. At Harvard he had decided that history rather than English was his true field, but his faculty adviser wouldn't approve the switch, and he had come home to Norfolk, to the house where he grew up and where his parents still lived. He was a great-great grandson of Littleton Waller Tazewell, a Virginia governor and United States senator—a gangling young man, pigeon-toed, owlish, sensitive, and what Mr. Chambers, being old-fashioned, called sweet, meaning exactly that. As a solemn little boy going to a private school he had carried in his belt a baseball glove and in his head most of the batting averages from the Sunday paper's baseball stats; during an early year with me he went abroad, as he did every chance he got, and came back with one overwhelming impression: that a kid from the University of Connecticut he had seen playing basketball some-where, in Italy perhaps, had the damndest moves imaginable, a good-looking black kid named Julius Erving. He wrote with great precision, and was orderly, neat as a pin, and direct—mathematical, really. But he didn't care when he came to work or what he did when he got there, and if he couldn't coax an editorial from his typewriter one day he wouldn't worry because he knew he would make up for it sooner or later and that anyway the page would appear in good enough shape next morning, somehow. I suppose old Widdy was what you would call an egghead.

Bill Meacham became ill and took early retirement. He had been active in the English Speaking Union, and an information officer in the British embassy who came down from Washington from time to time, to Williamsburg and on to Norfolk, and who admired him, got him put on the Queen's honors List as a member of the Order of the British Empire.

Guy Friddell arrived from the *Richmond News Leader* to replace him. On his first day at the *Pilot* I gave Guy a batch of letters-to-the-editor that the secretary had retyped onto copy paper, which was cut from the stock that the newspaper was printed on, and asked him to put them in shape for publication. He undertook to edit them with a fountain pen—an old-timey fountain pen holding liquid ink in a rubber tube inside it that, as I would notice, already had stained the pocket of every shirt he owned—and it turned the first page he applied it to into a near-total blot; and I thought to myself: what in the hell have we here?

At the *News Leader* Guy had been a political writer and columnist, and about the best on any Virginia paper, whose political writers and columnists included a Charlie McDowell, the *Richmond Times-Dispatch*'s Washington man and, later, a popular panelist on the public television program "Washington Week in Review." Guy had a master's degree in journalism from Columbia University and soon would be honored by the University of Richmond, also his alma mater, with a doctorate of literature. Also, he had a profound understanding of Virginia, its history, its ways, its institutions, and its leadership.

A feeling existed in the Richmond press that Guy was too loose a cannon to fit into an editorial port. There was something to that. Covering a tree-planting ceremony in which President Eisenhower did the honors, he trampled down the tree rushing from the rite to get in a political question or two. And there was the time President Kennedy telephoned him at the *News Leader* to tell him how much he enjoyed *Jackstraws*, among the earliest of half a dozen books he wrote, and nobody could find him because he was goofing off in the wire room. An assistant at the Norfolk public library called me, when Guy didn't answer his phone, and asked what she should do with a paycheck made out by the newspaper to him that she found between pages sixteen and seventeen of a Yale University Press book on gender and ideology in early New England verse that had been returned two weeks late. I advised her to determine from the front desk how much he owed in overdue book fines, deduct that, and send the change to his wife for safekeeping.

Yet Guy's contribution to the *Pilot*'s editorial voice was mighty. If he might become starry-eyed over Thomas Jefferson, Robert E. Lee, and his friend and neighbor Colgate W. Darden, Jr., a former governor and former president of the University of Virginia, and also over Smithfield ham and Lynnhaven oysters, he wasn't fooled by the Byrd Organization or massive resistance, and he didn't eat his chit'lins at an annual breakfast in Richmond's Rotunda Club honoring the commonwealth's truest of the blue. Nor was he taken in by the Democratic party's elegant liberal wing or its rude new Populists. He got the point and he saw the comedy of things. And he gave the paper insight into the heart of Virginia affairs that it had lacked.

Nevertheless, the limits and anonymity of editorial work denied him and Landmark Communications, Inc., the *Pilot*'s corporate parent, the full range of his interests and abilities. With Landmark's acquisition of the newspapers in Greensboro and Roanoke, it reconverted Guy into a columnist and made him a special writer for them as well as the *Pilot*, free to choose his topics and where to travel. Few newsmen have held greater license and done better with it.

Soon after Guy's arrival, R. C. Smith left the *Pilot* to become editorial-page editor of the *Charlotte News* and to complete *They Closed Their Schools*, a book about the five-year public school blackout in Prince Edward County climaxing Virginia's massive resistance, which he had been writing for several years. I plucked Glenn Scott from the Sunday office to succeed him.

Glenn was from nearby Smithfield, where his family owned a weekly newspaper. As a sophomore at Washington and Lee University he had written a novel about campus life that E. P. Dutton and Company published. I was in Sanford at the time, and Elliot Graham, the Dutton publicity director, who wasn't aware that I knew Glenn and his father, sent me a copy of it with a note predicting that the author would prove to be "the new Scott Fitzgerald." But Glenn got the recklessness out of himself early and settled down into three-piece-suit conventionality. He and Widdy Tazewell, having escaped the more bruising aspects of newspapering, lent the joint an intellectual cast.

Widdy departed the year before I retired to teach noncreative writing—that's how it was listed in the catalogue—at the University of Virginia. In Charlottesville he met and married Mary Lee Settle, the novelist and National Book Award winner, who also was on the faculty. I had come to know her a little after hiring her son from a marriage in England as a science reporter on the *Pilot*. She was strikingly pretty. The wedding was held outdoors at a Charlottesville estate near a swimming pool. After the rituals the bride and groom boarded a flower-decked raft and drifted in the pool's calm, eating grapes and puffing the seeds over the side—or so George Tucker, the *Pilot*'s reporter of seventeenth- and eighteenth-century affairs, told me. I suppose he was there. I wasn't. The couple finished their University of Virginia commitments and settled into the old Tazewell house on a leafy Norfolk street near a pleasant tidal basin. There Mary Lee got back to fiction-writing and Widdy wrote *Norfolk's Waters*, a history commemorating his home city's entry into its fourth century. He asked me to do the introduction, and I was delighted to comply.

During the seventeen years I directed the *Pilot*'s editorial page I brought half a dozen members of the news staff, young men and women, into the editorial offices for temporary duty—to fill in, for example, during a year that Widdy studied at the University of

North Carolina on a Mark Ethridge scholarship sponsored by the Southern Newspaper Publishers Association. Each of them wished to begin by writing a stinging piece on a pet hate. My standard response was to quote Juvenal: *Si natura negat, facit indignatio versum.* "When talent fails, indignation writes the verse." The regular staff and I put our share of anger into the editorial page. But I was terribly wary of what my youthful newsroom colleagues had been itching to get off their chests.

James R. Henderson III, who took over Guy Friddell's office, suited me better, as a craftsman, than any other editorial writer of my experience. He was a semanticist and a stylist, and like Tom Wicker contributed a bit to the pulp industry under a nom de plume. A keglike, bald, and bearded fellow with a Phi Beta Kappa key from Chapel Hill hanging to his jeans, Jim had been a wartime Navy signalman in a gun crew aboard merchantmen making the Murmansk run. It figured, then, that he was a worrier—he worried when somebody got fired, when rumors of change floated through the newspaper building, when people messed up their lives. Not long after I left he was transferred back to the news department— where, heaven knows, he was needed and welcome. I asked what the hell had happened, and the answer came down that Jim lacked security. My response was that I wouldn't have traded his insecurity for all the arrogance in the corporate offices, which spread across an entire floor.

Kathryn Harris Morton, the *Pilot's* book columnist, came in temporarily when Widdy Tazewell went away; I was leaving the vacancy for my successor to fill permanently. Because she had a husband and a couple of babies to look after, her hours had to be irregular. I told her I'd be happy if she turned in a piece a day, no matter at what hour, and I became joyful. A few years after my departure a Norfolk literary society sent me about fifty essays to judge, none bearing a name or other identification. I chose the winner after a first reading of the lot and confirmed it upon closely studying the top half-dozen. It turned out to be Kathryn's entry. I felt like a blindfolded wine-taster who recognized a 1962 vintage.

Mary Ann Dilly, who was my secretary in the news department, went with me into the editorial offices. She was fresh from high school in Clarkton, West Virginia, eighteen I think, yellow-haired, apple-cheeked, and twangy. Also, she was bright and ambitious. Widdy laid out a course of reading for her, and I showed her how I wrote and edited. I escorted her down the aisle and gave her away when she married Edward W. Frede, a reporter, in Trinity Lutheran Church. She and her husband moved to Pomona, California, where he worked for a newspaper and she latched on as secretary to the dean of Claremont Graduate School and University Center and before long was running the student activities office for a boss bogged down with his doctor's dissertation, the first person without a degree to enter those precincts. Twenty years later, in Danbury, Connecticut, where her husband was an editor, she directed the city's tricentennial celebration to national acclaim.

After Mary Ann I had a good many secretaries, some good, some bad, some so-so. The last candidate to be sent to me by the personnel office was Beth Newton Williams.

Beth had been working for two years in one of the business offices, credit or purchasing or services, and was leaving unhappily. Personnel said she was unusually capable and that it wished to keep her in the organization, and besides she needed a job.

Although skeptical of a strictly business type, I interviewed her. Why, I asked, was she quitting if she wanted work?

Because, Beth replied, the twerp she was working for peeked into her lunch bag and into the packages she sometimes brought after shopping during her lunch hour.

Come on in tomorrow, I told her.

Her mother was a native of Hatteras Island, on the Carolina Outer Banks, and she had spent much of her girlhood there and married a Hatterasman who, after their separation, had died in a work accident, and she was rearing their two daughters. Her great-grandfather, an Englishman named John Eden, had come ashore at Hatteras in a pork barrel after being shipwrecked, and had married a Fulcher, who was mostly Indian. Telling about her ancestor's arrival to someone in Beth's presence, I said potato barrel. "No," she corrected me, "pork barrel is what they always said."

She was every bit as resourceful as her great-grandfather. Once the news and editorial offices switched to computers, I couldn't operate without her. She memorized the style book and mastered grammar. If I went back I'd make her an associate editor.

One day Widdy Tazewell came to see me. He was barefoot, and a security guard made him register before he'd let him on the elevator. The reason he didn't invite me to his wedding, Widdy said, was because it was held on a Labor Day weekend and he figured I'd much rather go fishing than drive all the way to Charlottesville for a cup of champagne I didn't care for.

31 A Cord of Cottonmouths

The routine of my *Virginian-Pilot* editorship was to complete the editorial page by 1 or 2 P.M., go to lunch, and shift over to the news operation upon returning to the newspaper plant. Usually I went back at night. Sometimes I would not take a full day off for a couple of months. Then I would disappear into Currituck Sound for the better part of a week.

Currituck Sound is a forty-mile-long stretch of water, an average of three miles wide, never more than twelve feet deep, lying between the barrier islands and the mainland south of Norfolk. I could reach favorite parts of it in an hour's drive from my house. Its head is in Virginia, along about Pungo village, and up there it's called Back Bay. In North Carolina it bottoms into the Albemarle Sound and, pretty far below that, is linked to the Atlantic Ocean at Oregon Inlet. Yet it is only mildly brackish these days, for storms have closed all the upper inlets, and it has no tide except that it floods on a southwest wind and ebbs—rushes out may be a better term—on a northeast blow.

Currituck is an Indian word for "land of the wild goose." It and Back Bay remain famous for goose and duck hunting, although the sport is in decline, as the deterioration of all but a few of the dozen or so old hunting lodges attests. Not shooting but fishing attracted me. Currituck is hard to beat anywhere in the world for largemouth bass.

I never fished in Back Bay without a companion or in Currituck Sound without a guide. You can get lost, stranded, or drowned in those waters. But in the Knotts Island marshes, where the Virginia-Carolina line runs, separating also bay and sound, I did not hesitate to fish alone in the well-protected shallow ponds, and I did not wait until I was weary to go there; indeed, I often slipped down that way with a johnboat, or drove on to Currituck to meet a guide where he kept his juniper skiff, for half a day's fishing.

So it chanced that upon a midsummer's dawn, having just stowed my trousers, shirt, and shoes in my old U.S. Navy meshed laundry bag in replacement of my wading gear, I was standing in the johnboat buck-naked when a cottonmouth moccasin came alongside. Gingerly I stepped into the rubber waders and tightened the webbed belt about my middle. If an infringement upon the Garden of Eden story made the tableau all the more ludicrous, the metal deck's heat briefly on my bare feet was as harsh as sin's wages.

The snake was nearly as thick and buoyant as the truck inner tube encased in green nylon, with saddle and pockets and straps, in which I prepared to launch myself. "I'll concede," I said to the intruder, "that I'm probably no more attractive to you than you are to me. I'll go so far as to admit that an impartial witness would find precious little inspiration in either of us at the moment. But if you'll lay off my heel I'll promise not to bruise your head. You leave me the shoreline from that little point with the tussock protruding to the entrance ditch and you can have the rest of this pond. Go catch yourself a bullfrog or a bird and I'll unlimber my flyrod and see if I can raise myself a bass or two. Now, dammit, shove off!"

The cottonmouth kept station as the boat drifted shoreward, showing about three strakes of freeboard forward and dragging aft, then sheered off and planed toward deeper water. I do not suppose it even heard my voice. Yet snakes despite an absence of ears are sensitive to at least some sounds. About a dozen miles on down

Currituck Sound I once came upon Elmer Merritt, his permanent bronze retouched at nose and cheekbones from another spring's guiding, and two anglers he had unnerved by whistling up a cottonmouth and coldcocking it at the gunwales with his pushing pole. The snake had responded to Elmer's summons as promptly as a well-trained hunting dog, the fisherman marveled.

Bud Lupton used to amuse himself by coaxing Currituck cottonmouths that way. On occasion I heard him produce such a warble that a remarkably robust snake, having slithered a couple hundred feet to the stern boards of his juniper boat, tried to come aboard. "If I miss," Bud vowed to it, raising his twelve-foot ash pole and taking measure, "you sure as hell can be the captain." His swing was perfect. I was pleased that there was no change of command.

Like Bud and Elmer, most guides and others who spend much time in the marshes from Back Bay to Albemarle Sound, including the Knotts Island pond where I was wading that morning, are inclined to regard cottonmouths dispassionately. I remain horrified, though, by Bud's stark account of a curse of snakes he escaped on a North River bank when a schoolboy. There were dozens, he said, tangled and bedeviled. H. B. Ansell, a long-ago clerk of Currituck County Court, in his recollections of growing up on Knotts Island, spun a worse tale yet as an example of improbable local lore:

"A certain family had built a new log house with a clay fireplace, and unluckily this fireplace had been built over a den of snakes; and the family went to bed leaving a hot fire in order to dry the clay; and the next morning the family were found all dead and swollen to a puff and snakes in the room a foot deep."

Mr. Ansell's memory went back to 1835. His manuscript is in the Currituck County Library at Barco. It includes a second snake story:

"The hoop snake too was a dangerous reptile. This snake when any living animal would appear near, would round up in a hoop-shape, give swift chase to the unfortunate subject and overtaking it would drive its stinging tail into the pursued man or beast; death followed instantly. Sometimes a man chased by this snake would get behind a tree for protection; in such case the sting would be driven into the tree, which would at once wither and die. The snake not being able to extricate himself from the tree, and thus would be killed."

Although Mr. Ansell was certain the hoop snake was a creature of fiction, he said that in his youth "I heard some knowing ones say that they had seen and killed this snake." Every country boy in the South must have been similarly misled. Sixty years ago Mr. A. P. Long, a farmer from the Shakerag community in Granville County who had come to Mebane and opened a dress shop that his wife ran, told some of us loafing at the hardware store that when a young man he had leaped behind a green aspen to avoid a hoop snake's stinger—"horn," he called it—which found the tree's trunk and brought upon his head a shower of dead leaves.

The hoop snake myth is of excellent vintage. John Lawson in his *History of North Carolina*, first published in London in 1706, included this report under the heading of "Insects":

"Of the Horn-Snakes, I never saw but two that I remember. They are like the Rattle-Snake in Color, but rather lighter. They hiss exactly like a Goose when anything approaches them. They strike at their Enemy with their Tail, and kill whatever they would with it, which is armed at the End with a horny Substance, like a Cock's Spur. This is their Weapon. I have heard it credibly reported, by those who said they were Eye-Witnesses that a small Locust-Tree, about the Thickness of a Man's Arm, being struck by one of these Snakes at Ten o'clock in the Morning, then verdant and flourishing, at four in the Afternoon was dead, and the leaves Red and Withered. Doubtless, be it how it will, they are very venomous. I think the Indians do not pretend to cure their Wound."

Mr. Ansell no doubt had read Lawson. On the back of his Knotts Island manuscript he penned a history of Currituck County, drawing heavily upon colonial records—good evidence of the range of his scholarship. More in point, he referred to Knotts Island largemouth bass as "brown perch, or welchmen." That's straight from Lawson's section on "The Fish in the Salt, and Fresh Waters of Carolina." (Lawson spelled it "Welch-men." He also wrote that "flat or mottled Perch . . . shaped almost like a Bream . . . are called Irish-men . . .")

The "Welch-men" of Lawson's account "grow to be larger than

any Carp, and are very frequent in every Creek and Pond." Large-mouth bass indeed are ubiquitous, although there have been plenty of times when you couldn't prove it by me. But "larger than any Carp"? Adult carp, according to *McClane's Standard Fishing Ency-clopedia*, "are 12-30 inches in length and average 10-15 pounds." In the Knotts Island pond where I coexisted with the cottonmouth, I've seen, wallowing in marshes flooded from southwest winds during the spring spawning season, carp that could pass for drum. If you land a bass there or anywhere else in and around Currituck Sound that goes ten pounds you've landed yourself a prize for stuffing.

Yet I wouldn't lump John Lawson among the mass of people who won't tell the truth about a fish's size. William Bartram, a trained naturalist who traveled from Florida into the Carolinas in the 1770s and carefully recorded much of what he observed, including men in canoes jigging with hooks concealed in "white hair of a deer's tail, shreds of red garter, and some pari-colored feathers, all of which form a tuft or tassel . . . called a bob," estimated that bass hauled aboard "frequently weigh fifteen, twenty, and thirty pounds." A thirty-pound bass would top by nearly eight pounds the record lunker that George W. Perry took on a plug in Georgia's Ocmulgee River in June 1932.

Bartram called a bass a "trout," but what he described was clearly a largemouth—"of a lead color, inclining to a deep blue, and marked with transverse waved lists, of a deep slate color, and, when fully grown, has a cast of red or brick color . . . and the opening and extending of the branchiostega, at the moment he rises to the surface to seize his prey, discovering his bright red gills through the transparent waters, give him a very terrible appearance." Bass remain "trout" in some localities, "green trout" especially. I also have heard them called chub, linesides, black bass, and, of late and to my distress, hogs. Only Lawson and Ansell appear to have listed them without explanation as welchmen (although Lawson's term has been noted, sometimes incredulously, by various ichthyologists, including Philip A. Murray, Jr., in *Fishing in the Carolinas*.

Mr. Ansell failed, unfortunately, to enter in his memoirs any claim as to the size of Knotts Island bass. The biggest I ever caught there missed five pounds by an ounce or two. I believe his figures would have been modest. He was persuaded, in any event, that wild creatures and exaggeration are inseparable. "I doubt," he wrote, for instance, "that there are over a cord of snakes . . . in the swamps, knolls and marshes of this Island."

A cord is a measurement of cut wood—128 cubic feet, as arranged in a pile eight feet long, four feet high, and four feet wide. A cord of cottonmouths would be horrendous. But as long as the components were fairly scattered over a few miles of swamp, knolls, and marshes, they wouldn't deter me one bit from wading into their favorite element to take a whack at a Lawson- or Bartram-size bass.

32 Hermits, Carps, and Turtles

When William Byrd of Westover and six other commissioners, two like him from Virginia and the other four from North Carolina, in the spring of 1728 undertook to fix the border between their colonies westward from Knotts Island, just inside the coast, they "were told that on the south shore not far from the [Currituck] inlet dwelt a marooner that modestly calls himself a hermit, though he forfeited that name by suffering a wanton female to cohabit with him. His habitat was a bower covered with bark after the Indian fashion, which in the mild situation protected him pretty well from the weather. Like the ravens, he neither plowed nor sowed but lived chiefly on oysters, which his handmaiden made a shift to gather from the adjacent rocks. Sometimes, too, for a change of diet, he sent her to drive up the neighbor's cows, to moisten their mouths with a little milk. But as for raiment, he depended mostly upon his length of beard and she upon her length of hair, part of which she brought decently forward and the rest dangled behind quite down to her rump . . ."

The dividing line that the Byrd commission fixed remains almost as set. But Currituck Inlet was closed by a storm's backlash early in this century. The nearest thing to a nude female form I saw during dozens of trips to that vicinity belonged to a young woman who, the halter to bathing suit removed, lay on her stomach upon a blanket in the sun, lulled by country music from a portable radio, while her companion, bearded but obviously worldly, sipped beer and tinkered with the outboard engine bolted to a low-freeboard fiberglass boat, getting ready for a bass tournament.

Knotts Island is really a peninsula, as William Byrd further noted in his journal, linked in his day by marshes to the Virginia mainland; now a causeway flanked by drainage ditches supports a Knotts Island-Virginia Beach highway. During most of my *Virginian-Pilot* years a companion and I traveled that highway every week or two of the spring and fall to fish for largemouth bass.

Often we would encounter a spiritual heir to William Byrd's hermit in a chain of ponds dredged long ago by Joseph Palmer Knapp, the magazine publisher, who built a hunting lodge on Knotts Island as a scaled-down version of Mount Vernon. Our hermit's habitat was not an Indian sort but an uncemented cinderblock hut set at the head of a ditch dug through the marshes to North Landing River, which merges with the upper end of Currituck Sound. No oysters were available for his plucking; they had disappeared with the inlet's closing and dilution of the water's salinity to a slight brackishness, but an abundance of shells vouched for the utility of the 1728 handmaiden's shift. In one of two stout pens he kept a pair of bluetick hounds for hunting raccoons, in the other two or three wild pigs he was fattening with indifferent success. His sparse whiskers would not have made him decent; for raiment he relied upon the Currituck County Welfare Department and a social worker who kept an eye on him.

This hermit was a wiry, bent little man of perhaps sixty, so darkened by the sun and the water's tannic acid that the tattoos on his forearms were barely visible. Gathering no oysters, and neither plowing nor sowing, and no doubt wearying of pork and game, he supplemented his diet with canned food bought with cash paid him by a Campbell Soup Company agent for turtles—turkles, old watermen pronounce it—that he trapped.

He tended his basketlike pots from a leaky skiff powered by a 2½-horsepower Martin engine, which a pressure-cooker company briefly manufactured just after World War II. A favorite bait for his pots was carp.

A lot of carp feed on Currituck Sound's bottom. Oddly—to me, at least—carp go on jumping sprees, hurtling themselves well into the air as if to deny their stigma as trash fish. They like to spawn when sound water, pushed by spring's southwest winds, floods the Currituck marshes and ponds. Seeing their swirls, newcomer anglers are likely to become unduly excited. "Hell, they're only perch," Bud Lupton, a fishing guide operating out of Poplar Branch, used to tell them. "We're looking for bass."

My fishing partner and I came upon the Turkle Trapper one May in a flooded stretch of marsh fairly teeming with carp. I threw a landing net over a big one that immediately tore it apart. The Turkle Trapper was using a better tool—a pitchfork.

He held up for us to see a whopping carp impaled on the tines.

"Sure is an ugly son-of-a-bitch," I said in some awe. Carp have scales the size of big toenails, and as thick. Their color resembles the mud they favor.

The Turkle Trapper squinted his eyes a little tighter. Bulges formed under the stubble at his jaws. "Who you talking about?" he asked.

Fishing with Bud in Currituck Sound in that period I fared better with my hands on a turtle than I did with a landing net on a carp.

Bud spotted the turtle's head extending, periscopelike, above the slick surface of a shallow cove. Quickly he poled his juniper boat to it. "Mama'll cook that sucker," he said.

The turtle sounded. But the water was clear and we could see it on the sandy bottom. Bud made several passes at it with his push pole but missed. The turtle moved erratically, in tight circles and short runs, as if confused. Soon Bud pinned it down. It was about as big as the lid of a garbage can.

"I got him," announced Bud. "Now you reach down and grab

him by the tail and pull him up. No need to worry about his mouth; he can't bite you if you lift him when you've got him by the tail real good."

We were in about three feet of water. I took off my shirt, leaned over the side, and extended my right arm into the water, up to my shoulder. Cautiously I felt along the sand for the turtle's tail. When I found the claws on the turtle's hind feet I almost lost my nerve. But soon enough I sorted out the tail, got a purchase on it, and hauled away. That turtle must have weighed thirty pounds.

Once I had dropped it on the deck, Bud made a loop in a mooring line, passed it into the turtle's mouth, and snubbed the line's ends behind the turtle's haunches, immobilizing it. He placed the turtle on a forward thwart, on its back, and we returned to fishing.

Several hours later we knocked off and headed for Poplar Branch landing. I sat on the middle thwart, between the turtle and Bud. Neither of us had paid much attention to the turtle since Bud secured it.

Perhaps the slight chop, which wasn't enough to knock the turtle off the seat, stirred it into resentment. At any rate, it discharged ballast. A stream of water struck my face and chest. I was properly doused.

Bud naturally was amused, and after drying myself with a towel from my ditty bag I discerned some of the humor. Later I thought of checking into the biological details of turtles but never got around to it.

A few weeks later I joined Bud at sunup at the landing, where we chatted with two impressive-looking men from Pennsylvania who were waiting for their guide to stow their tackle. Bud introduced me to them. "Mr. Mason is a newspaper editor," he told the visitors. "He is editor of the morning newspaper in Norfolk. He is the only editor to fish regularly with me. He is, moreover, the only editor I know who has been pissed on by a turtle."

33 -30-

The Morse man was still around when I entered newspaper work in 1933. Although teletype machines clanging out all-caps copy were in general use by the wire service, telegraphers sent and received— in caps and lowercase—leased-wire stuff, which we called overhead. When I took down my slug forty-five years later I had no idea how computers collected, stored, and regurgitated news matter.

I used to think I could do—indeed, had done—every job in a newsroom and editorial office. I have been telegraph editor, state editor, Sunday editor, news editor, city editor, associate editor, managing editor, and, for seventeen beautiful summers and very mild winters, editor of the *Virginian-Pilot* in Norfolk. As swing editor on two newspapers in succession, I managed a different desk each night, including sports and, so help me, society. As a reporter on five newspapers, morning and afternoon, I covered everything from local police to state legislatures to the United States Navy. I put in time as rewrite, rim, and slot man. For a total of twenty-three years, off and on, I wrote editorials routinely. Early on I learned to print. Yet during my last three or four years, from the time video display terminals were installed in the news and editorial offices to the day I asked my secretary to help me with my coat and show me to the door, I was unable to prepare, without aid from a typist or editorial assistant, a take of copy acceptable to the composing room—or what passed for a composing room now that the Linotypes, type cases, and stones were gone and the chapel chairman didn't care who touched what, the type having disappeared. Two factors protected me against my final ineptitude: (1) I was the boss, and (2) I was getting out in the nick of time.

When I was young, a newspaper in these parts was a fairly simple operation—except for the noisy mechanical department, which the publisher, in his mystification, was likely to contract out to the printers', stereotypers', and pressmen's unions, probably with a handshake. The editor was a distant and, to the handful of reporters, recondite figure who, without advice or consent, wrote all the editorials. Under the managing editor, who ran the show, would be four desk editors who essentially were copyreaders and headline-writers: telegraph, city, state, and sports.

And, oh, yes, there was the society editor—don't forget that old girl, God bless her. Or, rather, God rest her. She didn't last long—from about 1920 until reader sophistication, egalitarianism, and the American Newspaper Guild pay scale ran her out in the sixties and seventies. She never was much esteemed by the newsroom working stiffs, although at the *News and Observer* in Raleigh during the mid-thirties she filled half the Sunday paper with weddings and engagements and was the only departmental editor with an assistant. Lenoir Chambers, who after retiring as editor of the *Virginian-Pilot* wrote a centennial-year history of his paper, in it paid tribute to an early society editor: "Miss Bessie was the embodiment of inherited and inherent elegance. She knew the family lines of Norfolk like some people know their Bible. By her very presence, as well as her need for someone to tell her how to spell, she commanded attention and dignity even in rough newsroom moments." A successor to Miss Bessie at the *Pilot* confided to me that she felt perfectly able to write a piece about a lady going to Petersburg for a little visit but had trouble getting her on the train and back to Norfolk.

A decade after inheriting Mr. Chambers's office, I presided over the dismantling of the *Pilot*'s society desk, which had been pushed into a corner of the women's department. For that I have no regret. But let me hasten to add that all the Miss Bessies of my acquaintance—and there were a good many of them—performed at least one service that is sorely missed today, which was to explain to the police reporter, the obit writer, and the city desk itself what names made more news than other names, dead or alive, for good reason or bad.

I meanwhile oversaw the introduction of some editorships of which I now have occasional doubts. While the tags given the added or revamped sections typically were tailored to the locality, none was totally original and each had become, if it wasn't already, fairly standard across the land: opinion, entertainment, household, business, travel—by whatever synonym dreamed up. Jack Knight, the press baron who looked more like one than the reporter he affected, said newspapers never were better than when they were stealing from each other. Although they couldn't possibly be that good, he had something.

As a student, I was admonished to avoid words and phrases that usage had made trite—to steer clear of clichés. As a reporter assigned to police courts and instructed to write funny pieces about the drunks, pickpockets, and whores paraded there, I developed an abiding distaste for cliché stories. Lately I have come to realize that it is demonstrably possible to turn an entire newspaper into a cliché.

Even so, only an idiot would contend that today's newspapers are not vastly better than the fire-starters and mullet-wrappers of my early years. If the trend to news monopolies and extensive chains is regrettable for many reasons, it ought to be recognized that local ownership and intracity competition never did guarantee excellence. No newspaper could be sorrier than one being choked to death by a rival able to fool around with advertising and circulation rates and to manipulate production costs with featherbedding union contracts. Quality depends more on orderly planning than gimmickry, and certainly on a budget that the old newspaper wars—the fabled ones in New York and Chicago and San Francisco and the shabby ones closer to home—did not encourage.

As newspapers have changed their section headings, so have they changed the editorial corps. They have confused it, too. On some newspapers the features editor, with dominion over all non-deadline matter, ranks with the managing editor in responsibilities, authority, and pay; on others he works for the managing editor. Where the buck stops—and how it travels—differs from paper to paper. There are executive editors, executive news editors, news editors, editorial-page editors, and senior editors, as well as associate, assistant, and departmental editors, and editors period, each subject to ground rules. I knew a managing editor who was kicked upstairs and anointed associate editor for public service. Within six months flawed and burned-out managing editors up and down the country were converted into associate editors for public service, public affairs, and public relations.

Editor of a newspaper is all I ever wanted to be, and a newspaper editor I became. It pleases me that all my life I was paid, as a working man in the newspaper tradition, by the week—in cash for a long time; if I had become a corporate assistant or shunted into a phony office I would have been paid as an executive, by the month. It suits me, too, that I never held a company title or sat on a board of directors or was called upon to make a judgment in an area where I was inexperienced.

Having moved through reporter's slots and across all the desks, and having been involved in the news end while presiding over editorial pages, and at no time having thought of myself as first an editorial man, I developed and kept the habit of detachment. I wrote a lot in behalf of reform in juvenile courts and juvenile corrections, for instance, and harped on Virginia's disgraceful prisons system, and attacked flaws in justice when they appeared in the naval courts-martial I monitored, but I never considered reinforcing my comments with personal appeals to the authorities concerned, such as the letters that the admirable Louis Jaffe, when editor of the *Pilot*, addressed to Governor Harry Byrd advocating anti-lynching legislation. I denounced social unfairness wherever it appeared, and quarreled with the Vietnam hawks and the book-burners and the gun cranks and the fiscal tightwads and the tobacco lobby and the school-closers and the flat-earth diehards generally, but I never became immersed in a crusade. My way was to consider the facts that I could collect and to wring from them the truth to the best of my ability at that time and under the circumstances that existed, including what time it was, and to keep my emotions out of the issue, whatever it was, and not to care too much what happened next. I had to get on with other things. Meanwhile, I took as much satisfaction in my associates' ideas and appeals as anything I ever managed to accomplish, and I put a lot of stock in laughter.

J. Harvie Wilkinson III succeeded me as editor on September 1, 1978, my sixty-sixth birthday. Frank Batten and I, who informally held a veto over each other on such matters, agreed on his appointment. He not only was outside the *Pilot*'s sixty-year line of succession, going back to Louis Jaffe; he was outside the newspaper field.

A Richmond native, thirty-four years old, he was a graduate of Yale, magna cum laude, Phi Beta Kappa, and Scholar of House with Exceptional Distinction, and of the University of Virginia Law School. At Yale he won the William Clyde DeVane Prize for the outstanding paper in the university's 1967 Scholar of the House program, which he expanded into a book, *Harry Byrd and the Changing Face of Virginia Politics, 1945-1966*. He was working on the book and, between law school sessions, writing editorials for the *Richmond Times-Dispatch* as a summer intern when I met him.

He was toying with the idea of going into journalism after receiving a law degree. But at about the time of his graduation his neighbor, Lewis F. Powell, was appointed to the United States Supreme Court and named him a law clerk. After two years in Washington he became an associate professor of law at the University of Virginia. There he wrote a second book, *Serving Justice: A Supreme Court Clerk's View*, and began a third, *From Brown to Bakke*, which he completed during a year off just before arriving at the *Virginian-Pilot*.

As editor, Jay Wilkinson was responsible only for the editorial page, as the *Pilot* reverted to its old separation of "church and state"—of editorials and news. His lack of news experience was no great handicap and his legal knowledge was a major asset. Jonathan Daniels, who was editor of the *News and Observer* during my Raleigh years, and Robert L. Gray, editor of the Raleigh *Times* when I was there, were lawyers, and Mr. Gray had practiced law. So had Douglas Gordon, editor of the *Ledger-Dispatch* in my first Norfolk period. At one time at the *Pilot* we had three lawyers on the news staff (one of whom became also an Episcopal priest). I was used to lawyer-journalists.

It concerned me that Jay had taken a fling at politics, but the circumstances were mitigating. While in law school he had run in futility for Congress as a Republican against the incumbent Democrat, David Satterfield, who was to the right of him and practically everybody else, and had been encouraged in the caper by Governor Linwood Holton, a Republican of such moderate impulses that he had attracted one of my more liberal newspaper colleagues into his administration. I never mentioned Jay's candidacy to him, equating it to college panty-raiding and goldfish swallowing, and figuring it might embarrass him.

The *Virginian-Pilot* had a reputation for liberalism, which grew largely from its consistent insistence on social justice and human dignity. But in some areas it was pretty conservative—on labor, for example, and the old virtues. Until I was editor, it was skeptical of liquor-by-the-drink, which prohibitionist-inclined Virginia did not legalize until the sixties. I honored its longtime opposition to legalizing gambling. Jay adhered to all its basic principles despite his political label.

The University of Virginia Law School tried to keep him and then to woo him back, and after three years succeeded. If ever he had taken the political veil, he did not cotton to the view from behind it. He departed teaching again upon being appointed deputy assistant attorney general for civil rights in the Reagan administration. In 1984 the President appointed him a judge of the United States Fourth Circuit Court of Appeals, embracing the Carolinas, Virginia and West Virginia, and Maryland. He was forty years old and had appeared as counsel in a court of law one time.

Much of the press in the fourth circuit states protested. Even the *Virginian-Pilot* thought he was in too great a hurry. The *News and Observer* railed against his inexperience, particularly after the American Bar Association, which had pronounced him qualified for the appellate court, conceded that it would not have endorsed him for a federal district bench, a long rung down.

A trial and an appeals court are vastly different. To say a judge of the latter would not be suitable for the former is like saying an architectural critic would not be a good police reporter. Higher courts require scholars, not magistrates. To my mind, the Supreme Court would profit from the presence of a historian who never saw the inside of a law school. I expect Jay to distinguish himself as a U.S. Circuit Court judge.

But if ever he feels on the high and mighty side and in need of a dose of humility, he might return to the *Virginian-Pilot* editorial suite and inquire whether he's been missed.

A year after Mr. Chambers hung it up his old friend Jonathan Daniels called at night from his own retirement home in Hilton Head, South Carolina, and asked a *Pilot* switchboard operator how he might get in touch with him. After a long pause the operator told him she was sorry, the newspaper didn't have a Mr. Chambers in its employ. Outraged, Jonathan telephoned me at home and said it was a hell of a note for a distinguished editor to be forgotten in a matter of months at the newspaper he had served for thirty-five years. I advised him to ring the *News and Observer* and ask for himself and find out what sort of impression he had left at his old stomping ground.

I've made no attempt to keep up with the *Pilot* and the custodian of its conscience since Jay. As I worked for no ghosts, I expect nobody to work for mine—or for anybody else's. My wish for my current successor and all his successors is that they will labor with the freedom and the satisfaction and the pride that I enjoyed.

During a month that I spent winding up my affairs at the *Pilot* and transferring the editorial command, I chanced to be in Winston-Salem with my brother Walter, a retired mathematician and textile industrial engineer living in nearby Mt. Airy, North Carolina. We visited a crafts fair and there came upon George Bryant, Jr., who had been at Chapel Hill with us and was displaying waterfowl he had carved and his wife Elsie had painted.

George headed the *Wall Street Journal's* Washington bureau before transferring to McGraw-Hill there. He took early retirement, left his Maryland farm, bought a place in Chincoteague, on the Virginia Eastern Shore, and spent a good bit of time in North Carolina. In our student days he and I split a few bootlegger pints of corn whiskey.

"I hear you're getting out, Bobby," he said. Only old schoolmates call me that.

He heard right, I assured him. "I'm looking for a good whittling knife," I said.

George grinned. His shoulders are drawn from lying at too many cold dawns in the marshes, shooting ducks. Sometimes he is crotchety.

"Just remember this," he said, solemnly. "If you hadn't done any of it, it wouldn't make a goddam bit of difference."

You can make a case for that.

I dug out a little news, now and then, and I evoked a few chuckles, and counted out a good many headlines, but I made no great discoveries and did not change the world or any of its parts. On the other hand, I plied my trade through three great periods of history— the Depression, World War II (I wrote my ship's battle diaries and war history), and the Race Revolution—when information was as vital as government and essential to it. If a democracy is dependent upon an uninhibited press, as I believe it to be, I find some gratification in having advanced it a trifle or two during trying times.

In any event, it was a good feeling to be driving down a street in an early morning, on my way to some fishing spot when I was older and on my way home from work when I was younger, and to see stacks of newspapers at corners and to observe carriers making their rounds, and to know that all over the city and throughout the countryside people would read headlines I had scribbled or news or editorials I had written before they did much of anything else, even sipped their coffee.

I would remember then, and I never would forget, that evening in Sanford, when I was new on my first job and was still what Professor Oscar Coffin called "one of the neighbors' children," working on a country semiweekly that paid me $10 a week and was late coming out that Thursday, and Mr. Dan C. Lawrence stormed into the basement office and demanded to know why he hadn't got his paper, he having had his supper and being more than ready to read the news. For Mr. Dan C. Lawrence, as I already have said, was an important man in that town.

Epilogue

Sam Potts, who was sports editor of the *Virginian-Pilot* from the Lord knows when till the late twenties, is remembered principally for two things. One is that he had a medical degree. He did not care for medicine and never had practiced it, and people did not call him Doctor. What they called him was, for reasons unrecorded, Governor, or Gov.

The other thing he is remembered for is that he was in the press box at the High Street field off Portsmouth's edge in May 1927 when a hurricane-force squall blew away the grandstand. The Portsmouth Cubs and Petersburg Broncos, of the old Virginia League, were the luckiest people in the ball park. They had dugouts. Everybody else took an awful buffeting. Two were killed and ten injured. Among those escaping unhurt was Baseball Commissioner Kennesaw Mountain Landis, a guest of honor. Gov Potts reported this horrendous event with half a line of agate type:

Game pp; rain

My great friend Sonny Tilghman, who preceded me at the *Pilot* by about six years, worked with Gov Potts for a little while. By then Gov had been superannuated into writing church notes and lodge items. I never knew him, but lately have seen a picture of him. It is a group photograph of the news staff, and he is sitting up front, with the managing editor and city editor and telegraph editor; standing behind these old desk bulls are six or seven reporters, most of them young men wearing hats and smoking cigarettes. Gov Potts stares through steel-rimmed glasses; his hair is gray and brush-cut, and seems to be charged with lightning, as though it never recovered from that terrible afternoon at the baseball field. He is heavy-shouldered and thick-waisted, and sits in the slumped, relaxed way that old people on porches acquire. He is coatless, and wears suspenders. His socks are white, his shoes high-laced and sturdy. His ankles seem to be swollen.

One of the things that Sonny Tilghman was forever going to do

25:25

was write a play set in the *Virginian-Pilot* city room. He had the opening scene firmly in mind.

As the curtain rises, there sits Governor Potts. He is all alone, leaning over his desk on his elbows, reading *Spinks' Sporting News*. It is early in the day or late at night, either before working time or after the presses have started. Gov had little home life. He spends most hours at the office.

As Gov reads, a telephone rings. It is on another desk, on the other side of the stage. Gov ignores it. He has a friend managing in the Three-I League, or the Sally League, or the Kitty League, or maybe the Western Association, and he is studying the team standings and line scores. The phone rings again.

Telephones in that period did not ring automatically. Operators in the telephone building rang them. When the phone rings a third time, it is in a staccato series, in urgency.

Gov now looks up, scowling. He does not otherwise move. Then he turns a page in the *Sporting News*. He knows a kid who has moved up the Yankee chain from Norfolk to Kansas City, which is Triple-A and has its box score printed. He is searching out the kid's name.

Again the phone rings. This time it keeps on ringing, with hardly any pauses, and Gov at last hauls himself out of his chair. He has dropped his suspenders from his rounded shoulders, and as he shuffles toward the noisy telephone he hauls his britches over his hips. He has on bedroom slippers. His ankles indeed are elephantine. He sighs.

As he reaches the phone, it becomes silent. He eyes it warily. Then he picks it up and gingerly lifts the receiver from the hook. "*Pilot*," he whispers. "*Virginian-Pilot* city room."

There is no answer. The phone is dead. A beauteous smile works its way through the Governor's broad and craggy face.//

Well, Sonny never got around to writing his play set in the *Virginian-Pilot* city room. His opening scene, I fear, wasn't much of a start.

But it is enough to serve me in telling you something I learned about the newspaper business during the forty-five years, one month, and three days I pursued it. Here it is:

When a telephone rings in a newspaper office, go ahead and answer it. It's probably some damn fool with some wild-ass rumor, but you never can tell. *You never can tell!*